W9-CNN-480

DISCARDED
UNIVERSITY OF WINNIPEG
LIBRARY
515 PORTAGE AVENUE
WINNIPEG, MAN. R3B 2E9

THE HABSBURGS AND EUROPE

1516–1660

Portrait of Philip IV, by Velázquez, 1631–1636.
Reproduced by courtesy of the Trustees,
The National Gallery, London.

THE HABSBURGS AND EUROPE

1516–1660

by H. G. KOENIGSBERGER

Cornell University Press / ITHACA AND LONDON

First published 1971

International Standard Book Number 0-8014-0624-2
Library of Congress Catalog Card Number 73-145868

PRINTED IN THE UNITED STATES OF AMERICA
BY VAIL-BALLOU PRESS, INC.

To

Dorothy, Francesca, and Laura

⁂

Preface

THERE ARE SEVERAL excellent histories of Europe, of Spain, and of individual Habsburg rulers of 1516–1660. So far as I know, however, there is none that treats specifically the history and aims of the house of Habsburg in its relation to the rest of Europe during the century and a half of Habsburg predominance. Although these three chapters were written over a period of ten years and were each meant to fit with other chapters in large, composite volumes, together they form a coherent whole, and I kept this in mind while writing them.

It seems to me that there was an element of tragedy in the transformation and decline of Charles V's imperial ideal. This transformation and decline set in as soon as the ideal was formulated; it was inherent in both the characters of the principal actors and in the political circumstances of the age, but it took four generations to play itself out. The stress on the tragic element of this story is not, I think, the result of romanticism on my part but, I hope, of a recognition of some basic elements of the human condition that the history of Habsburg predominance exemplifies.

I wish to thank the Syndics of the Cambridge University Press for permission to reprint Chapters I and II from *The New Cambridge Modern History*, Volumes II and III, respectively, and Messrs Thames and Hudson Ltd. and McGraw-Hill, Inc., for permission to reprint Chapter III from *The Age of Expansion*, edited by H. R. Trevor-Roper. Those who wish to read further on this subject should return to these scholarly volumes, the last of which is also superbly illustrated.

H. G. K.

Ithaca, New York
January 1971

Contents

Illustrations

Maps

❧

Introduction

FROM THE ELECTION of Count Rudolph of Habsburg as German king, in 1273, until the abdication of the last Austrian emperor, Charles I, in 1918, the house of Habsburg, or house of Austria as it was more commonly called, never ceased to play a prominent role in the politics of Europe. But for nearly one hundred and fifty years, from 1516 until 1659, it actually dominated European politics, as France, Germany, and the Soviet Union were to do in later periods. It is not difficult to see how this dominance came about. Charles V's inheritance of the crowns of four major dynasties, Castile, Aragon, Burgundy, and Austria, the later acquisition by his house of the crowns of Bohemia, Hungary, Portugal, and, for a short time, even of England, and the coincidence of these dynastic events with the Spanish conquest and exploitation of the New World—these provided the house of Habsburg with a wealth of resources that no other European power could match. In such circumstances, Habsburg domination of European politics, although not necessarily of Europe, was inevitable; i.e. the politics of all other European powers were to a considerable degree, and in western Europe almost completely, determined by their relations with the house of Austria.

It is much more difficult to be certain what this dominance meant to those who experienced it and what the aims were of those who exercised it. These aims were probably never a simple domination of Europe by one man or one power. The Habsburgs were not Napoleons or Hitlers. But if Charles V defined his position and his aims in chivalric, religious, and dynastic terms, rather than in terms of political domination, he set no limits to them. His emblem was the columns of Hercules, Europe's gateway to the wider world, and his device was *plus ultra*—always further. No wonder that both the emperor's supporters and his opponents saw his aims as a *monarchia universal*, a world empire. But what seemed to his supporters a God-given opportunity, holding out the promise of universal peace and unity among all Christians and Christianized heathens, appeared to his enemies as a sinister quest for universal domination. The history of this dialectic is the theme of the first chapter of this book.

Charles V's transcendental and universalist aims remained unfulfilled. His son Philip II, without his father's imperial title, neither could nor wished to revive them. By temperament peace-loving and conservative, he would have been content, or so it seemed to many of his contemporaries in the early years of his reign, simply to preserve his inheritance. He was not allowed to do so. As the ruler of the greatest Catholic power, he slid inevitably, and not altogether unwillingly, into the role of the principal champion of a Catholic Christendom that appeared to be in mortal danger from the dual attack of the Moslem Turks and the Protestants. But while Charles V's cause was embodied in his own position and aims, Philip II's was outside himself. He could never fully resolve the dilemma which faces all great powers that set themselves to champion a universal cause: the impossibility of harmonizing the limited but imperative demands of reason of state which impose themselves on all secular governments with the limitless demands of the universal cause. To Philip it seemed that the power and authority of his own monarchy had to be defended before all else; for without this power and authority, Catholic Christendom would assuredly be lost. But to both his allies and his enemies, it seemed equally clear that the king was, time and again, preferring the interests of Spain and of his house to those of the Church or of Christendom.

This dichotomy became particularly evident in the last twenty years of Philip's reign; for then he conquered Portugal and attempted to conquer England and France —all for the best of legal and religious reasons, and in defense of his justified and justifiable rights. Yet to Englishmen, Frenchmen, Dutchmen, to many Portuguese, and even to the popes themselves, the Spanish king's policies seemed only too plainly the embodiment of a Spanish will to dominate Europe and the world. In the end, all the diverse, complex, and originally autonomous struggles and ambitions of the peoples of western Europe came to center on the problems generated by the ambivalent aims of Philip II as champion of the Counter-Reformation and

Philip II as ruler of the greatest power of the age. This is the theme of Chapter II.

Habsburg championship of the Counter-Reformation did not die with Philip II; but, in the seventeenth century, its center shifted from Madrid to the Vienna of Ferdinand II. Here, it tended to become narrowly legalistic and backward-looking. When Wallenstein's victories opened the prospect of a Catholic *monarchia* in Europe more powerful than Charles V could have imagined, the court of Vienna not only failed to grasp this opportunity but deliberately sabotaged it.

In Madrid, the Spanish Habsburgs and their ministers also still talked in terms of their customary championship of Catholic Christendom. But this was little more than a traditional attitude. After the Protestant fiasco in Bohemia and, even more clearly, after the death of Gustavus Adolphus, Catholic Christendom was no longer in serious danger. Spanish policy no longer differed substantially from that of other powers: it was commanded by "interest," as contemporaries put it, i.e. by reason of state. Charles V's transcendental imperialism had deteriorated into a mere Spanish imperialism. Objectively, Philip IV and Olivares no longer had to face Philip II's dilemma; for one of its horns, the championship of a universal cause, had shrunk to insignificance from a growing disbelief, both in the sincerity of the house of Austria as the champion and even in the very need of any such championship. Subjectively, however, Philip IV and the Castilian ruling class could not free themselves from the patterns of thought generated by an earlier, idealistic imperialism, and hence they consistently pitched their political aims beyond the physical capacities of Castile and beyond the psychological capacities for imperial co-operation of the other Spanish dominions. Thus the Habsburg predominance over the politics of Europe dissolved in a European "civil war" in the course of which the remnants of earlier religious and idealistic aims disappeared beneath the brutal realities of power politics. This is the theme of Chapter III.

☙ I

The Empire of Charles V in Europe

THE SIXTEENTH CENTURY was an age of prophets. Luther, Zwingli, and Calvin interpreted the Word of God, challenging the claim of the Roman Church to its own uniquely valid interpretation. These prophets found their armed champions in Knox, Coligny, and William of Orange. The Catholic Church countered them with her own arms, with Loyola, with Philip II and the Inquisition. But for more than a generation, before the religious conflicts erupted into open war, the political and religious life of Europe was dominated by a very different fighter for God: the Habsburg emperor Charles V, the last medieval emperor to whom the religious and political unity of Christendom was both the ideal purpose of his life and a practicable object of policy. "Caesar is not a doctor of the gospels," wrote Erasmus in his dedication to Charles of his paraphrase of St. Matthew; "he is their champion." "God's standard bearer," the emperor called himself when, in June 1535, he weighed anchor at Barcelona to wrest Tunis from the Turks.

§ 2

The formation of the Habsburg empire

Charles had good reasons for his belief. "God has set you on the path toward a world monarchy," said the grand chancellor Gattinara, in 1519. Marriage alliances and inheritance had given Charles this unique opportunity. In the fifteenth century, the houses of Austria and Burgundy had become united in northern Europe, those of Aragon and Castile in the south; but the marriage of Philip of Burgundy and Joanna of Castile, at the beginning of the sixteenth century, produced a similar union between the northern and southern houses only through a series of unexpected deaths. As a result, Charles inherited the Habsburg possessions of Austria, Tyrol and parts of southern Germany, the Netherlands and Franche-Comté, and, south of the Alps, Spain with her new American colonies and the Spanish dominions in Italy, Sicily, Sardinia, and Naples. To Charles V, this inheritance was a sacred trust, the evidence of a divine intention as well as the material means to carry out this intention. Others had jealously claimed some of his provinces without just title; but, with God's help and his own unceasing efforts, he had always managed to preserve his inheritance undiminished for an heir. Thus wrote Charles to his son in his secret instructions and testaments. At one time or another during his reign, Charles himself or a member of his family sat as ruler or consort on nearly every royal throne of Europe. Dynastic alliances had appeared as the effective instrument of God's will, and dynastic alliances remained the emperor's favorite policy throughout his life, the only type of policy he chose freely

THE HOUSE OF HABSBURG

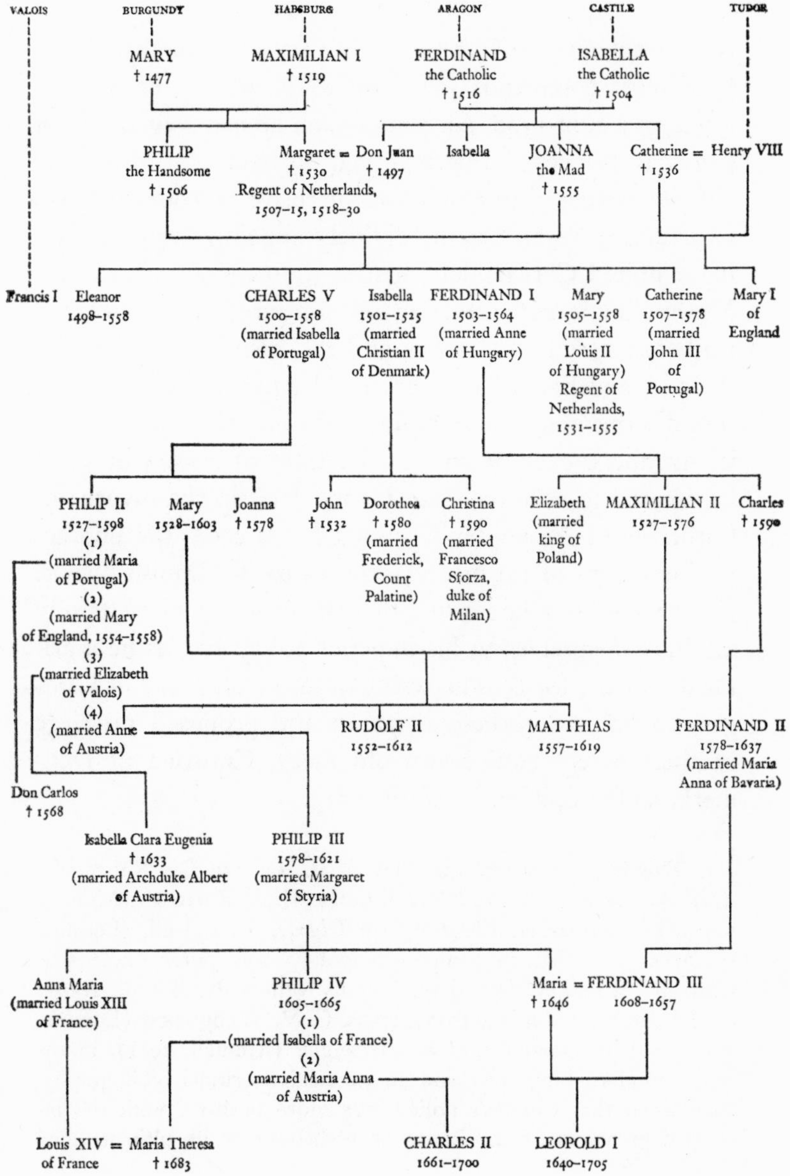

for the enhancing of his power in Europe. "For that which God most commends [to princes] is peace," he admonished his son in 1548. All wars which he had waged against Christian princes had been forced on him.

Only against the infidel was offensive warfare justified. Charles saw his task as the divinely appointed one of leading a united Christendom against the external enemy, the Muslim Turk and, later, against its internal enemies, the Lutheran heretics.[1] To this end the houses of Burgundy, Austria, and Spain had been raised and united in his person. To this end Charles supported the legitimate rights of its members, even against the dictates of reason of state; he refused to accommodate Henry VIII in the divorce of Catherine of Aragon and pressed for decades the impracticable claims of his niece Dorothea to the Danish throne. To this end, too, he insisted that the members of his family sacrifice themselves to his imperial policy just as he sacrificed himself; for thus he wrote to his sister, Mary of Hungary, who had protested against the proposed marriage of their barely twelve-year-old niece, Christina of Denmark, to the duke of Milan in 1535.

1. This is substantially the view of P. Rassow, *Die Kaiser-Idee Karls V* (Berlin, 1932); *Die Politische Welt Karls V* (Munich, 1947). E. Armstrong, *The Emperor Charles V*, 2nd ed. (London, 1910), argued that the emperor's policy was purely defensive, with all his actions forced on him by others. K. Brandi, *Kaiser Karl V*, vol. I (Munich, 1937), trans. C. V. Wedgwood (London, 1939); vol. II, *Quellen und Erörterungen* (Munich, 1941), in the fullest modern biography and an exhaustive critical bibliography, maintained that Charles's policy was more positive, with the increased greatness of the house of Habsburg as its ultimate aim.

For most of Charles's contemporaries, his imperial position had no such transcendental significance, least of all for the men responsible for the young prince's smooth entry into the inheritance of his many lands. Charles had lost his father in 1506 at the age of six and had inherited from him the possessions of the house of Burgundy: Franche-Comté with the claim to the duchy of Burgundy (since 1477 in French hands) and the provinces which were then called *les pays de pardeça* and which came to be known as the Netherlands (*les pays d'embas*) only from the 1530's. These were the duchies of Luxemburg and Brabant, and the counties of Flanders, Holland, Zeeland, Hainault, and Artois, together with a number of smaller counties and lordships. Charles's mother, Joanna of Castile, who survived until 1555, was insane and incapable of government. In consequence, the regency for the child was undertaken by his grandfather, the emperor Maximilian I, acting through his daughter, Margaret of Austria, dowager duchess of Savoy. Margaret's regency was brought to an end in January 1515 when the estates bribed Maximilian to have the young prince declared of age.

Within a year of this event, Ferdinand of Aragon was dead (January 23, 1516). The whole inheritance of the Catholic kings, Ferdinand and Isabella, now fell to Charles of Burgundy. To Guillaume de Croy, lord of Chièvres, the effective head of Charles's government, the problem was neither new nor unexpected. Little more than ten years before, the Burgundian nobility had accompanied Charles's father, Philip, to Spain and had helped him to make good his claims to the crown of Castile. Since then, Spanish grandees had lived at the Burgundian court and had been admitted to the Order of the Golden Fleece. Spanish merchants were familiar figures in Bruges and Antwerp. For Chièvres and the great seigneurs in his council the question of whether or not to accept the Spanish succession never arose; it was only a question of how to achieve it. Chièvres was the leader of the old Walloon nobility. By culture, family ties, and the possession of estates near or even across the French border they were traditionally francophile. Now, Chièvres had to reconcile the "English" party with whose help Margaret had governed. He had to win over Maximilian and Henry VIII into full co-operation and induce Francis I to maintain a benevolent neutrality (Treaty of Noyon, December 3, 1516).

Having none of Gattinara's or Charles's sense of imperial mission, Chièvres could afford to leave France in control of northern Italy if this meant peace and amity with his powerful neighbor. When finally, in September 1517, he concluded a truce with the old enemy of the Habsburgs, Charles of Guelders, Burgundian diplomacy had won its major objectives—peace in Europe and freedom from all interference with the Spanish succession.

The situation in Spain itself was much more problematical. The union of the Spanish crowns had not meant the union of the Spanish kingdoms, and there were still powerful forces in each which would gladly have seen a return to separate rulers. The Castilians would not suffer the appointment of an Aragonese as Spanish ambassador in Rome; the men of Navarre said they would rather see a

Turk than an Aragonese as commander of the fortress of Pamplona. In Castile, despite the efforts of Isabella, the power of the crown was still far from firmly established. At every royal death, the old antagonism between grandees and towns broke out into open strife. Since Isabella's death, the regency of Castile had been in the hands of her old minister, Cardinal Ximenes de Cisneros, archbishop of Toledo. After Ferdinand's death, Ximenes was well aware that only the early arrival of Charles in Spain could assure him a smooth succession. The nobles, trying to profit by the interregnum, were attempting to regain their old control over the towns. Toledo and Valladolid were in revolt against their corregidors, the royal representatives in the city administration. The cardinal's attempt to raise a militia of thirty thousand was sabotaged by both towns and grandees who feared for their own power. Ximenes had to give way for fear of more serious trouble. Most difficult of all, and most embittering, was the problem of royal appointments. The Spaniards accused the Netherlanders of greed and place-hunting. In fact, the court at Brussels was careful to hold its hand in all but a few cases; but, in Spain itself, Ximenes' secretary wrote that government was impossible without giving benefices and rewards (*mercedes*) and that the Flemings were hated even before they had arrived.

The eighteen months which it had taken Chièvres to prepare for Charles's departure had been too long an interregnum for Spain. When Charles landed there, in September 1517, his supporters were already disillusioned, while nobles and towns were sullenly apprehensive of the expected rule of the foreigner. The cardinal regent lay dying, for joy at the king's arrival, as Charles's court jester maliciously said. Charles himself, young, ugly, and inexperienced, speaking no Spanish and surrounded by Burgundian councilors and courtiers, did not initially make a good impression. The Spaniards contrasted the magnificence of the Burgundian court, its tournaments and balls, with the sober and inexpensive habits of the Catholic kings. Only three bishoprics were given to foreigners, but these included the see of Toledo, for Chièvres's nephew, and it was easy to regard this as plunder for the Burgundians. Moreover, it appeared that those Spaniards who had been in the Netherlands were preferred to those who had served the king's cause in Spain. In February 1518, the cortes of Valladolid presented Charles with far-reaching demands and much pointed counsel as a condition of the country's homage and of a grant of 600,000 ducats payable over three years. The court was accommodating and, if relations were not cordial, Charles was now the acknowledged king of Castile.

The estates of the realms of the crown of Aragon had preserved even greater liberties than those of Castile. It took much longer than in Castile to come to terms with the cortes of Saragossa and Barcelona and to obtain from them 200,000 and 100,000 ducats respectively. Chièvres preferred not to repeat this delay in Valencia. With the crown of Aragon, Charles had now inherited the old Aragonese empire, the Balearic Islands, Sardinia, Sicily, and Naples. It was a union of kingdoms each with its own history, its own traditions, obligations, and enmities. The necessity of defending southern Italy from the Turks inevitably brought Charles V's empire into collision with the Ottoman empire, quite apart from Charles's view of himself as the champion of Christendom. The rival Aragonese and Angevin claims to Naples brought Charles into collision with France, a collision which the purely Burgundian policy of Chièvres had at least temporarily been able to avoid. Defense against the Turks inevitably turned into a struggle for the control of the central Mediterranean. Defense against the French inevitably turned into a struggle for the control of Italy and hence, as the emperor's advisers Gattinara and Granvelle were later to argue, into a struggle for the dominant position in Europe. Even without Charles's election as emperor, Castile's traditional friendship with France (maintained despite the francophobia of the Castilians) was now irretrievably broken, and similarly broken was the Walloon nobility's policy of Franco-Burgundian amity.

There remained the final step in Charles's succession, the succession to the Austrian and South German dominions of the Habsburgs and his election as king of Germany which carried with it the crown of the Holy Roman Empire. Even before Maximilian's death, January 12, 1519, the Habsburg courts in Spain, the Netherlands, and Austria were busy with their preparations for the election. When Francis I entered the field as a candidate, the rivalry between the two rulers appeared for the first time openly, and with Charles took that curiously personal and moral flavor based on his conviction of the divinely ordained nature of his claims. With the pope supporting Francis I and the electors still undecided, Margaret of Austria suggested that both pope and electors might be more easily induced to accept Charles's younger brother, Ferdinand, than the powerful ruler of the Netherlands, Spain, and half of Italy. Charles's sharp reaction from Barcelona reads like a program for his reign. "It seems to us," he wrote to his aunt, "that if the said election is conferred on our person . . . we will be able to accomplish many good and great things, and not only conserve and guard the possessions which God has given us, but increase them greatly and, in this way, give peace, repose and tranquillity to Christendom, upholding and strengthening our holy Catholic faith which is our principal foundation." Experience had shown, he continued, that even such a virtuous and victorious prince as the emperor Maximilian had been in constant trouble to safeguard his patrimony and imperial rights; but he, Charles, with the power of all his great kingdoms and dominions, would be feared and esteemed among other princes, would obtain true obedience from the subjects of the Empire and defeat the enemies of the faith. This would be greater glory for both Ferdinand and himself than acquiring dominion over Christians. Charles promised, however, to work for Ferdinand's election as king of the Romans, that is as heir presumptive to the imperial title. In the end, Charles was elected unanimously by the German electors (June 28, 1519).

The election was peculiarly the triumph of the new grand chancellor, the Piedmontese Mercurino Arborio di Gattinara who had been appointed to his office in 1518. A brilliant lawyer and superb administrator, an enthusiastic humanist and admirer of Erasmus, he had risen in the service of Margaret of Austria. For the next twelve years he did more than any other person to shape the development of his master's political ideas, then still in the youthful stage of the chivalrous quest for personal glory in the tradition of the Burgundian court. In his own memoirs, in speeches to the Spanish cortes and the Netherlands states general, in memoranda for the emperor and his council, Gattinara reiterated his belief that the imperial title gave Charles authority over the whole world, for it was "ordained by God himself, foretold by the prophets, preached by the apostles and approved by the birth, life and death of our Redeemer Christ." It was Dante's imperial idea revived. Like Dante, Gattinara, his learned and historically conscious compatriot, saw the center of imperial power in Italy. Not the personal possession of Milan or of other territories, but the friendship and support of the Italian states and all Christian princes (guaranteed, no doubt, by Habsburg military power) were to assure the emperor his position as moral and political leader of the world. In time Charles made these views his own, with little of the Italian's humanist learning, but with an even greater emphasis on the religious and dynastic aspects of his position. When Gattinara died in 1530, Charles had grown up to intellectual and moral independence. From thenceforth he dispensed with a grand chancellor. Long years of power had heightened his sense of responsibility and had developed his slow and unoriginal mind to self-assurance and mastery of politics, making him tower over his contemporaries both in the constancy of his ideals and in the flexibility and shrewdness of his tactics. At thirty-four he wrote to his younger sister Mary, dowager queen of Hungary and recently appointed regent of the Netherlands, to console her over the troubles of her task: when she had had as much experience as he, she would no longer despair over difficulties. Years later, Mary was to complain to their brother, Ferdinand, "that the emperor is difficult and does not always think well of a matter if it does not come from him." Thus, self-assured and masterful, in his later years a little sceptical, the emperor appears in Titian's famous portraits.

Not all contemporaries, not even those in his own dominions, could accept Charles's and Gattinara's view of the empire as standing for peace among Christians and the defense of Christianity against Muslims and heretics. Gattinara's Italian policy was ascribed to his possession of estates in the duchy of Milan. His policy of moral leadership for the emperor became suspect when, after the battle of Pavia, he urged the annexation of Dauphiné and Languedoc. With an imperial niece married to the duke of Milan and imperial troops in control of its fortresses, the emperor's claim that he was preserving the independence of the duchy had a hollow ring to the Venetians and the French. Europe saw Charles V's empire primarily in terms of power, and in this view originated the permanent hostility of the only other European power of comparable strength, France, and the intermittent hostility or at best cool friendship of the lesser independent powers, England, Denmark, and the Italian states. Moreover, Charles's very insistence on his religious aims and their fusion with his political ends helped to make insoluble two problems which were difficult enough in any case: his relations with the German princes and his relations with the pope. To the Protestant German princes, the emperor's policy represented the double threat of imperial and religious coercion; and since the Catholic princes were equally alarmed about the emperor's political power, they never gave him the political support which alone would have enabled him to solve the religious question.

The pope seemed to be the natural ally of "God's standard bearer," and Charles never ceased to hope that such he would prove to be. But Clement VII and Paul III, in their capacity of Italian princes, were as alarmed as their twelfth- and thirteenth-century predecessors at seeing Naples and Milan united in one hand. They therefore never stopped intriguing with France against the imperial power in Italy. Of this fact Charles was fully aware. What he never fully understood was that the popes, as spiritual heads of the Christian Church, could never entertain the emperor's claim to be the ultimate arbiter of the religious troubles which afflicted Christendom. It was unacceptable that at Augsburg and Regensburg the emperor's theologians should attempt to reach a compromise with the Protestants binding on all Christians; it was intolerable that a secular prince should take the initiative in reforming the Church and should threaten to summon a general council. The threat of the Turks and Protestants held pope and emperor together in uneasy alliance and only once, in 1527, did the underlying hostility break out into open and disastrous warfare; but the emperor's inability to induce the Papacy to co-operate whole-heartedly in his policies was one of the major weaknesses of his position.

Imperial administration and imperial policy

The very existence of Charles V's empire—the uniting of a number of countries under the rule of one person—thus raised problems which the individual countries either would not have had to face at all, or, as the histories of France and England demonstrated, would have had to face in a much more tractable form. Added to these difficulties was the unprecedented problem of governing this diverse collection of states. In the last analysis, the empire of Charles V existed only in the person of the emperor. It was not even called an empire. That name was reserved for the old Holy Roman Empire, here distinguished by a capital letter from the empire of Charles V, a term which should be clearly understood as a purely modern designation; when Charles V's contemporaries used a collective name for his dominions at all, it was *monarchia*. There was much confusion in the minds of contemporaries as to the significance of even that venerable institution, now that it had suddenly acquired such a powerful head. To Gattinara, at least, it was clear that the personal union of the states of the empire must be matched by a functional union. By training and experience, Gattinara belonged to the school of Roman lawyers, mostly natives of Franche-Comté, who had helped the dukes of Burgundy to weld the Netherlands into a functional union by the establishment of the councils and courts through which they governed the provinces. His authority as Burgundian grand chancellor was now extended to cover all of Charles's dominions. The Council of State, the only one of the councils to which great nobles were admitted and which advised the emperor on all imperial matters, was extended to include Spanish and Italian members, as well as the Burgundians. Characteristically, Gattinara saw his emperor as legislator for the whole world, "following the path of the good emperor Justinian," reforming the laws and simplifying legal procedures, so that all the world would want to use them and that "it would be possible to say that there was one emperor and one universal law."

Nothing came of this vision. Nor did anything come of Gattinara's plan for a treasurer general to whom the treasuries of all the emperor's dominions should render account. After Gattinara's death and the abolition of his own office of grand chancellor, the other all-imperial institutions regressed even from the very modest level they had attained. The central control of the empire became more and more a matter of personal control by Charles and those advisers whom he chose to consult on any particular issue. The enormous amount of paper work (of which only a small part has been published) was handled by two distinct institutions: a Spanish secretariat of state, continuing traditions inaugurated by the Catholic kings and responsible for the affairs of Spain, Italy, and the Mediterranean; and a French secretariat, based on Burgundian traditions and responsible for all affairs north of the Alps. The old German imperial chancellery continued to function independently in purely technical matters, but politically it was dependent on the Franco-Burgundian secretariat. Inevitably, these developments led to a great increase in the power of the secretaries of state. Both the Spanish secretary, Francisco de los Cobos, and the Franco-Burgundian secretary, Nicolas Perrenot, seigneur de Granvelle, another Franche-Comtois, were men of great ability; but neither their functions nor their personalities made their position and influence comparable to that of Gattinara before 1530.

More than ever Charles, and Charles only, represented the empire. He governed it like the head of one of the great sixteenth-century merchant houses where the junior members of the family served as heads of the foreign branches of the firm. There were great advantages in having members of the Habsburg family as governors general, regents, or even kings in his dominions. They were locally more acceptable than even the greatest nobles of nonroyal blood and much less likely to be involved in local feuds; their employment as his personal representatives accorded with Charles's own views of the central role of the dynasty in his whole position. The Netherlands, the Empire, and Spain after 1529 were always, at least nominally, entrusted to a Habsburg or his consort. Only for the Italian dominions had nonroyal viceroys to be appointed. In the event, the emperor's policy proved a success in all but one disastrous case, and his family served him loyally and, in the persons of his two governors general of the Netherlands, his aunt Margaret of Austria (1518–1530) and his sister Mary of Hungary (1531–1555), with more than common skill and devotion.

If Charles V trusted his governors and viceroys and if

he, unlike his morbidly suspicious son, Philip II, was prepared to keep them in office for decades and uphold them against local opposition, he yet reserved the ultimate control over policy and over the administration entirely to himself. He and his secretaries were in weekly correspondence with his governors. Despite the delays caused by the enormous distances the couriers had to travel, despite the emperor's notorious tardiness in taking decisions, despite the frantic appeal of governors and generals for fuller powers to cope with an emergency—despite all these difficulties, the emperor insisted on taking all important decisions himself, relying only on those councilors who were traveling with him on his constant journeys from dominion to dominion. The system achieved the control he desired, but at the cost of lost opportunities and great inefficiency. Once, at least, during the revolt of the Comuneros, it came near to ruining his power in Spain.

Apart from the regular political correspondence, the viceroys and governors were bound by the instructions they received when they entered upon their office. They had to follow the advice of the privy councils which Charles appointed for them. He reserved all important appointments to himself, and the administration of any one of his dominions was therefore never the governor's administration but always the emperor's. In his political testament of 1548, he counseled his son not to let his viceroys usurp more authority than he had given them; while Philip should not believe all complaints which were leveled against them, he should never fail to listen to such complaints so that governors should not become absolute and his vassals despair of obtaining justice. It was sound advice, followed fairly and reasonably by Charles himself, but was later pushed to extremes of suspicion and duplicity by Philip II.

The emperor was determined to keep control not only over public appointments, but also over all other forms of patronage. He had the reputation of being slow to reward service; but a minister or a servant could always hope that, in the end, he would be given a *grazie* or *merced:* an ecclesiastical benefice, a title, a pension, a castellanship, or one of the host of minor offices and sinecures with which the emperor could make a man rich without loss to himself. Great lords and ministers were willing to serve the emperor in the hope of such rewards, and lesser men, in turn, attached themselves to the lords and ministers. Viceroys and governors, sometimes even provinces and cities, had their agents at the emperor's court to represent their interests by a judicious distribution of gifts among councilors and secretaries. Some of these grew rich. Cobos, so Charles himself thought, did not take presents but had received many *mercedes* and desired more. The younger Granvelle, who succeeded his father as one of the emperor's principal advisers, was not above taking presents, though he liked to appear to refuse. The Granvelles, father and son, were reputed to have accumulated property to the value of a million ducats.

The position of Charles as the dispenser of all patronage explains much of the passionate longing of his subjects to have him reside within their particular country. As patronage had been Ximenes' most important problem before

Charles's first visit to Spain, so it remained a key problem of all his viceroys and governors. Margaret and Mary, in the Netherlands, were given lists of persons to whom, and to whom only, benefices and offices were to be allotted in strict order as they fell vacant. In vain Margaret protested. She could not obtain the support she needed for the emperor's service if she could never reward those who supported and worked for her. Her reputation, she said, had suffered badly when such appointments and grants as she had made had been revoked by the emperor. In the end, she pleaded at least to be allowed to dispose of a third of the benefices. But the emperor refused even this request.

Undoubtedly, the emperor's policy was effective in concentrating political control over his dominions in his own hands, but it remained a constant source of grievance to his subjects and made the work of his governors extraordinarily diffcult. The subjects will more readily obey the prince himself than his governor, wrote his sister Mary at the end of twenty-four years of this experience, for, however much good sense the latter has, he is not as useful to them and hence there will always be a greater number opposing than assisting him.

The emperor's failure to develop a nonpersonal institutional organization for his empire was not, however, the result only of the very personal view he took of his office, but also of the attitude of his different dominions. He was no Alexander or Napoleon who had conquered his empire, but the hereditary and legitimate ruler of each of his states whose laws and customs he had sworn to maintain. The Sicilians prided themselves on their voluntary allegiance to the house of Aragon and alarmed the Spaniards by dark hints of another Sicilian Vespers, should their privileges not be observed. The Spaniards maintained that the title of king of Spain was better than that of emperor of Germany and desired Charles not to use this latter title when he was in Spain. The Germans were particularly suspicious of foreign troops, and their fear that the emperor was arranging the "Spanish succession" of his son was one of the main reasons for his loss of authority in Germany at the end of his reign. The Netherlanders, the original architects of his empire, resisted even attempts to bring their own provinces into closer union. In 1534 the governor general proposed to the states general a defensive union with regular financial contributions from each of the provinces for a standing army. The proposal was rejected; "for if we accept the project," the states general said, "we shall undoubtedly be more united, but we shall be dealt with in the manner of France," that is, lose our liberties. The particularism of the emperor's dominions was a fight not only against centralization but also against autocracy. While Charles seized all opportunities which presented themselves to strengthen the crown's authority in each of his dominions, he never attempted a full-scale attack on the liberties of his subjects in any of them. Any attempt to create an imperial administration would have been regarded as just such an attack.

In these circumstances, it is not surprising that Charles failed to develop an economic policy for his empire or even to conceive of an economic unity of his dominions in the way in which contemporary rulers of single states were beginning to think of the economic unity of their kingdoms. In this field, as in others, only Gattinara understood the full implications of empire. He had proposed a common imperial currency. But nothing ever came of this proposal.

The emperor's policy in economic matters consistently followed the line of least resistance, a line determined by vested interests, local traditions, and the overriding financial necessities of the imperial government. The monopoly of the oceanic trade was, indeed, firmly upheld; but, characteristically, it was reserved to the Castilians. A request by the Flemings for a spice staple at Bruges was rejected by Charles because "this commodity was first found at the expense of this kingdom (Castile) and, in fairness, I have granted the staple to the port of Coruña." Yet Castile was quite unable to provide the manufactures which the Spanish colonists overseas demanded. So far from taking advantage of the excellent colonial market which paid for its imports in solid gold and silver, the Castilians were alarmed at their own exports to which they ascribed the high prices in their kingdom. The cortes of 1548 even petitioned for a prohibition of exports to the Indies, now that the colonists should have had sufficient time to build up their own industries. It was the very reverse of a mercantilist or imperialist attitude. The emperor did not accept this petition; nor did he accept an earlier one (1542) for the prohibition of the export of all raw materials from Spain, a prohibition which would have broken the most important economic link joining his two greatest dominions, the Spanish wool trade to the Netherlands. Admission of all the emperor's subjects to the Spanish colonial trade would have benefited all parts of his empire. The effect of the Castilian monopoly was that French, English, Venetian, and Genoese merchants and manufacturers competed on equal terms with the Catalans and Netherlanders in supplying Castile with goods for re-export to the Indies. Nor was there any attempt to maintain what was left of the economic links of the old Aragonese-Catalan empire, once, in its heyday, the rival of the Venetian and Genoese commercial empires. Barcelona had declined from its former greatness. Her merchants still bought grain in Otranto and Palermo, salt in Trapani, and silk in Naples and Messina. But the Genoese, Venetians, and Ragusans, with more ships and greater capital resources, had broken Catalan pre-eminence, and the Neapolitans and Sicilians preferred to sell their raw materials to Venice and Florence whose industries could supply them with finished goods.[2]

The expulsion of the Jews by the Catholic kings in 1492 had deprived Spain of the only important group of her citizens who might have played the role in the economic life of the empire which Spanish soldiers and administrators were increasingly playing in its political life. Into the void left by the disappearance of the Jews stepped, first, the South German bankers. In 1524 the Fuggers, already the owners of most of the mineral wealth of Tyrol and

2. F. Braudel, *La Méditerranée et le Monde Méditerranéen à l'époque de Philippe II*, 2nd ed. (Paris, 1966), I, 110 ff. This is the most comprehensive modern work on the political, social, and economic history of the Mediterranean countries in the sixteenth century.

Hungary, leased Spanish crown revenues from the three orders of knighthood, Santiago, Calatrava, and Alcántara. By the end of the reign, the Fuggers also controlled the silver mines of Guadalcanal and the mercury mines of Almadén. The Welsers, the second greatest banking firm, also had occasional interests in these leases and tried to build up their own colonial empire in Venezuela, in the classic style of the Spanish *conquistadores.* More important still than the Germans were the Genoese. Andrea Doria's change from French to imperial service, in 1528, gave them their opportunity. In the next decades, the Centurione, the Pallavicino, the Spinola, the Grimaldi, and many others established themselves not only as the emperor's bankers, but as the greatest traders in the Spanish Mediterranean area. Colonies of Genoese merchants settled in every important Spanish and South Italian port. Their economic services were as indispensable to the emperor as the naval services of Doria's galleys. It was the final and decisive victory over their old rivals, the Catalans.

In the north, the Netherlands undoubtedly profited economically from the Spanish connection. Imperial finance dominated the Antwerp money market. But imperial policy did not prove as effective a help to the Netherlanders' economic interests as they had hoped. Nowhere was the divergence of interests within the empire more apparent than in the complex and tortuous relations between Holland and the Baltic powers after the expulsion from Denmark of Charles's brother-in-law, Christian II, in 1523. To Holland the free passage of her ships through the Sound meant prosperity; its closing spelled heavy losses, unemployment, and hunger, for the Netherlands were dependent on Baltic grain. For the merchants of Amsterdam, it was vital that Denmark should not fall into hostile hands, especially those of their deadly rivals, the Lübeckers. For the merchants of Brabant and Flanders, Holland's difficulties meant their own opportunities, since the Lübeckers were subtle enough to offer them far-reaching concessions when they themselves were at war with Holland. For the emperor, the Danish problem was above all a question of the rights of his family. He supported first Christian II's attempts to regain his throne and, later, those of Christian's daughter, Dorothea, and her husband, Frederick of the Palatinate. Through them he hoped to extend imperial influence in northern Europe, even if this involved Holland in costly and unwanted wars. Only Mary of Hungary's government in Brussels did its best to reconcile the parties, at times bluffing effectively with the threat of the engagement of all the emperor's forces. Such an engagement, however, Charles was unwilling to make. For him Denmark was a side issue compared with the problems of France and the Turks; rather would he allow the Netherlands to treat on their own with Denmark and Lübeck, reserving for himself the right to support the claims of his niece. Hence it was more than twenty years before the relations between the Netherlands and Denmark were finally settled in the Peace of Speyer (1544), and it was the Danes who insisted that the emperor sign for all his dominions. It was a victory of the political and economic over the dynastic concept of empire; but the emperor accepted it only with great reluctance.

Within the different parts of the empire there were powerful forces willing to support Charles and his imperial policy. The Burgundian high nobility who had done so much to secure their prince the effective succession to his kingdoms remained loyal to the end even if, for most of them, Gattinara's and Charles's Christian ideals meant little more than the fashionable commonplaces of their knightly upbringing at the Burgundian court. When Philibert de Chalon, prince of Orange and Charles's viceroy of Naples, appealed to him for support against the French invasion of Naples in 1528, he wrote, "The king of France is sparing no effort. It would be very shameful and damaging to you, Sire, if you did not do your utmost; for it is by this that the world will see which one of you two will remain the master." There was no imperial ideal here. Chalon and many of his fellow nobles saw the emperor's policy as simply a quest for personal honor and reputation. It was enough for them to serve the most powerful prince in Christendom and to have the opportunity of appointments to provincial governorships or even viceroyalties, or to win fame by leading his armies against Frenchman, Turk, or heretic. Thus, too, thought the Spanish nobility. Their early hostility to Charles soon changed to enthusiastic support. More than the Netherlanders, they were in sympathy with Charles's crusading and imperial ideals. Had not the Castilians fought the Moors on their own soil? Had not the Aragonese achieved power and renown by their Italian conquests and wealth by the easy acquisition of Sicilian and Neapolitan estates or ecclesiastical benefices? The double lure of knight-errantry and plunder made the

Spaniards imperialists in Europe as it made them *conquistadores* in America. Nor did the chances of promotion and high office hold less attraction for the Italian nobility. As king of Sicily and Naples, the emperor was their own prince as much as he was ruler of Spain and Germany. The Gonzaga, the Pescara, the del Vasto preferred the role of an imperial viceroy or captain general to that of a provincial condottiere.

Next to the high nobility, the lawyers were the emperor's most enthusiastic supporters. Trained in Roman law with its imperial and absolutist traditions, many of them humanists and Erasmians, they found it easy to combine their sympathy for Charles V's imperial claims with the prospect of dazzling careers in the imperial councils. For the rest of the populations of the emperor's dominions the advantages of belonging to a world empire appeared more doubtful. There were those, especially among the merchant class, who were able to take advantage of the political connections between Italy, Spain, and the Netherlands. But, as we have seen, the economic links between the parts of the empire depended little on its political structure or on the emperor's policies. The Spanish hidalgos, the lower nobility, who flocked in their hundreds to serve under the emperor's standards in the Spanish *tercios*, represented a Spanish, rather than a universal, imperialism. For the mass of the population, the empire seemed to be the last chance of peace within Christendom —that passionate longing which had attached itself for centuries to the name of the Roman Empire. Now, in Charles V, it seemed to find its fulfilment. Or so it appeared to the crowds who cheered the emperor's, or his son's, entry into their city on his journeys from country to country; and so it was presented on the triumphal arches which greeted him—arches on which local Latinists displayed their learning and enthusiasm for the "restorer of the Roman Empire" and the "future ruler of the whole globe." But it was just this longed-for peace which the emperor failed to give his subjects. When the court had passed on its way, the taxes remained to pay for wars which often seemed no concern of the single provinces. If loyalty to the emperor seldom wavered, his governors, foreign or native, were often hated, and the ruler's absence on his imperial duties was deeply resented. Ultimately, local interests and loyalties remained predominant in every case; the feeling of imperial solidarity never developed sufficiently to become an effective political force.

Warfare and taxation: the Netherlands

Wars and ever-increasing taxes seemed to be the lot of the emperor's subjects. They pressed on millions when the benefits of empire seemed to be reaped by a few hundreds. Every letter that passed between the emperor and his viceroys, every memorandum presented to him by his ministers, was directly or indirectly concerned with problems of finance; for only ready money would keep in the field the emperor's armies, keep afloat his galleys, the instruments on which, in the last resort, all his policies and the very existence of his empire depended. The emperor's financial needs became more and more the fulcrum around which his relations with his separate dominions revolved.

Nowhere was this clearer than in the Netherlands. Their great towns, as they were never tired of insisting, lived by trade and industry; they wanted peace. Their nobility, though personally as avid for glory in the field and as bored by peacetime pursuits as the rest of the European nobility, were sufficiently involved in their country's economic life to support this desire. In 1536 the governor general herself, Mary of Hungary, pleaded with her brother to keep the Netherlands neutral in an approaching war with France. Charles declined. Such apparent weakness would only encourage the French and the Guel-drians to attack the provinces, he wrote.

If the wars with France were the more expensive and potentially the more dangerous, the wars with Guelders were the more destructive and the seemingly more senseless. Charles of Egmont, duke of Guelders, was perhaps the most determined enemy Charles V ever faced. Against the centralizing policy of the Brussels government he stood for the independence of the small princes. With French money and support he equipped his marauding bands. His marshal, Maarten van Rossem, "Black Martin," the bogey-man of Dutch children, spread fire and destruction through Holland and northern Brabant. In 1528 he sacked The Hague and barely failed to capture Antwerp and Louvain in 1542. Time after time, Holland and Brabant petitioned a willing governor general to negotiate peace with Guelders. But Egmont, urged on by France, broke every truce and treaty. In the end his policy defeated itself. Friesland, Groningen, Drenthe, Overijssel, and Utrecht came to hate the would-be defender of their liberties more than the emperor. One after another they allowed themselves to be conquered by the governors of Holland and Brabant. In 1538 Egmont died, still undefeated in his own duchy. His successor, William of Cleves, tried to continue his policy when the political basis for it had disappeared. In 1543 the emperor was for the first time free to turn his full powers against Guelders and bring the long, anomalous warfare to an end by the annexation of the duchy. The northeastern frontiers of the Netherlands were now secure; but the war had lasted too long and had shown the Netherlands how little advantage they derived from the great power of their prince.[3]

Charles V pursued the traditional policy of the dukes of Burgundy of bringing the provinces into closer unity and providing them with more efficient and powerful government. Against these centralizing policies the provincial estates and the states general set their traditional privileges and autonomy. Ultimately, the relationship between crown and estates was one of power which in the reign of Philip II had to be resolved by open warfare. Under Charles V, neither side was as yet willing to push its claims to extremes, nor even to pursue a consistent policy of attacking the powers of the other. The estates did not seriously question the right of the "natural prince" to govern, nor his right to demand money for the defense of the country. The government regarded it as a matter of pride, or, at least, an effective propaganda point, that the Netherlanders lived in greater freedom than the French and that

3. A. Jacopszoon, "Prothocolle van alle de reysen," MS. in Amsterdam Stadsarchief, transcript by E. van Bienna.

their prince did not arbitrarily impose taxes on them. Nevertheless, every new financial demand was stubbornly resisted and whittled down by the estates. Every government proposal had to be reported back to the provinces and towns. In Brabant, and before 1540 in Flanders, the petty bourgeoisie of craftsmen and guilds were represented in the town councils and had to approve all proposals. Since, in general, unanimity was required, the artisans of Louvain, for instance, were perfectly capable of holding up the decisions of the whole states general. Failing to induce the town councils to give their delegates full powers the emperor pursued a consistently antidemocratic policy toward the towns. Wherever the opportunity arose, he excluded the gilds from municipal government. He did this in Tournai in 1522, in defiance of his own promises; he did it again in Brussels in 1528, and in Ghent in 1540, following rebellions by these towns against his goveror general. The patriciates who were left in control of the towns were, on the whole, more accommodating to his financial demands. But he and his governors failed completely in their attempts to make the estates give up their insistence on the redress of grievances before the discussion of new taxes. He did not even try to prevent the provincial estates from building up their own administrative machinery to control the collection and expenditure of the taxes they voted.

The estates prevented the establishment of absolute royal power as it existed in France. But the interests of the urban patriciates, and therefore the states general, were local and sectional; the privileges they defended were equally local and often opposed to the interests of other provinces. Thus, Holland insisted on her privilege of freely exporting grain even when there was famine in the rest of the Netherlands. In consequence, Charles V's regents were never faced with a general revolt. The states general remained a conservative force, capable of blocking important government policies, such as the union proposed in 1534–1535, but unable and unwilling to challenge the crown's control of government. Nevertheless, the position of the imperial government in the Netherlands was unstable and tended to deteriorate, especially after about 1530. For this deterioration the increasing financial demands of imperial policy were largely responsible. No one has yet attempted to work out in detail the history of Netherlands finance during the emperor's reign, nor is this surprising: sixteenth-century methods of accounting were haphazard in the extreme, accuracy in arithmetic was rare, and the imperial finance officers frankly admitted the general confusion. But there is plenty of evidence of heavy and increasing taxation and of the intermittent, but steadily increasing, groundswell of the discontent it caused. Twice, in 1522 and 1525, the regent Margaret of Austria feared the imminent outbreak of rebellion. In 1525 there were riots in Bois-le-Duc; in 1532 in Brussels. Relations between the estates of Holland and the governor, the count of Hoogh-straeten, grew steadily more strained. The abbots of the great monasteries of Brabant, normally the steadiest supporters of the government, formed a secret federation in 1534 to resist the imposition of further taxes. Most serious of all was Ghent's refusal to contribute her share of the taxes voted by the states general in 1537. By 1539 the town was in open rebellion against the government, though protesting its loyalty to the emperor. As so often before in the city's stormy history, the gilds set up a democratic dictatorship and inaugurated a reign of terror against patricians and government supporters. The emperor himself had to arrive with a large army to reduce the town to obedience (February 1540).

In the last years of the emperor's reign the wars with France demanded larger sums than ever. Charles left his son debts amounting to four and a half million livres. Even so, the Netherlanders claimed that in five years they had given him eight million ducats in extraordinary grants. They complained that they were being made to conquer Italy for the emperor; they believed, rightly or wrongly, that he kept Spanish troops in the Netherlands to hold down the people. Rising prices, the decay of older centers of the cloth industry, such as Ghent and Leiden, the growth of a new rural and small-town textile industry in Walloon Flanders—all these changes were upsetting the equilibrium of Netherlands society and creating a revolutionary situation, immensely aggravated by wars and high taxation. From about 1530 onward, Lutheran and Anabaptist preachers found a ready following among the artisans and laborers of the old industrial towns. Shortly after the emperor's abdication, Calvinist preachers were even more successful in Antwerp and Walloon Flanders. The country nobility, at least in some parts of the Netherlands, saw their rental income dwindle with rising prices. Few of them could supplement it, like the high nobility, from government officers. Their traditional local influence suffered from the encroachments of the central government and its courts. As yet, they were still completely loyal; but the ground was already prepared for their opposition in the following reign. Charles V's Burgundian origins and personal popularity to some extent masked the seriousness of the situation. But when the emperor pronounced his abdication in the great hall of the palace of Brussels, before the deeply moved states general and the weeping knights of the Golden Fleece (October 25, 1555), the Habsburg political system in the Netherlands was already near to dissolution. A few months later (1557), the government had to declare its financial bankruptcy and the states general became all but unmanageable. A few years later, the religious and social troubles came to a head, and the Netherlands embarked on the eighty years of civil, religious, and national war which broke up not only the empire they had so lightheartedly helped to create, but also their own country.

Warfare and taxation: Spain

The history of Spain in the empire of Charles V stands in sharp contrast to that of the Netherlands; at the same time, it was equally dominated by imperial finance.

Earlier than any other dominion, Castile was faced with these demands, and her immediate reaction could scarcely have been more hostile. To finance Charles's return journey to the Netherlands and his imperial election, Chièvres summoned the Castilian cortes to the remote Galician town of Santiago (March 1520) to demand a new *servicio* even while the grant of 1518 had not yet expired. From the beginning there were difficulties. The court insisted that the delegates should have full powers. The towns, rightly fearing that their deputies would be bribed with money from the taxes they were asked to vote, tried to bind the deputies with definite instructions. The Toledans did not appear at the cortes at all. The other towns demanded the discussion of grievances before supply. Gattinara then adjourned the cortes to the port of Coruña where the court was already embarking (April 1520). By a mixture of bribery and concessions, eight of the eighteen towns represented in the cortes were now induced to vote the *servicio*; five maintained their opposition; the others were divided and did not vote. As the ships weighed anchor, on May 20, 1520, the revolution had already begun.

No one in Spain, not even Charles's own council, thought that the new taxes were legal or that they could be collected. Mobs attacked the houses of deputies who had voted for the *servicio* and, in Segovia, murdered them. Royal authority broke down in most Castilian towns. The council's ineffective efforts at repression, especially the burning of Medina del Rio Seco by royal troops, only added to the bitterness of the opposition. Throughout the summer and early autumn of 1520, the nobility raised no finger to help their king. They had not yet forgiven him his Burgundian councilors and their alleged plunder, and they were particularly angered by the appointment of a foreigner, Adrian of Utrecht, as regent. The rebellious towns, led by Toledo, formed a league and set up a junta that was in effect a revolutionary government. Adrian was driven out of Valladolid and had to seek refuge on the estates of the admiral of Castile, Fadrique Enríquez. The rebel leader, Padilla, captured Tordesillas and the insane queen mother. It looked as if Charles's authority in Spain would collapse completely. Only full powers to pardon and to negotiate with the Comuneros could save the situation, Adrian wrote in ever more despairing letters. His demands were echoed by the admiral, Enríquez, and the constable of Castile, Iñigo de Velasco, both of them appointed co-regents with Adrian in the autumn of 1520. "Your Majesty should not be afraid of paper and ink," Velasco wrote. Oaths and pledges, he continued, could always be broken with those who had broken far more; and thus the emperor should allow his regents to make decisions which, if necessary, he could later repudiate.

At no time were the problems of effective imperial control over distant dominions more evident. In the end, however, Charles's and Chièvres's policy of making only such concessions as did not touch the basis of royal authority proved successful: suspension of the collection of the *servicio*, the appointment of Enríquez and Velasco, with the promise of no further foreign appointments, and Charles's speedy return to Spain. But for many months the issue hung in the balance, and it was no direct effort of his own which saved the situation for Charles.

In the towns, radical and popular elements were more and more gaining the upper hand. When the revolt spread to the estates of the grandees, these latter began to take alarm. The old antagonism between towns and nobles flared up again. In Andalusia, the nobles with their vast estates and large numbers of Morisco tenants were aware of their danger earlier than the Castilian nobility. From the beginning they prevented the spread of the Comunero movement to the south. Within the Comunero camp, rival factions maneuvered for control of the movement. During the winter of 1520–1521, one after another of their moderate leaders from among the urban nobility deserted to the royalists. On April 23, 1521, at Villalar, the Castilian nobles and their retainers routed the Comunero army. Valladolid and the other towns of northern Castile at once made their peace with the king; only Toledo, the prime mover in the revolt, held out until October 1521.

The power of the monarchy was thus restored in Castile, never to be seriously shaken again during the reigns of the Habsburg kings. The towns kept much of their autonomy; but royal control was safeguarded by the reestablishment of the powers of the corregidors. The deputies to the cortes had now to arrive with full powers, and their salaries were paid from the taxes they voted. All attempts to revive the principle of redress of grievances before supply met with a firm refusal; after their defeat of 1521, the towns had lost their power to insist. Charles did not need to attack the cortes any further. They were willing to vote taxes, and their petitions, often repeated session after session, could be granted or refused as the emperor chose.

Although the nobles had won the civil war, they could not, for that very reason, break their alliance with the monarchy. The monarchy, now that it could manage the cortes and afford a standing army, was the stronger partner. Charles systematically excluded the grandees from the government of Spain, much to the duke of Alva's chagrin. But he still had many prizes and titles to give to the nobles as a compensation for their loss of political power. More immediately important still was the nobles' exemption from taxation. It was not a privilege which the emperor admitted willingly. At the cortes of Toledo, in October 1538, to which nobles and clergy were summoned together with the eighteen towns, the government proposed an excise tax on foodstuffs from which there should be no exemptions. The nobles voted against it almost unanimously, Velasco dropping dark hints of commotions which always happened in Castile when any "novelty" was introduced. To avoid an open rupture, Charles gave way; but he never summoned the nobility again to meetings of the cortes. The monarchy had won its political victory in Castile only at the cost of letting the nobility contract out of the financial obligations of the state and the empire.

The consequences for Castile were tremendous. Together with the Netherlands, it was Castile which supplied most of the financial needs of Charles V's wars. Government revenue from taxation rose by about fifty per cent during the emperor's reign.[4] During the same period,

4. The pioneer work of Ramón Carande, *Carlos V y sus banqueros*, vol. II (Madrid, 1949), has given us a better picture of Charles V's finances in Castile than we have of any other of his dominions. Leaving aside the revenues which the government obtained from the import of precious metals from Mexico and Peru, the taxes from the clergy and the *cruzada* (sale of ecclesiastical absolutions), and some internal tolls whose yields were either very uncertain or did not increase substantially during the reign,

prices roughly doubled. Since the population was rising, it is clear that the total burden of taxation diminished, rather than increased; but its distribution between the different classes of society changed radically. By far the greater part of ordinary revenue had originally been derived from the *alcabala*, a sales tax paid by all classes, nobles included. At the request of the towns, the *alcabala* had been converted into the *encabezamiento*, a quota payment by each town or village. This quota remained constant, and its real value tended to diminish as prices rose. On the other hand, the yield of the *servicio* rose much more rapidly than prices. The hidalgos, who dominated the town councils and represented the towns in the cortes, willingly voted taxes from which they themselves, as nobles, were exempt. The weight of parliamentary taxation fell entirely on the *pecheros*, the nonprivileged classes. As shown by the index in the table, "Revenues of the Crown of Castile," the money yield of these taxes nearly quadrupled against a mere doubling of prices, and the proportion which they formed of the total burden of taxes in the table rose from 8 to 19 per cent. The crown's alliance with

---

we can construct a table, "Revenues of the Crown of Castile" (in million maravedis):

Type of revenue	Circa 1516		Circa 1553	
	Amount	Index	Amount	Index
Ordinary revenues (mainly *encabezamiento*)	380	100	500	132·8
Maestrazgos (leases of revenues of the estates of the orders of knighthood)	51	100	89	173·7
Servicio (grants by the cortes)	37	100	136	370·0
Totals	468	100	725	155

the nobility was shifting the burden of empire to the shoulders of those least able to bear it.

The emperor's governments in Spain were perfectly aware of this situation. "The common people who have to pay the *servicios*," wrote Prince Philip to the emperor in 1545, "are reduced to such distress and misery that many of them walk naked." The poverty was so universal, he continued, as to extend not only to the emperor's direct vassals but also to those of the nobles to whom they could no longer pay their rents. Yet, the nobles as a class do not seem to have suffered. They were, in most cases, able to raise their rents at least as fast as their prices.[5] Together with the foreign merchants and bankers, they were the chief buyers of *juros*, the life annuities funded on government revenues. When, in 1558–1559, the government sold land and villages belonging to towns on the royal demesne, it was the nobles who bought them.

With the influx of precious metals from America, prices rose more steeply in Spain in the sixteenth century than elsewhere in Europe. The stimulus afforded by this influx of money and by an expanding colonial market might have been expected to promote a rapid economic development. But Spanish agriculture was backward. The armed shepherds of the powerful sheepowners' guild, the Mesta, drove their flocks over hundreds of miles, from upland to lowland, and from lowland to upland pasture, through the whole length of Castile, trampling down cornfields, breaking down fences, and spoiling much cultivated land in a country whose arid soil was, in any case, wretchedly poor

5. Braudel, *La Mediterranée*, II, 53. This view is also supported by Carande in a letter to the author, January 30, 1956.

compared with the soil of England or France. Despite the violent hostility of the landowners, the government upheld the Mesta's privileges, since the Mesta paid generously for them. Much more than in England, it was true in Spain that sheep were eating men, and the dark side of the flourishing Spanish wool exports to Flanders was an impoverished Spanish peasant unable to buy the manufactures of his urban industries. The towns were unable to flourish because of the shortage of agricultural products and the unwillingness of those gaining by the influx of precious metals to invest in trade. Thus the Castilian towns had remained small compared with those of Italy and the Netherlands. Their industries were underdeveloped and unable to compete with foreign industries for the dazzling opportunities of expanding trade. Imperial taxation, falling more and more heavily on the *pecheros*, thus had reached the point, wrote Philip to his father in 1546, where the natives of this kingdom were abstaining from all manner of commerce.

If heavy taxation tended to discourage investment and economic enterprise by the Spanish middle and lower classes, the nobles did not suffer from this handicap. But the inclinations and traditions of grandees and hidalgos, formed in the centuries of struggle against the Moors, made them even more averse to economic activities than the rest of the European nobility. Church and army and, for the hidalgos, the study of law at Salamanca and Alcalá de Henares, followed by a career in the king's service, these offered more attractive opportunities than the ignoble occupations of commerce. The cortes constantly complained of the activities of foreign merchants; but when, in 1552, Philip raised the question of the gradual redemption of the *juros,* then amounting to a capital sum of some 6,200,000 ducats, the holders of the *juros* objected violently; they would not know where else, except in land, to invest their money, and they feared that the price of real property would rise too much.

Thus, to the amazement of foreigners, all the silver from Peru could not make Spain a rich country. American treasure helped to pay for the emperor's wars and made the fortunes of Genoese bankers, but far too little of it was invested in production so as to overcome the country's economic backwardness. As Charles V's empire became more and more a Spanish empire, the economic weakness of Spain became an ever more serious handicap in her struggle with her west European rivals.

It was the smaller and poorer of the emperor's Spanish dominions which resisted most successfully the inroads of centralized government and the pressure of imperial finance. If the Aragonese and Catalans had made greater difficulties than the Castilians in acknowledging Charles as their king, at least they did not rise in revolt against him. Only in Valencia, the one kingdom Charles did not visit during his first Spanish journey, did a revolution break out. At first it was directed, not against royal authority, but against the nobility. While the Valencian nobles were reluctant to do homage to an absent king, the artisans and laborers of the city of Valencia hastened to protest their loyalty. The Valencian populace, already armed and trained to resist the danger of Moorish invasions, now organized in a *Germanía*, a popular Christian brotherhood, directed against the nobles and Moors (1519). Charles could not remain the ally of such a movement; but, as in Castile, he did little more than appoint a Castilian grandee, Diego Hurtado de Mendoza, as governor. For more than eighteen months, the *Germanía* controlled most of the kingdom; but they failed to co-operate with the Comuneros, nor were they able to arouse the sympathy of the lower classes in neighboring Catalonia. Their slaughter and forcible conversions of Moorish tenants on noble estates cut across the class appeal of their revolt without gaining them sympathy from the country nobility or from the clergy. The forces of the *Germanía* leader, Vicente Peris, were defeated by the nobles' troops in October 1521, and Valencia immediately voted in its municipal elections for a return to the lawful authorities; but it was not until 1523 that all resistance outside the capital was finally overcome.

The defeat of the *Germanía* did not, however, affect the older rights and privileges of the kingdoms of the crown of Aragon. The Aragonese nobles ruled over their vassals like kings, having power of high and low justice. In Catalonia they had the right to wage private war. In the cortes they successfully maintained the principle of redress of grievances before supply, "so that it was in the power of a cobbler, smith or suchlike person to hold up everything until he was satisfied." Thus wrote the shocked Venetian ambassador, Contarini.

If in Aragon a person was arrested by royal order, he could put himself under the jurisdiction of the *justicia*, the highest judge of the kingdom who held his appointment for life and therefore was independent of royal pleasure and displeasure. Contarini claimed that Charles had asked the pope to release him from his oath to maintain this particular privilege. But there is no evidence that this step proved effective or that Charles at any time attempted a full-scale attack on the Aragonese and Catalan privileges or freedoms. If the grants of the Aragonese, Catalan, and Valencian cortes were comparatively small and often hedged about with onerous conditions, it was doubtful whether these small kingdoms could be made to pay so much more as to make it worthwhile running the risk of a head-on clash. Moreover, his Aragonese and Catalan subjects had long been accustomed to shouldering imperial responsibilities and, at least for his Mediterranean policies, he found their traditions more helpful than those of the Castilians.

These traditions were the rivalry with Genoa for the trade of the western Mediterranean and with France for the control of southern Italy. In the first half of the sixteenth century, two new problems appeared: the problem of North Africa and the Barbary pirates, and the rise of the Ottoman empire as a naval power. These problems, originally quite separate, became so interwoven during Charles V's reign that they finally resolved themselves into a struggle between the Spanish and the Ottoman empires for the control of the Mediterranean.

The North African problem was largely the result of the Spanish conquest of Granada (1492) and the forcible conversion of the Moors of Castile (1502). Almost for the first time in history the two shores of the western straits of the Mediterranean were now under separate and hostile political control, their commercial and cultural links broken. But, although the Christian reconquest of the Iberian peninsula was now complete, Spain remained a multiracial society, the only one in western and central Europe. Within her borders, the forcibly converted Moriscos were a constant threat, for the African Moors—many of them refugees from Andalusia thirsting for revenge—raided the Spanish coasts and often received help from the Spanish Moriscos. Christian Spain reacted in two ways: by internal assimilation and by external conquest. In 1525 the emperor extended the Castilian edict of forcible conversion to Valencia, and the Inquisition helped him to use it against the "new Christians" of both Muslim and Jewish origin. Externally Spain reacted by the attempt to conquer North Africa. This was the policy of Queen Isabella and Cardinal Ximenes. It was broken off after initial successes because Spanish energies were side-tracked by Aragonese policy in southern Italy.

Until the early 1530's, Spain's problems in the western Mediterranean were still largely separate. The oldest, the Genoese-Catalan rivalry, had been solved by the Spanish-Genoese naval alliance which made Andrea Doria captain general of the emperor's galleys in the Mediterranean and which sealed Genoese commercial supremacy over Catalonia. In the meantime, however, Spain's failure to complete her North African conquests had brought a bitter revenge. In 1516 the Moorish rulers of Algiers called on the pirate brothers Barbarossa to capture from the Spaniards the Peñon, the fortified rock at the harbor entrance.

It took Khair ad-Din Barbarossa thirteen years to achieve this aim; but, long before, he made himself master of Algiers and acknowledged himself the vassal of the sultan at Constantinople. For the first time in centuries, the Christians were faced by a really powerful hostile naval force in the western Mediterranean, a force whose raids were a constant terror to the small coastal villages and towns of Spain and Italy. Worse was to follow. As a counterstroke to Doria's capture of Coron in the Morea (1532), the sultan appointed Khair ad-Din Barbarossa pasha and grand admiral of the whole Turkish fleet. With more than one hundred ships, he ravaged the coasts of southern Italy in 1534 and then threw his forces against Tunis and expelled its Moorish king, an ally of Spain.

The emperor's Italian provinces were now seriously threatened, not only by pirates but by the full naval strength of the immensely powerful rival empire of the Turks. Effectively, it became a struggle for the control of the central Mediterranean; under Spanish domination, it would protect Sicily and cut off Barbarossa from Constantinople; under Turkish domination, it would keep the Muslim forces united and open the road to attacks on Italy and the western Mediterranean. Concentrating all his forces for the first time and leading his troops in person, Charles conquered La Goletta and Tunis in 1535. It was perhaps his greatest personal triumph, his vindication as a Christian knight and crusader. But Barbarossa was not crushed. Within weeks he retaliated by raiding Port Mahon in Minorca. More serious still was Doria's defeat at Prevesa, in September 1538, caused largely by distrust between the allied imperial and Venetian fleets. The Prevesa campaign had been the one serious attempt by the imperialists to carry the war into the eastern Mediterranean. There can be no doubt that this was the emperor's ultimate aim, with the conquest of Constantinople as the final prize. In August 1538, Mary wrote in great alarm from the Netherlands to dissuade her brother from his grandiose plans. The difficulties of operating over such distances were enormous, she argued; France, only recently reconciled, was quite unreliable; the pope and the Venetians would give little help; they risked little, while the emperor alone risked irremediable loss; his dominions needed peace above all, not further adventures. After Prevesa, Mary's views prevailed and the emperor's offensive actions had strictly limited objectives. Even these were often unattainable, as the disastrous failure of the emperor's own expedition against Algiers demonstrated in 1541.

The Turks, for their part, also made only one serious attempt, during the emperor's reign, to penetrate in force into the western Mediterranean. This was in 1543. The Franco-Turkish alliance, discussed as early as 1525 and openly acknowledged in the 1530's, was potentially the most deadly danger the emperor had to face in the Mediterranean. Yet the Turks did not follow up their 1543–1544 expedition. Even with French bases available to them, the distances were too enormous; the hazards of operating more than a thousand miles from the home base were as great for the sultan as they were for the emperor. The Spaniards completely failed to conquer a North African empire. Compared with the Indies, or even with Italy,

North Africa offered few attractions to Spanish soldiers in search of plunder. Economically, the Spanish strong points were a liability. The Venetians and other traders to the Barbary Coast preferred the Moorish ports. The Spaniards kept up their North African garrisons purely for strategic reasons. Yet they substantially maintained their naval supremacy in the western Mediterranean basin. The Turkish bases were too far from the heart of the Christian Mediterranean to challenge this.

Warfare and taxation: Italy

In sharp contrast to the deterioration of Spain's position in North Africa was her successful defense of the Aragonese empire in Italy against France. Sicily, the oldest Italian dominion of the crown of Aragon, was indeed never seriously threatened. As in Aragon itself, the emperor here succeeded to a small and relatively poor country whose estates enjoyed the most far-reaching privileges. In the Sicilian parliament, clergy, nobles, and towns had defended these privileges successfully against the encroachments of Spanish viceroys. At the very beginning of the reign, in 1516, they rose against a hated viceroy, Hugo de Moncada, and forced him to flee from Palermo. The nobles who led the rising protested their loyalty to Charles, and their envoys at Brussels obtained at least the replacement of Moncada by another viceroy, a Neapolitan, the duke of Monteleone. But, when neither Charles nor Monteleone showed any sign of revoking Moncada's unpopular edicts, a new rising broke out in 1517. This time it was led by members of the Palermo bourgeoisie, and it spread through most of the island. Amid murder and pillage, it soon became a social revolt against the nobility. The nobles reacted by assassinating the leader of the movement in Palermo and when, six months later, Spanish troops arrived, the situation was already under control.

Unlike the revolt of the Comuneros, the Sicilian revolts of 1516 and 1517 (and an abortive conspiracy of nobles in 1523) had little effect on the balance of political power. The Sicilian nobles and towns were fundamentally loyal to the crown of Aragon. They cherished the memory of the Sicilian Vespers of 1282, their one supreme assertion of national will; but, as the spirit of national unity disappeared in bitter party feuds and in the rivalry of Palermo and Messina, the Sicilians lost almost completely their capacity for united action. Whereas in the Netherlands the defense of sectional liberties and privileges led eventually to a revolution against the centralizing policy of the hispanicized monarchy, in Sicily the similar interests of nobles and towns only led to more internal wrangles and feuds. For, as in Aragon and Catalonia, the monarchy made no serious attempt to interfere with the country's privileges. Hampered in every action by these privileges and inadequately supported from Spain, successive viceroys fought a losing battle against the proverbial corruption of Sicilian officials, the venality of the Sicilian courts, the blood feuds of the barons, and the ubiquitous bandits who were often, like the modern Mafia, protected by the local nobility. No longer, as in the fourteenth century, could the noble factions plunge the whole country into civil war; but they and their armed retainers still attacked each other's castles and cities, and their feuds had to be settled by regular peace treaties, guaranteed by the viceroy.

Finance was the key to the government's policy, as it was throughout the emperor's dominions. After centuries of external peace, Sicily was now threatened with invasion by the Turks. Charles V's last two viceroys, Ferrante Gonzaga (1535–1546) and Juan de Vega (1547–1557), had to construct completely new coastal defenses, maintain the Sicilian squadron of ten galleys and the *tercio* of Spanish infantry in the country, and train a native militia to beat off Moorish raids. These raids made the Sicilians appreciate the naval protection which Spanish rule provided against worse calamities. But parliament increased its "donative" from an annual average of 100,000 scudi to only about 175,000 during the emperor's reign, a period when general prices rose in at least the same proportion. Apart from Aragon and Catalonia, Sicily remained the most lightly taxed of the emperor's kingdoms. When he abdicated, a new proverb became current in Italy: "In Sicily the Spaniards nibble, in Naples they eat and in Milan they devour."

The financial problems of Charles V's government in Naples were, indeed, relatively easier than in most of his other dominions. The kingdom's parliament was incomparably weaker than that of Sicily. The city of Naples itself had no vote in the granting of the donative; though it sent its deputies to the assemblies, it had its own representative institutions for this purpose. The clergy were not represented at all, and the nobles were too sharply divided into an Aragonese and an Angevin faction ever to have seriously thought of making parliament into an instrument of their political aspirations. There was no question of demanding redress of grievances before supply; the emperor and his viceroys dealt with petitions entirely as they thought fit. Thus Charles could draw large sums from the kingdom and send them abroad: 1,750,000 ducats between 1525 and 1529 for the imperial armies in northern Italy; 300,000 for his coronation, in 1530; 150,000 in 1543 and 175,000 in the following year, with another half million ducats in 1552—all sent to Milan and Germany. But there were limits to what even the strongest of the emperor's viceroys could screw out of the country. Repeatedly, the viceroy, Pedro de Toledo, refused imperial requests for money or declined to accept bills of exchange drawn on his government. The communes had anticipated two hundred and fifty thousand ducats on future taxes, he wrote in 1540; to do more would be expecting "to squeeze juice from a stone." With the increasing urgency of the Turkish menace, the cost of defense was rising steeply. From about 1530, the emperor had to help with Spanish money. But, if the coasts of Apulia and Calabria suffered at times from Khair ad-Din's raids, the Neapolitans were as conscious as the Sicilians of the protection afforded them by Doria's galleys.

There were, however, good political reasons for not exasperating the Neapolitans too far. The old feud between Aragonese and Angevins did indeed make co-operation of all nobles against the government impossible. The Aragonese faction had received much land confiscated from those who had supported Lautrec's invasion of 1528.

Many more estates had been given to Spanish and Genoese supporters of the emperor who settled in the kingdom and intermarried with the Neapolitan nobility. All these were loyal; yet they and the Neapolitan towns were as proud as the Sicilians of their voluntary allegiance; they prized their privileges just as highly; their wealth and the authority they wielded over their estates were perhaps even greater. The barons imposed arbitrary taxes on their vassals and prevented them from appealing to the royal courts. The very judges of these courts were subject to their pressure if they came from baronial territory. A revolt by even one of these lords could be dangerous, as the prince of Salerno demonstrated in 1552 when he tried to bring the French and the Turks into the kingdom at the most critical moment of the emperor's reign.

It was therefore both politic and just that the crown should take a stand against these excessive powers of the nobility. The protection of the poor and the weak against the rich and the powerful became the keynote of the instructions which Charles V gave to Pedro de Toledo in 1536. He had appointed this Castilian grandee in 1532 to rebuild a country ravaged by French and imperial troops, and to clear up the legacy of oppression and injustice left by a long period of weak government. A rapid succession of short-lived viceroys, some of whom, like the Netherlander Lannoy, did not even pretend to understand Neapolitan conditions, had been quite incapable of dealing with corrupt royal officials, tyrannous barons, and bandits protected by great lords. For twenty-one years, Toledo battled against these evils by edicts and executions. His success was very limited. Eighteen thousand persons had been condemned to death during his viceroyalty, he told the Florentine ambassador in 1550, and he did not know what more he could do. The instructions to his successor, in 1559, paint a picture of conditions in the kingdom almost as dark as those of 1536.

But Toledo's policy succeeded in keeping nobles and people divided. Only once did they combine, and immediately imperial rule in Naples was in the gravest danger. In 1547 Charles V wanted to introduce the Spanish Inquisition into Naples. In Sicily it had already been introduced by Ferdinand the Catholic and had, at first, been very unpopular. In 1516 the Palermitans chased the Inquisitors from their city together with the viceroy. Only toward the end of the emperor's reign did it become more popular through the immunities from royal jurisdiction which it offered to its thousands of lay familiars. The Neapolitans reacted even more violently than the Sicilians. False testimony was so common, they said, that the secret procedure of the Inquisition would lead to the destruction of all honest persons, and the emperor was only introducing it as a means to get hold of their property. Nobles and burghers of the city of Naples formed a union; the *seggi*, their representative assemblies, took over the city government; there were clashes with Spanish troops and the viceroy's warships fired on the city. Soon it was rumored that the "union" was negotiating with the French. Finally, Toledo offered the withdrawal of the Inquisition as a special favor granted to the burghers rather than to the city as a whole; enmity between burghers and nobles was a safer foundation for Spanish rule, he judged, than the Inquisition. In Naples, the very privileges of the nobility and their strength in local government redounded to the advantage of the viceroy; for much of the popular hatred of foreign rule was diverted to the native nobility. As a result, and despite the Neapolitan mob's taste for rioting, Naples remained, on the whole, a contented part of Charles V's empire.

In Sicily and Naples, Charles V was hereditary king; in Milan he had no such rights. When the last Sforza duke, Francesco II, died in 1535, imperial troops under the marquis del Vasto were already in control of the duchy; but for years the emperor was uncertain how to settle the succession. During the negotiations with France, the cession of either Milan or the Netherlands to a younger son of Francis I was discussed in the imperialist camp. Charles himself and his Burgundian councilors, notably Granvelle, wanted to keep the Netherlands and give up Milan. Castilian nationalists, such as Archbishop Tavera of Toledo, supported this view, both from a dislike of Spanish entanglements in Italy and from the dislike of giving up a hereditary dominion in favor of a conquered one. But the majority of Spaniards, such as the duke of Alva, and the Hispano-Italians insisted on the retention of Milan as the key to Spanish power in Italy.[6] In the end, the Netherlands were not given up and Milan was successfully defended. But, in practice, the Spanish party had won. Prince Philip was invested with the duchy (1546); its affairs in the emporor's councils were entrusted to Cobos;

6. F. Chabod, *Lo stato di Milano*, pp. 39 ff.

the command of its fortresses was given to Spaniards or Neapolitans. Milan become a military outpost of Spain.

The Spaniards did not materially change the administration of the country by its traditional authorities, any more than they did in Sicily and Naples. The Milanese nobility were relatively poor and politically weak through their division into the Guelph and Ghibelline factions. Hence, where in Sicily and Naples the viceroys' powers were limited and counterbalanced by the surviving powers of old feudal institutions, in Milan the powers of the governor general were similarly limited and counterbalanced by a more modern, semiautonomous civil service, consisting of the senate and the professional city administrations it supervised. Only at his peril could the governor general quarrel with the senate, as Ferrante Gonzaga found in 1554 when the senate induced the emperor to send an investigating commission to Milan and to recall his governor general.

Senate and city magistrates might limit the governor general's administrative authority; unlike the Sicilian parliament, they could not limit his powers to raise taxes. The large imperial army in Lombardy had to be paid, and it had the power to see that its pay was forthcoming. The protests of the towns, and even of the civilian governor general, Cardinal Caraccioli, were ineffective against the halberds of del Vasto's *Landsknechte*. After Caraccioli's death in 1538, del Vasto combined the two offices of governor and captain general (1538–1546), as did Ferrante Gonzaga after him (1546–1554). The Spaniards could now impose taxes at will, subject only to the fear of a rebellion in the duchy, with the immediate danger of renewed French intervention.

Yet, if the Spaniards "devoured" in Milan, Milan also devoured Spain. In 1535 Granvelle had hoped that the duchy would pay not only for its own defense, but would contribute to imperial expenses. The disillusionment was rapid. Seven Perus would not suffice to meet all the emperor's needs in Lombardy, wrote the Spanish ambassador in Genoa in 1537. Four decades of war had left a terrible legacy of poverty and ruin. In the war years of 1536–1538 Spain had to send more than a million ducats for the army in Lombardy, while Milan paid some six hundred thousand. In the last five years of the emperor's reign, Spain equaled the Milanese defense contribution of about two million ducats. The cost of the Spanish garrison left the government of Milan with an almost permanent deficit. The duchy itself, however, recovered under the peace which Spanish rule finally provided. In the second half of the sixteenth century, its population increased and vigorous reconstruction of its cities and industries gave Lombardy another fifty years of prosperity before the disasters of the seventeenth century.

The Empire and the imperial succession

It was his election as king of Germany which had given Charles V his right to the imperial title and with it the moral justification to pursue his imperial policy. It was in Germany that, in the end, his imperial policy met with the most complete and irretrievable disaster. Charles kept his promise to his younger brother, Ferdinand. He made over to him all his rights to his hereditary dominions in Germany (1521–1522) and also appointed him head of the *Reichsregiment*, the imperial government of Germany. In 1531, after his own coronation by the pope, Charles induced the electors to elect Ferdinand king of the Romans. Charles must have known that this step gravely prejudiced the prospects of his own son, Philip, to succeed him as emperor and that it even prejudiced the future existence of the combined power of the house of Habsburg. But Philip was only four years old. If Charles himself died prematurely—and his many wills and testaments show that he always bore this contingency in mind—it was essential to have a successor who would defend both the Habsburg claims in the Empire and the child Philip's rights in the Netherlands, Spain, and Italy. Most important of all, Charles needed the strongest possible representative in Germany. "At that time there were so many difficulties and intrigues with the electors," he wrote later in his memoirs, "that the emperor, seeing that the great kingdoms which God had given him prevented him from residing as much in the Empire as he desired, arranged to have the king, his brother, elected as king of the Romans." In his instructions to Ferdinand in 1531, Charles allowed him much wider powers than any of his viceroys or governors. But he demanded to be consulted over the bestowal of high noble titles, and he insisted that his own appointments should be maintained and all his commands observed. In practice, therefore, Charles continued to control imperial policy in Germany.

The crux of the German problem was the alliance of

Luther's reform movement with a number of the German princes. For more than twenty years Charles tried to minimize the importance of this alliance and to solve the religious question within the framework of a general reform of the Church. He changed his policy only when these attempts had definitely failed and when the Schmalkaldic League of Protestant estates began to intrigue with France. Still striving to keep the religious and the political problems apart, he struck at the Protestant princes, ostensibly as rebels against imperial authority, in order to deprive the reform movement of its political backing. His victory at Mühlberg was to have provided the basis for a solution of both the political and the religious problems of Germany. In fact, it solved neither. The Council of Trent and Bologna was the pope's council and remained unacceptable to the Protestants. The German princes, Protestant and Catholic alike, were more unwilling than ever to increase the constitutional powers of the emperor by a thorough reform of the imperial constitution. Despite his victory and immense prestige, Charles was not strong enough to coerce all the princes. He tried to bypass the problem by proposing a league of princes with the emperor at its head, in which each member was to pay a fixed contribution for a league army. The idea was not new. In 1519 the Swabian League, of which Charles was captain by virtue of his Austrian and South German possessions, had expelled the francophile duke of Württemberg from his duchy. The army of the league had been a most useful asset to Charles during the imperial election campaign and, in 1520, it had enabled him to acquire Württemberg. He did his utmost to keep the Swabian League in being; but since, in the eyes of the German estates, his power was dangerously great already, they were unwilling to continue it. On several occasions before the Schmalkaldic War, the emperor returned to the idea of forming a league, but never with more than partial success. His more comprehensive scheme in the autumn of 1547 fared no better. The Empire "would be reduced to servitude," said the elector of Brandenburg, and the princes rejected the scheme.

The failure of this plan precipitated the crisis over the imperial succession. Philip was now a man. The war against the Protestants had shown that only with the help of money and troops from Spain and the Netherlands could the emperor uphold his authority in the Empire. More than ever, Charles was convinced of the correctness of his analysis of 1519. There is no direct proof that in the winter of 1546–1547 he contemplated asking his brother to resign his title of king of the Romans in favor of Philip; but Ferdinand's extremely sharp reaction to rumors of such an intention leaves little doubt that this was the ideal solution that Charles was contemplating. Ferdinand's attitude and that of his son, Maximilian, and the extreme hostility of the Germans to the idea of a "Spanish succession," induced Charles to give up the idea. In acrimonious debates between the senior members of the Habsburg family, a compromise was finally arrived at, in 1551. Ferdinand was to remain king of the Romans and succeed Charles to the imperial title, but was himself to be succeeded by Philip, with Maximilian succeeding Philip in his turn.

Neither side was satisfied and, for the first time, the unity of the Habsburg family was seriously impaired. In 1552 Maurice of Saxony and other German princes, in alliance with Henry II to whom they promised Metz, Toul, and Verdun, attacked Charles and forced him to flee from Innsbruck for his life. Their success was at least partly due to the equivocal attitude of Ferdinand. The flight from Innsbruck and the Treaty of Passau with the rebellious princes undid the results of Mühlberg. The virtual collapse of his authority in Germany, together with his failure to retake Metz from the French (winter of 1552–1553) convinced him that his imperial program, as he had conceived it in 1519, had failed. The Church had not been reformed in such a way as to bring the Protestants back into the fold; neither had the Protestants been finally crushed by force of arms. Italy was secure, but France remained as threatening as ever and, so far from joining in a crusade, was the ally of the infidel. The Empire remained intractable, and the next emperor, while still enjoying the alliance of the Spanish-Burgundian branch of the house of Habsburg, would no longer himself dispose of its full powers. His position would, inevitably, be much weaker than that of Charles; his interests would be purely central European. Charles V's abdication, in 1555–1556, was his own recognition of the failure of his imperial idea, the failure of the last attempt to re-establish the medieval concept of Christian unity under the leadership of emperor and pope.

Charles himself retired to a country palace built against the monastery of San Jeronimo de Yuste in Estremadura. There he held court and continued, amid his devotions, to take a lively and often active interest in the fortunes of his empire until his death in 1558. For the empire itself did not break up with his abdication. Its nature, however, was already beginning to change. From a universal, Christian empire, with a Burgundian core and inspiration, it was becoming a Spanish, Catholic empire with a Castilian core and inspiration. The inadequacy of the all-imperial administration was one of the weaknesses of Charles V's empire. But the old Aragonese empire possessed at least the rudiments of an imperial administration in the Council of Aragon, the supreme court for the realms of the crown of Aragon in Spain and Italy. The Council of the Indies, for the Castilian overseas empire, functioned in a similar way, but with much wider competence in administrative and political matters. It was on these models that, in 1558, Philip II founded the Council of Italy. This provided Spain and her Italian dominions with a much closer administrative integration than any other group of states had possessed since Roman times.

The Netherlands were economically the most advanced and wealthiest of the emperor's possessions. "These are the treasures of the king of Spain, these his mines, these his Indies which have sustained all the emperor's enterprises," wrote the Venetian Soriano in 1559. But even as he wrote, it was no longer true. Against the greater wealth of the Netherlands, Spain provided its rulers more willingly with money. From about the middle of the century, the flow of American silver to Spain increased rapidly beyond all previous expectations. The wars in Italy and Germany showed more and more clearly the superiority of Spanish

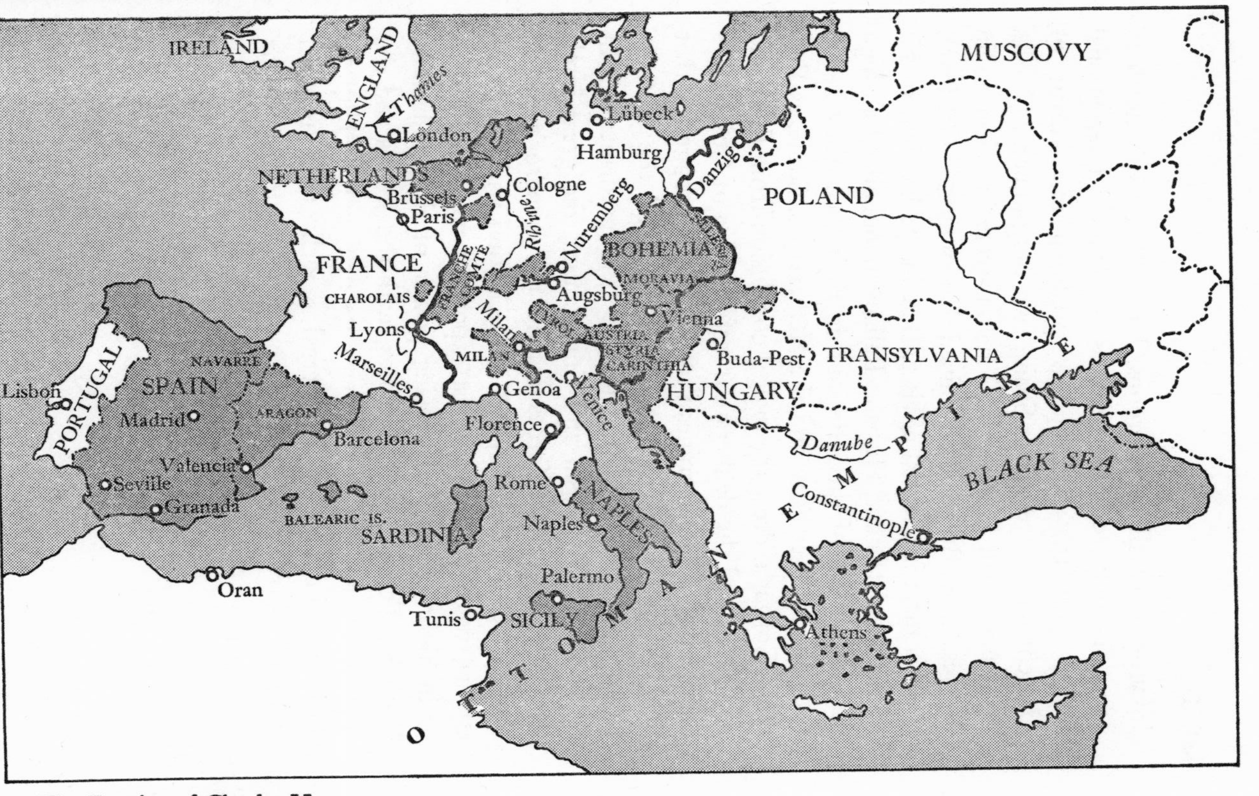

The Empire of Charles V.

infantry over all other troops. Until Gattinara's death in 1530, the emperor's council was a genuinely international body, with the Burgundians predominant. Adrian of Utrecht was his regent in Spain; two Burgundians, Charles de Lannoy and Philibert de Chalon, were his viceroys in Naples. The Burgundian-trained Piedmontese, Gattinara, was his most influential adviser. But, in the last half of his reign, Spaniards and Hispano-Italians monopolized all high positions south of the Alps and, in their turn, they began to appear in Germany and the Netherlands. Some, as Ferrante Gonzaga, drew the logical conclusion from this trend and advocated the deliberate transformation of Charles V's empire into a Mediterranean monarchy. He suggested that Spain should withdraw from Germany and the Netherlands, neither of which could be held permanently. In Spain itself, Illuminism and Erasmianism, the great intellectual and spiritual forces behind the emperor's earlier vision of Church reform and reconciliation with the Protestants, were dying; their last exponents were imprisoned or in flight before the growing power of the Inquisition. With St. Teresa and St. Ignatius, with the Jesuits and the Inquisition, and above all, with its new king, Philip II, Spain now became the intellectual as well as the financial and military spearhead of the Counter-Reformation in the age of the wars of religion.

II

Western Europe and the Power of Spain

THE TREATY OF Cateau-Cambrésis (April 2–3, 1559) was a belated recognition of the end of the imperial plans of the late emperor Charles V. The last phase of the war between Habsburg and Valois had been precipitated by the octogenarian Pope Paul IV in his hatred of Spanish dominion in Italy. The principal combatants had fought it almost unwillingly, but the struggle had been as bitter as it was inconclusive and even more costly than previous wars. Now a new era was to dawn with the marriage of Philip II to Henry II's daughter, Elizabeth.

O Paix, fille de Dieu, qui nous viens réjouir
Comme l'aube du jour . . .
Et joindre étroitement l'Espagne avec la France
D'un nœud qui pour jamais en amour s'entretient . . .

sang the poet Ronsard.

The change was even greater than men realized at the time. In less than ten years from the abdication of Charles V

(1555–1556), all political problems moved on to a completely different plane. Until the middle of the sixteenth century, the Reformation had been successful only where it had been allied with the state. When it became revolutionary, as it did in the German Peasants' War and in the Anabaptist movements of the Netherlands and northern Germany, it had been easily put down, because it had been supported only by the lower classes in town and country. Now, for the first time and quite suddenly, revolutionary movements became nationwide and included classes, or elements of classes, ranging from artisans to princes of the blood. Determined minorities tried to impose their views on whole countries. They had to build organized parties to match the power of the state. They either acted through a parliament or assembly of estates, or else, at one time or another, they became openly revolutionary. Only religious belief, held either from fanatical conviction or political expediency, could bring together the divergent interests of nobles, burghers, and peasants throughout the whole kingdoms. Thus it was with the Huguenots and the Holy League in France, with the Calvinists and Sea Beggars (*gueux de mer*) in the Netherlands, and with Knox's "brethren" and the Lords of the Congregation in Scotland. After the third session of the Council of Trent, with its clear definitions of Catholic dogma and of heresy, only those excessively optimistic, or as obtuse in matters of religion as Catherine de Medici, could still believe that Catholic and Protestant views might yet be reconciled. Two alternatives remained: toleration or annihilation of the opposition. For a long time neither side was prepared to accept the first alternative.

At the moment when these formidable forces were beginning to emerge, the governments of western Europe were themselves overtaken by a severe crisis. The long wars between Charles V and his opponents had overstrained the resources of their governments. While the economic life of western Europe was expanding, that part of it which could be touched by taxation had been overburdened. The fall in the value of money had reduced the value of government revenues and had at the same time pushed expenditure to unprecedented figures. In five years the Netherlands had paid eight million ducats for the war, and Castile eleven million in three years. Both the Spanish and the Netherlands governments went bankrupt in 1557, forcibly reducing interest payment on all their debts to 5 per cent. A few months later, the French government was compelled to follow suit. These crises caused the first big international banking crash. Antwerp and Lyons were hardest hit, but Augsburg, Genoa, and Florence did not escape disaster. With credit difficult to obtain and expensive, governments had to look for new sources of revenue. In the Netherlands these could be obtained only through grants by the estates. Ruler and subjects alike looked to Spain for relief; but when Philip II returned to Madrid in 1559, he found that the financial situation there was even worse than in Brussels. It soon became apparent that in France, too, the crown could not increase taxes further without the consent of its subjects. As so often in the history of the *ancien régime*, financial crisis led to political crisis. The clash between the ruler's demands for money and the unwillingness of his subjects to pay opened up the whole problem of political power.

Firm and experienced leadership was now essential. But in France and the Netherlands it disappeared at this very moment. In both countries the government passed into the hands of women, as it had already done in England and Scotland a few years earlier. In a political society whose ethos was masculine and military, and whose habits of loyalty were still to the person of the sovereign, the "monstrous regiment of women" made the political crisis all but unmanageable. Only Elizabeth I overcame it, and she had the immense advantage over Catherine de Medici and Margaret of Parma of being a reigning sovereign in her own right.[1]

The crisis of the governments of western Europe was bound to affect international relations. The old rivalries did not die with Charles V and Henry II. France still had a foothold in Italy through her occupation of Saluzzo and five Piedmontese fortresses. At any moment she could threaten Spanish predominance in the peninsula and, as before, she would not lack Italian allies. Her old border quarrels with the Netherlands were dormant, not settled. Both Spain and France had their allies and clients among the German princes. England had not forgotten nor forgiven the loss of Calais. More serious still, neither the English nor the Scottish government appeared to be stable. Both France and Spain might intervene and seriously upset the balance of power in western Europe. These were the bare bones of the Habsburg–Valois struggle, stripped of

1. So was Mary Queen of Scots; but much of the damage to the authority of the Scottish crown had been done during the regency of her mother, Mary of Guise.

the idealistic motives of Gattinara and Charles V. Ministers and ambassadors saw them as such and were under no illusions. But few had the strength of mind to follow consistently the austere logic of reason of state. They and their sovereigns were not immune from the religious emotions which dominated their subjects. They were convinced that their religious opponents were moved by purely material and political considerations, and these convictions have misled some modern historians. But they were equally convinced of the honesty of their own religious convictions as a motive force for their politics, and of no one was this more true than of Philip II. In practice, therefore, the springs of political motivation were muddy and policies were not pursued consistently. The national rivalries of the great powers became entangled in the social, political, and religious struggles within the different states and in the international patterns of religious loyalties. France, the Netherlands, England, and Scotland, all had "fifth columns" within their boundaries—a deadly weakness which Charles V, Francis I, and Henry VIII never had to face, despite occasional rebellions against their rule. Thus, for more than twenty years, the great powers shrank from open war, though they were often on the brink. The internal weakness of France seemed to present Philip II with the opportunity for which his father, the emperor Charles V, had striven all his life in vain: the alliance of the Catholic powers, under the leadership of the Habsburgs, against the enemies of Catholic Christendom. If, later, William of Orange overdramatized the Habsburg–Valois marriage alliance of 1559 into a conspiracy of the kings of Spain and France against the religious liberties of their subjects, he was at least correct in his appreciation of Philip II's religious policy. But the weakness of France depended precisely on these enemies of Catholic Christendom, the Protestants, who were such a deadly danger to Philip's own authority. Philip II never managed to resolve completely the ambiguity of his aims of keeping France both weak and Catholic, and this ambiguity accounts for much of his tortuous policy during the French Wars of Religion.

Spain still had to face the external enemy of Christendom, the Ottoman Turk. Philip II was the only western ruler who, in the twenty years after Cateau-Cambrésis, was still fighting a major war. He might persuade the French crown to co-operate with him against the Protestants. He could never persuade it to help him against the Turks. The Turks, moreover, had their own potential allies inside Spain, the Moriscos. If the Moslem "fifth column" could never hope to capture the whole country, as the Huguenots and Sea Beggars might, yet in alliance with the greatest naval and military power of the time they might still be a terrible danger. The political crisis in Spain was therefore only little less severe than in the other countries of western Europe.

Spain

Charles V had failed to secure the imperial succession for his son. But the fact of empire was not changed by this failure. Philip II still ruled over Spain and her dependencies in Italy, Franche-Comté, the Netherlands, and the

Indies. These had been the main sources of Charles V's imperial strength, of his money, and his soldiers. Materially, at least, it was to Philip's advantage to disengage Spanish policy from the problems of central Europe while, at the same time, keeping on amicable terms with his uncle and cousins of the Austrian branch of the Habsburg family. His marriage to Mary I of England (1554) was the logical complement to such a policy, and even after Mary's death (1558), it was not immediately obvious that England would not remain, or become again, a Habsburg satellite. But the absence of the imperial title raised its own difficulties about the nature of Philip II's empire. Charles V's views of the transcendental nature of his position and of his destiny to create a Christian world monarchy had depended on this title. What was left for Philip II was another part of his father's mission, the defense of the Catholic Church. "You may assure His Holiness," Philip wrote to his ambassador in Rome in 1566, "that rather than suffer the least damage to religion and the service of God, I would lose all my states and an hundred lives, if I had them; for I do not propose nor desire to be the ruler of heretics." Even the popes, however, found it sometimes difficult to distinguish between Philip's views as to what was the service of God and what the service of the Spanish monarchy.

This formulation of purpose still left out the empire itself. Neither Philip nor any of his contemporaries ever worked out a comprehensive theory of empire to take the place of the now outlived ideas of Charles V's time. In America the Spaniards had conquered and converted heathen populations. Spanish theologians and jurists debated their rights and those of the conquerors, and the Spanish government codified them as laws. But in Christian Europe, Philip himself, and almost everyone else, saw in his empire only a *monarchia*, a collection of states under one ruler. From the latter part of Charles V's reign, it had become more and more a Spanish empire. Philip's succession gave Spain and Castile an even greater predominance; for Philip spoke only Castilian, fixed his residence in Castile, and preferred Castilians to all his other subjects in positions of power.

Inevitably, the Castilians came to regard themselves as the rulers of the empire, though they were well aware of the growing hostility of other nations. The marquis of Ayamonte, governor of Milan, wrote to Philip (February 2, 1570): "I do not know whether there is anyone in the world who is subject to the Spanish nation and empire and who is devoted to them, but does not rather abhor their name." This, he added, was especially true of the Italians. His view was endorsed by an unsigned comment scribbled on the letter: "For these Italians, though they are not Indians, have to be treated as such, so that they understand that we are in charge of them and not they in charge of us." A typical note of a master race.

In practice, however, Philip's empire could not be run in quite this way. Philip, like his father, rested his claims to the sovereignty over his different dominions on the laws of these states. When Bernardino de Mendoza, his ambassador in France, tried to reassure the French about a possible Spanish succession to the crown of France after the death of Henry III, he likened Philip's monarchy to one of the great monastic orders which were under one head, but in which no one nation commanded another. Such advances as there were in imperial unification were made to meet the demands of defense and of a more efficient administration, not as the result of any advance in imperial ideas. Thus the Spaniards kept a tight hold on all important military positions in their Italian dominions. The captaincies of the local militia and of the feudal levies were generally reserved to natives, for it was Philip's policy to keep the Italian nobility contented. But only Spaniards commanded the regular *tercios* and the castles and fortresses. The greatest administrative advance in imperial unity was the creation of the Council of Italy in 1558. Philip did not want to see the old Aragonese empire continue as a separate structure within his possessions. It was compromised, in his eyes, by its Catalan traditions. Its supreme organ, the Council of Aragon, was staffed by Aragonese, Catalans, and Valencianos. The new council, with its mixed Castilian and Italian personnel, was to act as supreme court for Sicily, Naples, and Milan, and as their administrative link with Madrid. Formally, at least, it was a striking advance over Charles V's system. No other European government was now as well informed about its dependencies, nor able to supervise their administrations with such attention to detail and such concern for the welfare of its subjects. Yet its councilors were nearly always mediocrities, with little understanding of imperial problems. All important political decisions continued to rest with the king and his closest advisers. Philip did not set up a Council of Flanders until 1588, although the Netherlanders petitioned for it as early as 1574. It does not appear to have been very effective. The same was probably true for the Council of Portugal, founded in 1582–1583. Even the administrative advance in imperial unity therefore remained a very partial one.

The most effective link between the center of the empire and its members remained the system of weekly, sometimes daily, correspondence between the king and his secretaries, on the one hand, and the viceroys and governors, on the other. Changes from Charles V's system of personal control were the result less of organizational advance than of changes in personnel. Philip II was less fortunate than his father, who had been able to appoint loyal and capable members of the Habsburg family to rule his dominions in his absence. Like the great merchant houses, the Habsburgs were beginning to suffer from the "problem of the third generation." Philip's half-sister, Margaret of Parma, proved herself loyal and not unintelligent, as governor general of the Netherlands. But she lacked the political insight of her aunt, Mary of Hungary, who had held the same position for Charles V. Philip's half-brother, Don John of Austria, was still too young for office when Philip succeeded to the throne. His brilliant though erratic gifts later gave the king his greatest triumph, the victory of Lepanto. But Don John was a failure as governor general of the Netherlands and his early death, at 31, may have saved him from disgrace at court. Philip tried to make use of his Austrian relatives by carefully bringing up several of the young archdukes at his court. They proved loyal, but of such depressing mediocrity that their political services consisted in little more than the fading magic of their imperial names.

The king's most terrible disappointments were his own sons. Don Carlos (born 1545), child of Philip's consanguineous first marriage with Mary of Portugal, showed early signs of mental instability, perhaps the legacy of Joanna the Mad which he inherited through both his parents. His tragic death has provided generations of historians, dramatists, and librettists with splendidly romantic plots, especially about the prince's supposed love for his young stepmother, Elizabeth of Valois.[2] The truth is more simple. For years Philip tried to induce Carlos to take a responsible interest in affairs of state. Eventually he had to admit that the prince's criminal paranoia, his murderous rages, his physical assaults on the citizens of Madrid and the king's councilors, and his treasonable contacts with the rebels in the Netherlands rendered him unfit for any authority and a danger to the state. On January 18, 1568, he arrested him. He could do no less if he was to fulfil his duties as a Christian prince to his subjects. Thus he wrote to his sister, the empress, and the agony of a father speaks through the stilted prose of a king. Six months later, Carlos was dead. There is no evidence that he was murdered, by Philip's orders or otherwise, though within a few days suspicions were whispered in the court itself.

Philip's only surviving son, the later Philip III, was not mad. But the old king was rightly under no illusions as to

2. Thus especially Schiller, and Verdi's librettists J. Méry and C. du Locle.

his abilities. The one outstanding member of Philip's family and his only successful governor general of the Netherlands was Margaret of Parma's son, Alexander Farnese. His career, as that of Don John, was to show the greatest weakness in Philip's own character, his almost pathological suspiciousness and duplicity.

Philip therefore had to fall back on the Spanish and Italian high nobility to fill his viceroyalties and governorships. He could employ lawyers, ecclesiastics, and professional administrators in his councils and as secretaries of state and, in general, he preferred to do so, just as his father had done. In the viceroyalties and military commands, this was not possible. The native nobility hated the men of the long robe. "They do not know what it is to be a king," wrote Juan de Vega, viceroy of Sicily, "nor wherein lies the greatness and authority of monarchy . . . nor of chivalry and honor." The Castilian grandees, naturally, had the lion's share of these appointments. Six of Philip's nine viceroys of Sicily were Spaniards; so were all of his viceroys of Naples, with the single exception of Granvelle, and ten out of thirteen of his governors of Milan. In the viceroyalties of Aragon, Catalonia, Valencia, and Navarre, and in the captain-generalcy of Granada, the question of appointing non-Spaniards did not arise at all. The days of Adrian of Utrecht were long since past. But for the old Italian nobility, too, there were still splendid prizes if they chose the service of the Catholic king. Gian Andrea Doria was commander in chief of the king's Mediterranean fleet. The marquis of Pescara and Marc Antonio Colonna were viceroys of Sicily. So was the duke of Terranova, who also became a grandee of Spain and governor of Milan. Alexander Farnese was governor general of the Netherlands and, in Philip III's reign, Ambrogio Spinola was commander in chief.

Philip II appointed only one northerner to high office south of the Alps: the Burgundian Antoine Perrenot, Cardinal Granvelle, son of Charles V's secretary of state. Granvelle came from the same school of Franche-Comtois lawyers as Gattinara. He had little of the old grand chancellor's imperial vision, yet he had a clearer conception of the nature of the Habsburg monarchy than either Philip himself or any other of his ministers. Philip, like his father, tried to rule his empire through his personal control of official appointments and all forms of patronage. The emperor had tried to overcome the weaknesses of this system by constant traveling throughout his dominions. Thus his subjects could always hope that their grievances would be relieved and their services rewarded. Philip failed to understand this. He criticized his father for having wasted his time, health, and money in his constant travels. Margaret of Parma and Granvelle pleaded with him to revisit the Netherlands. Philip found ready and logical excuses not to do so. If he came with insufficient money and troops, he said, his authority would suffer rather than gain. But, as his subjects' hopes gradually turned to disappointment, the old bands of loyalty wore out. Men ceased to believe in the time-honored distinction between the wise and good prince and his wicked ministers who could be blamed for all ills. They turned against the prince himself. Thus it happened in the Netherlands, and thus it happened nearer home, in Granada and Aragon. Granvelle, from his vantage point in Brussels, saw the storm signals. The general dissatisfaction with the Spanish nation, he wrote to Philip in 1563, arose from the suspicion that the king wanted to reduce the Netherlands to the status of his Italian provinces. Yet he was the common lord of them all, and it would be well to show that he did not regard only the Spaniards as his legitimate sons; for these were the words people used, both in Flanders and in Italy. A few ecclesiastical offices and grants (*encomiendas*) given to Netherlanders in Spain would confirm the loyalty of the recipients, their families, and clients, and would keep another twenty-five thousand in hope of future rewards. Some of the great lords might be given positions of command in Italy. Orange, for example, would serve well as viceroy of Sicily, far from the bad influences of Protestant Germany, and with greater contentment through advancement in the king's service.

Here was perhaps the clearest appreciation of the nature of the empire in the whole reign of Philip II. In contrast to similar appreciations in the first half of the sixteenth century, it arose, not from a theoretical justification of empire by a humanist scholar or statesman, but from the practical insight into its political problems by a brilliant administrator. In the event, Philip found it, as usual, easy to shelve his minister's suggestions. He could not satisfy even all legitimate Spanish claims for *encomiendas*, he answered, and it would be too dangerous to experiment, in such important positions as the Italian governorships, with anyone whose religious beliefs were not absolutely above suspicion. Moreover, would Orange not be disappointed after the end of a three-year term as viceroy? For Philip, again unlike his father, was usually unwilling to renew appointments, for fear that his viceroys might become too independent. Thus he lost the opportunity of retaining the loyalty and services of the man who was to become his most able and determined enemy.

In practice, the king did not exercise as much control over patronage as he thought he did. His system of personal government is well known. All work was done on paper, on the basis of *consultas*, that is, memoranda, reports, and advice presented him by his ministers. In Madrid or in the gloomy magnificence of his monastic palace of El Escorial which he built on the slopes of the Sierra de Guadarrama, the king worked alone in his small office, annotating reports, poring over maps and figures, giving his decisions or, as often, deferring them. We know nothing of his order of work, of his selection of documents or of his system of priorities, if indeed he had any. Philip never attended council meetings for fear that his presence would inhibit the councilors from speaking their opinions. The effect was the opposite of the one he desired. The councilors knew that their opinions were reported to the king by the president or secretary of the council. They knew that Philip might pretend to accept their advice, yet take a contrary decision. Thus they tried to conform their views to the yet unknown wishes of the king; their advice became conservative, their statements of opinion half-hearted and qualified. Inevitably, a strong president of the Council of Castile or the Council of State, a Cardinal Espinoza, or a Cardinal Granvelle, dominated policy-making. Equally inevitably, the already strong position of the secretaries of state was further strengthened in the hands of astute men, like Antonio Pérez, who knew the king better than any councilor. It was such men who effectively dominated royal and imperial patronage; for even such a hard-working and well-informed ruler as Philip II had to rely on their advice. The result of this system was that those whose requests were not granted blamed the king for having specially invented the procedure of the *consulta* to be able to refuse them more easily, while those who obtained what they wanted were more grateful to the ministers and secretaries than to the king himself. Philip's ministers and secretaries, as long as they lasted, tended to become rich men.

The Habsburgs had perfected a courier and postal system which was, perhaps, the best in Europe. Even then, communication between the king and the governors of his dominions remained dangerously slow. But much worse than the geographical handicaps were Philip's own habits. He was notoriously painstaking and conscientious, but his craving for ever more information hid an inability to distinguish between the important and the trivial and a temperamental unwillingness to take decisions.[3] His much admired self-possession covered an occasional tendency to panic, as in 1571, when he suddenly ordered the evacuation of the whole population of the Balearic Islands from

3. Many historians have, however, overdone their disapproval of some of Philip's foibles. Cf. H. G. Koenigsberger, "The Statecraft of Philip II of Spain," *European Studies Review,* vol. I, 1971.

fear of a Turkish invasion, or as in 1587, when he ordered the marquis of Santa Cruz to set sail against England in November, regardless of the weather and the number of ships which were seaworthy.[4] In both cases his ministers refused to carry out his commands. But the reverse was much more common. It was of lack of orders that the viceroy of Sicily, García de Toledo, complained when he wanted to relieve the siege of Malta in 1565. It was the lack of clear and timely decisions from Madrid which helped to undermine the authority of Philip's government in the Netherlands.

Motion, but little movement, was the characteristic of the internal history of Castile, as it was that of Philip's system of government. Charles V had effectively solved the internal political problems of the kingdom. The nobility supported the crown enthusiastically. The political power of the towns was broken. Their representatives in the cortes continued to discuss freely all matters of state, from the baleful influence of foreigners on the country's economy, from overheavy taxes, to the excessive powers of the Inquisition, and even the king's own methods of government. Philip was always willing to receive memoranda and petitions on all these matters; but he would not even grant an audience to the representatives, and he accepted or rejected their petitions entirely as he saw fit. He even abrogated the one really important privilege which

4. For a more rational explanation of this order, cf. A. I. I. Thompson, "The Appointment of the Duke of Medina Sidonia to the Command of the Spanish Armada," *Historical Journal,* vol. XII, 1969.

the cortes had managed to hold on to, that of refusing consent to the revocation of laws passed in previous sessions.

The political conflicts of the days of Cardinal Ximenes and of the revolt of the Comuneros had degenerated into the intrigues of court factions and the jurisdictional quarrels between the different law courts and councils of the kingdom. Two men dominated the now all-Spanish Council of State during the first part of Philip's reign: the duke of Alva and the Hispano-Portuguese Ruy Gómez de Silva, prince of Eboli. Since the Venetian ambassadors first wrote about the rivalry between these two, historians have generally spoken of two parties or factions at the court of Madrid, the Gómez "peace party" and the Alva "war party." Recently, these parties have been identified, perhaps a little too imaginatively, with a "conservative" Comunero tradition (Alva) and a "liberal" monarchical tradition (Gómez).[5] They were not so much parties as groups, bound loosely together by family connections, patronage, and clientage. In the absence of genuine political conflicts they represented little but their own interests and the clash of personalities. Owing to family intermarriages and personal rivalries, there were many crosscurrents. With the rise of Cardinal Espinoza in the king's favor and, even more, after Gómez's death (1573), the earlier groupings tended to break up. The factions became more complex, but their struggles no less bitter.

The results of these rivalries were only a little less disastrous for Spain than similar rivalries were for France and the Netherlands. They slowed down government business

5. See G. Marañon, *Antonio Pérez* (Mexico, 1947).

in an already excessively dilatory system, for each party tried to block the proposals made by the other. The connections of the family clans of Silva and Mendoza, Toledo (Alva) and Figueroa, Córdoba, Enríquez, and Guzmán, covered the whole country and involved every quarrel over a sheep run in the power politics at the court of Madrid. They became entangled in the jurisdictional quarrels between military commanders and civil courts, and of both with the claims of ecclesiastical courts. In Calderón's play, *El Alcalde de Zalamea*, Philip II appears as the *deus ex machina* to settle the dispute between the noble colonel of a regiment and the peasant mayor (*alcalde*) of a small town in the *alcalde*'s favor when the latter declares that the king's justice must be one and indivisible.[6] This certainly accorded with Philip's own views. He was unceasing in his efforts to bring the benefits of efficient centralized government and equal justice to subjects suffering under the privileges and petty tyrannies of the nobility. Yet, precisely because Philip saw himself as the sole fountainhead of justice, he was slow to interfere in the quarrels of his courts. They each had their spokesman at court and in the king's councils. Philip fostered their rivalries. His fear of treachery led him into betraying his own ministers and friends. "Kings use men like oranges," said the duke of Alva; "they squeeze out the juice and then throw them away." His own career showed the justness of his words, though he never wavered in his loyalty. The king's unreliability poisoned the politics of his court and turned political and personal rivalries into deadly struggles for power

6. "Toda la justicia vuestra / Es sólo un cuerpo no más."

and survival. "No decent man can suffer it," said the marquis de los Vélez; "for if you do not have the king's favor, they all will trample on you, and if you have it, they will take your life and your honor." Philip's system of government was directly responsible for the revolt of the Alpujarras of Granada, for the revolt of Aragon, and, at least indirectly, for that of the Netherlands.

Outside Castile, Philip was faced with two major problems: the independence or autonomy of the peripheral states of the Iberian peninsula and the religious and racial diversity within these states. When Philip returned from the Netherlands in 1559, the Inquisition had just saved Spain from a "most terrible conspiracy," discovered only just in time to prevent the whole country from being lost. So said the Inquisitors of the arrest of a handful of poor "Lutherans" in Seville and Valladolid, probably Erasmian or Illuminist survivals from the freer atmosphere of the emperor's reign. Apart from these, the mighty Inquisition, with its courts and councils, its theologians, judges, prisons, and thousands of lay familiars, inquired into the Protestant opinions of about 325 suspects during the half century from 1550 to 1600. Many of even this small number were very doubtfully Protestant. All Spanish traditions, formed in the centuries of struggle against the infidels during the *reconquista*, worked against the success of Protestantism. Heterodoxy had a Moorish or Jewish taint in the eyes of every pure-blooded caballero or townsman. No other nation remained as impervious to Protestant propaganda.

If the Protestants were never a serious problem, the "New Christians" were. The policy of assimilating the Moriscos into Spanish Christian society had been started soon after the conquest of Granada; but, in more than two generations, it had met with only very limited success, not least because of language difficulties and because the Spanish government was unwilling to spend money on an effective system of Christian education. Nor did the policy of assimilation command universal support among the Spaniards themselves. No Morisco could become a priest because he was not accepted in the seminaries, reserved for those with *limpieza*, purity of Christian blood without taint of Mohammedanism, Judaism or heresy in the family. Moriscos could not enter the army nor follow a legal career. They remained second-class subjects and, typically, were hated more by the poor Christians than by the great nobles who employed them on their estates and who, in earlier generations, had almost all mixed their blood with that of Jews and Marranos. Equally typically, large numbers of Moriscos drifted into crime and outlawry.

From the beginning of Philip's reign, the position of the Moriscos in Granada suffered a gradual deterioration.[7] This was not originally due to any policy decision. The silk industry on which many Moriscos depended for their livelihood suffered under export prohibitions, imposed in a vain attempt to halt the rise of prices in Spain. Between 1560 and 1565, the tax on silk was more than doubled and the tax-farmers, to whom the Moriscos were fair game, surpassed even the generous limits of corruption which were generally expected from their activities. A govern-

7. This account of the causes of the Morisco revolt is based largely on K. Garrad, *The Causes of the Second Rebellion of the Alpujarras (1568–71)*. I would like to thank Professor Garrad for letting me see his typescript and for permission to use it here.

ment commission under the efficient Dr. Santiago, set up to inquire into all titles of land, confiscated in fact mainly Morisco land. When the Turks launched their great Mediterranean offensives in the 1560's, North African Moors took the opportunity to make raids on the coast of Granada. Every time they were joined by large numbers of Morisco outlaws from the province itself. Spain was swept by rumors of an elaborate spy network, covering the whole country, and of a planned rising by all Moriscos, supported by the Turkish fleet.

The captain general of Granada, Iñigo López de Mendoza, marquis of Mondéjar, was experienced and respected, even by the Moriscos, who saw in him their only protector against both the rapacious Christians and the murderous *monfís*, the bandits of the Sierra Nevada. But for years he had been quarreling with the municipal council of Granada and with the royal *audiencia*, the supreme court for the south of Spain, over precedence, rights of jurisdiction and the ownership of the Sierra Nevada pastures. The *audiencia* was at odds with the Inquisition over similar questions, and the Inquisition, in its turn, had quarreled with the captain general. Archbishop Guerrero of Granada supported Mondéjar in his liberal policy toward the Moriscos, but was engaged in a law suit with his own cathedral chapter. Everyone quarreled with Dr. Santiago and his land commission. As usual, these local quarrels were transferred to Madrid, where the captain general's enemies found a spokesman in the marquis de los Vélez, who had a private feud with Mondéjar over some disputed land.

At this point, the government in Madrid decided to solve, once and for all, both the Morisco problem and the political crisis in Granada. Espinoza, the president of the Council of Castile, persuaded the king to re-enact an edict of 1526, forbidding the Moriscos the use of Arabic, their Moorish names, dresses, and ornaments, and the possession of arms, besides ordering the destruction of all Moorish baths, so as to make an end to all Moorish ceremonies. The edict was published on January 1, 1567, despite Mondéjar's protests and warnings. Espinoza's protégé, Pedro Deza, had already been appointed president of the *audiencia* of Granada several months before. The *audiencia*, supported by Madrid, now claimed the jurisdiction over the Moriscos which the captain general had formerly exercised. Its own soldiers took over from those of the captain general, but they were inexperienced. They failed to hunt the bandits and only oppressed the peaceful Morisco farmers. Public security, precariously maintained by the captain general's forces up till then, now collapsed. Seeing that their only protector, the captain general, had lost his struggle with the *audiencia*, the Moriscos threw in their lot with the *monfís*. From 1567 they began to plan their rising. Increased taxation for the purpose of coastal defense, coming on top of a bad harvest in 1567, made rebellion seem the only means of escape from the growing misery of life under Spanish rule. On Christmas Day 1568, they struck, at the very moment when most of the captain general's troops had been ordered to the coast to guard against Moorish raids.

Spain's Morisco policy, both assimilative and repressive,

lay in ruins. The Spanish system of divided authority had caused the paralysis of the Granada administration at the most critical moment. The war of suppression which followed showed up unexpected military weaknesses. Mondéjar won early and brilliant successes. By February 1569 he seemed to have already pacified the province. But the robberies and cruelties of the Spanish soldiers drove the Moriscos to renewed resistance. The behavior of Philip's soldiers toward civilian populations, especially those who were not regarded as good Catholics, proved to be a recurring and deadly weakness in nearly all Spanish campaigns. Mondéjar's personal enemies persuaded the king to replace him in the supreme command by the young Don John of Austria, under whose nominal leadership the Spanish generals continued to quarrel. The war was waged with appalling cruelty by both sides and it took another two years and much voluntary support from the Spanish towns before it was won.

But Spain had not completely failed. The Moriscos of Aragon and Valencia had remained loyal. When the revolt was over, one more heroic effort was made to make the policy of assimilation a success. The Moriscos of Granada, in their thousands, were sent inland to be distributed in small groups among the Christian population of Andalusia and Castile. As a feat of organization it was a remarkable achievement. In its execution it seems to have been rather less harsh than some similar forcible shifts of population in the twentieth century. Many Moriscos seem to have done reasonably well in their new homes and some even intermarried with Old Christians. But as a means of assimilating the two races, the policy was a failure. The lack of Spanish and Christian education was not remedied, and, in consequence, mutual misunderstanding between the two races persisted. Both sides remained unforgiving.

The unification of the Iberian peninsula

From the end of the fifteenth century, it had been the policy of the Spanish crown to unify the whole Iberian peninsula. The preferred method, for the Christian kingdoms, was marriage alliance rather than conquest. Only Portugal still remained independent. There was no hurry about changing the status quo. Up to about 1580, Spain's resources were fully extended in her great war with the Moslems and by the revolt of the Netherlands. Portugal was a friendly power. Some Spanish grandees preferred it independent, for where else could their children flee from the king's wrath if the occasion arose? Alva had the temerity to say this to Philip himself and the king never forgot, even though Alva eventually conquered Portugal for him.

King Sebastian of Portugal was, from early youth, determined on a crusade in Morocco. Nothing that cautious and realistic advisers, including his uncle Philip II, could say would dissuade him. Portugal made a tremendous effort. But her naval power and the wealth of the Lisbon merchants were committed to her overseas empire. The country itself was poor, and royal finances had been in a precarious state for decades. Sebastian's forces were pitifully inadequate for his ambitious plans. His own leadership was rash and incompetent. On August 4, 1578, the Portuguese army was annihilated by the Moors on the field of Alcazar-el-Kebir. The last Christian attempt, before the nineteenth century, to conquer North Africa had ended in complete disaster. The childless king was among the slain, and the Portuguese succession question suddenly became acute.

Sebastian's successor, his 67-year-old great-uncle, Cardinal Henry, was not expected to last long. But it was immediately clear that neither the Portuguese nor the European powers would willingly accept a Spanish succession. Philip had to prepare his ground carefully. He called Granvelle to Madrid, recognizing at last the cardinal's political gifts and imperialist spirit. He signed a truce with the sultan March 21, 1580) which he had started to negotiate, without enthusiasm, three years earlier. Both in the Netherlands and toward England, Spanish policy became more accommodating. In Portugal itself, the catastrophe of Alcazar-el-Kebir had caused an almost complete collapse of public morale. All the nobility had lost relatives. "The traders and handie-craftsmen who had not their kinsmen there (and yet many of them had) did venture their wealth in it [i.e. the campaign]." [8] The nobility was divided, mostly for purely personal reasons, between support of Philip and of one or other of the Portuguese pretenders, the duke of Braganza and Antonio, prior of Crato, the illegitimate son of the cardinal king's brother. The representatives of the towns in the cortes were similarly divided. King Henry tried to play his own game and added to the confusion.

8. I. de Franchi Conestaggio, *The Historie of the Uniting of the Kingdom of Portugall to the Crowne of Castile*, (trans. E. Blount (London, 1600), p. 55.

Philip cleverly exploited this situation. His pamphleteers insisted on his hereditary rights. His Portuguese agent, Christóvão de Moura, worked successfully to win over nobles and townsmen, bishops and university professors. When one of Henry's ministers proved impervious to bribes of money or titles, Moura provided him with relics for the nunnery he had founded. Could His Majesty steal some from the monastery of the Escorial? Moura wrote to Philip; otherwise he would get hold of corpses and say they were those of holy virgins. Philip thought the matter could be arranged without going to quite such lengths. But when Cardinal Henry died on January 31, 1580, it became apparent that resistance to the Spanish succession was still too strong. Philip would not succeed without a show of force. Antonio, the prior of Crato, became the recognized leader of the resistance to Spain. His pamphlets proclaimed the disasters that had befallen nations which had accepted Spanish rule. The mass of the common people and the lower clergy supported him enthusiastically. But in Castile, nobles and towns now rallied to the support of their own king. The Italian provinces sent ships, money, and munitions. Granvelle, who had organized the Castilian war effort, induced Philip to recall Alva from retirement. On June 27, 1580, Philip finally allowed his army to cross the frontier into Portugal.

The Portuguese had no chance. Their troops were no match for Alva's generalship and superior forces. Some of their defenses were sabotaged; too many of the upper classes favored the Spaniards. France and England gave good words but failed to intervene. Lisbon fell on August 25, and Oporto in October. That was the end of organized fighting; but it had been fierce while it lasted, and Alva's troops had committed their usual outrages.

Philip could now claim the rights of a conqueror. He found it prudent not to do so. At the cortes of Thomar in 1581, and in a subsequent statement of 1582, he promised to uphold Portuguese laws and privileges, to appoint only Portuguese to official positions, and not to introduce Castilian taxation. He abolished the customs barriers between Castile and Portugal so that his new kingdom could freely import much-needed grain. It was Philip's only major move in the economic unification of his empire; but he regarded it less as such than as a special privilege granted to his new subjects. In 1593 the customs points were set up again, mainly for financial reasons. The Portuguese colonial empire continued as a separate empire under the crown. For the moment, the Portuguese were well enough satisfied with this arrangement. Only later, from the last years of the century, the disadvantages of this separatism became apparent. Then Portuguese colonies and shipping were attacked by the enemies of Spain, by Holland, England, and France, while the Spaniards made only halfhearted efforts to protect them. They were not altogether displeased to see the Portuguese weakened and attacks diverted from their own colonies.

The prior Antonio escaped from Portugal and continued to direct a stream of propaganda against Spain, doing his best to spread the "black legend" of the Spaniards' and Philip's cruelty and perfidy. In fact, he was little more than a pawn in the politics of England and France. His name, however, remained a symbol for anti-Spanish feeling in Portugal. The common people, indeed, had profited by the introduction of Castilian ideas of equal justice, for their nobles had treated them "like black slaves," as the Venetian ambassador Matteo Zane said. But the nobles themselves were disappointed in their extravagant claims on Philip's patronage; the clergy remained hostile, for fear Philip would fleece them like the Castilian clergy; and the educated classes now turned deliberately away from Castile and began to look toward France. Gil Vicente and Camoëns had written some of their work in Castilian. This bilingualism now went out of fashion. The union of the crowns of Portugal and Castile did not produce the hoped-for unification of the peninsula. In 1640 even the formal union broke up again.

Isabella the Catholic once said that she hoped for a revolt in Aragon; it would give her the opportunity of establishing the power of the crown there as firmly as in Castile. Philip II showed no such desire. The eastern kingdoms of Spain were poor and sparsely populated. It would have been much too dangerous to interfere in Valencia where one-third of the population were Morisco. Catalonia was difficult but loyal. Her old imperial traditions fitted well with Philip's Mediterranean policies. The shipyards of Barcelona provided him with galleys and experienced seamen. But Barcelona had little part in the expanding trade of the sixteenth century, and the Catalan nobility was allowed little share in the fruits of empire. They ruled their estates like miniature kingdoms, engaged in constant feuds and often made common cause with the ubiquitous bandits. The convoys of American silver, en route from

Seville to Barcelona and Genoa, were frequently and sometimes successfully attacked. The stolen silver was then used in a profitable smuggling trade across the Pyrenees. The Spanish government suspected, not without cause, that the Catalan robber barons of the northern frontier were in close contact with the French Huguenots. But Philip did little more than appoint some of his most faithful and competent Castilian grandees as viceroys to battle with these problems as best they could.

In Aragon, the king could not even appoint Castilians as viceroys. Here the unfortunate country population looked to the king to protect them from the arbitrary powers of a tyrannous nobility. Philip was very willing to respond to such an appeal; yet the nobles and the townspeople clung fiercely to their privileges. The old hatred of the Castilians had not abated, and Philip had not helped his cause by refusing to visit Aragon. When he finally did so, in 1585, it was at least partly to settle the succession to the large county of Ribagorza whose inhabitants were in revolt against their feudal overlord, the duke of Villahermosa. The Aragonese cortes, the nobles, and the court of the *justicia* were alarmed at this Castilian interference. New quarrels arose over the appointment of a Castilian viceroy, and in the years after 1585 tension in the kingdom was rising rapidly.

The explosion of 1591, however, was sparked off by events at the court of Madrid itself. After the death of Ruy Gómez, his widow, Doña Ana de Mendoza, princess of Eboli, tried to maintain the Eboli influence at court with the help of Philip's secretary, Antonio Pérez. It is very unlikely that Pérez and the one-eyed princess were lovers, as historians and novelists have often thought; but the upstart secretary was hated both by many of the grandees and by his rivals in the Spanish civil service. The king's favor was unstable and Pérez knew it. To safeguard himself, he intrigued with all parties: with Don John of Austria and his secretary, Juan de Escovedo, against the king; with the king against Don John; perhaps even with the Netherlands rebels against both. Philip was deeply suspicious of Don John and his romantic ambitions. He vetoed his plans of invading England to liberate and marry Mary Queen of Scots. In 1577 he had determined on a policy of appeasement in the Netherlands and Don John was once more involving him in war. When Don John sent Escovedo to Spain to press his warlike policy, Pérez began to fear for his influence on the king and was in a panic that Escovedo might expose his intrigues. He reacted in the same way as Catherine de Medici in a similar situation on the eve of the massacre of St. Bartholomew. It was easy to represent Escovedo as Don John's evil genius, plotting treason against the king. Philip gave his consent to murder (March 1, 1578), just as Charles IX had done. It was not a massacre, as in 1572. But Philip never forgave Pérez for having forced his hand. On July 28, 1579, he had his secretary and the princess of Eboli arrested without warning. Granvelle had just arrived to prepare the Portuguese campaign, and the king no longer needed the Eboli faction.

For the next ten years, Pérez remained a prisoner. But the Escovedo family and his enemies at court wanted his complete destruction. Philip now made his second mistake; he fell in with these plans, having convinced himself both that Pérez had misled him and that he had compromising documents in his hands. All efforts to extract these and a confession failed. In April 1590 Pérez escaped from prison, fled to Aragon, and claimed the protection of the *justicia*'s court. In this court, he now answered Philip's case against him, for the first time, by directly accusing the king of the murder of Escovedo. It was a situation which has become familiar in the twentieth century, that of a man who is driven to treason by a system of arbitrary government in which he himself has played a prominent part. Philip had one more card which could overtrump Aragonese privileges. On a fabricated charge of heresy, the Inquisition now demanded that Pérez be handed over to its prison in Saragossa. Never before had the hated Inquisition appeared so blatantly as the tool of royal absolutism. Twice, in May and September 1591, the populace of Saragossa prevented the transfer of Pérez to the Inquisition prison. The king's special representative was killed in the riots. To the Aragonese it meant the defense of their liberties; to Philip it meant open rebellion which had to be put down by force. In November 1591 a Castilian army marched into Aragon. Aragonese resistance collapsed within a few days and Pérez fled to France, there to continue his polemic against the king.

Philip had the *justicia* and many ringleaders of the rebellion executed, but was remarkably moderate in the constitutional changes he imposed. The *justicia* was, from now on, to be removable at royal pleasure; the viceroy could be a foreigner that is, a Castilian; and majority voting was substituted for the principle of unanimity in the Aragonese cortes. These changes, together with some very reasonable reforms of the legal system, gave the crown the ultimate power of decision in Aragon, but they preserved the kingdom's autonomy.

The Mediterranean and the Turkish wars

The Treaty of Cateau-Cambrésis had left Spain free to concentrate on her most formidable enemy, the Turk. The emperor's campaigns had shown that the Christians could not seriously dispute Turkish supremacy in the eastern Mediterranean, nor the Turks Spanish supremacy in its western basin. A stable balance of power, however, had not yet been reached. Spain was in a much more precarious position than her enemies. The sultan's vassals and allies on the Barbary Coast were always a potential threat to the Christian flank. Their raids on shipping and on the luckless fishing villages and small ports of Italy and southern Spain were a constant reminder of this threat. Their contacts with the Moriscos in Granada carried the Moslem danger to the very heart of Spanish power. As long as the Barbary kingdoms remained relatively isolated, the danger they presented could be kept in check. Everything therefore depended on the control of the central Mediterranean and both sides developed their strategy accordingly. For the Spaniards it had to be defensive. They were committed to two naval fronts, the Mediterranean and the Atlantic, on which, for technical reasons, warships were not easily interchangeable. Galley for galley, the Turks could out-build them. An attempt by the combined squadrons of Spain's Italian dominions and allies to recapture Tripoli for the Knights of St. John (1560) ended with the loss of more than half the Christian ships and showed the danger of undertaking even a limited offensive operation without naval superiority. The preservation of his fleet therefore became the main object of Philip's naval strategy. It had the disadvantage that Spain might be forced into a naval action when she least desired it or lose a vital strategic position. This dilemma became painfully apparent during the Turkish siege of Malta in 1565. The Knights of St. John were sending more and more desperate appeals for relief as the Turks closed in. Philip's own captain general, García de Toledo, viceroy of Sicily, was in despair at the silence from Madrid. Without definite orders he could not risk his fleet against the stronger Turkish armada. After weeks of hesitation, Philip decided against it. The island was saved by the heroic defense of the Knights and by the brilliant operation in which Toledo landed reinforcements without engaging his fleet.

It had been a near thing, but it was the turning point in the Mediterranean war. The Turks had lost the fight for the control of the central Mediterranean. But this was not immediately clear. The Turks were still formidable. On both sides, the shipyards were building warships at full pressure. Uluj Ali, the Calabrian renegade and king of Algiers, did little to help the Moriscos of Granada during their rebellion, but he took the opportunity to overthrow the Spanish vassal king of Tunis (January 1570). Once the Morisco war was won, Philip was bound to react to this setback. With the Netherlands temporarily pacified, he could afford to concentrate on the Mediterranean and join Pius V's Holy League with Venice against the Turks (May 1571). Philip had little of his father's crusading ardor. For him, the League presented the chance of meeting the Turks for once on equal or superior terms and securing the Spanish position in the central Mediterranean and on the Barbary Coast. The gamble paid off brilliantly. At Lepanto on October 7, 1571, the League's fleet, commanded by Don John of Austria, virtually annihilated the Turkish fleet. Yet the effects of Don John's famous victory were moral rather than material. To the Spaniards, from the common soldier Cervantes to the commander in chief Don John, Lepanto was their St. Crispin's day, with the added glory of having fulfilled Spain's destiny as God's champion against the enemies of His Church. This mood explains much of the continued willingness of the Spaniards to support their king's religious and imperial policies, even in the face of ruinous costs and mounting disasters.

The political and strategic consequences of Lepanto, however, were slight. Bickering between the allies about the direction of the next move wasted most of the sailing season of the next year. Cyprus had fallen and there was no chance of retaking it. In March 1573 Venice concluded a peace with the sultan. The Holy League might help her to win battles, but it could not protect her possessions. The defection of Venice at least left Don John free to concentrate on the central Mediterranean. In October 1573 he took Tunis; less than a year later it was lost again to Uluj Ali, commanding a Turkish fleet of such superior strength that the Spaniards could not risk engaging it in open battle. It seemed as if Lepanto had never been fought. The brief period when Philip had been able to concentrate his forces in the Mediterranean was past. It had badly overstrained his resources. From 1571 to 1573, the small kingdom of Sicily had spent 1,200,000 scudi on Don John's armada, and in 1575 Philip was forced to send 75,000 scudi as a direct aid to the Sicilian government to prevent its financial collapse. The financial position of Naples was even worse, and the Spanish government itself staggered toward its second bankruptcy (1575). Spain was now heavily engaged in the Netherlands. The strategic position in the Mediterranean, back where it was after the siege of Malta, presented a tolerable equilibrium. The naval and financial resources of the Ottoman empire, though still superior to those of Spain, had also been overstrained and the Porte, too, had to turn its attention to problems on its other borders. It was time to conclude a truce. The great struggle between the Spanish and Ottoman empires changed into a "cold war," with only occasional and indecisive forays. Its final outcome was to be determined, not by the clash of arms, but by the internal development of both empires.

Spain and Italy

Just as in the emperor's reign, so in that of Philip II, the problem of defense dominated Spain's relations with her Italian dominions. But after 1559 Naples and Sicily, rather than Milan, were in the front line of imperial defense. It is therefore not surprising that a viceroy of Sicily, Marc Antonio Colonna, gave the clearest formulation of the problems of imperial defense. Nor is it surprising that, again, imperial arguments were put forward by an Italian rather than a Spaniard. Members of old and famous Italian families like the Colonna, Doria, and Pescara could not accept for themselves any inferior status to the Spanish grandees in the service of the king of Spain. It followed that they had to regard Milan, Naples, and Sicily as states ranking equally with the Spanish kingdoms in an international, rather than a Spanish, empire. Characteristically, Colonna's remarks centered on finance. The Sicilians, as he knew from experience, haggled about every ducat to be sent to Spain; yet, in case of a serious Turkish attack, the defense of the island would not depend on some two hundred thousand ducats more or less. Only the combined resources of all the king's dominions could provide safety for each one; for they were all members of one body and must help each other. "I have never seen Your Majesty's affairs in danger, or lost, for lack of money, men and munitions," Colonna wrote to Philip in 1582, "but because there was abundance in one part and want in another," and because the vanity of ministers prevented them from giving full support to their colleagues.

When García de Toledo's galleys set sail from Messina for the relief of Malta, or when Don John's victorious ships returned from Lepanto, it was easy for the Sicilians to see the advantages of the Spanish connection, and their parliament contributed willingly to imperial defense. But when the Sicilian galleys were called from the defense of the island's shores against corsair raids to take part in Alva's expedition against Lisbon, the advantages of empire seemed to be all on the side of Spain. Up to about 1580, Sicily's imperial connection served as a stimulus for the reform of her administration and the extension of royal power and justice at the expense of turbulent barons and Mafia-like bandits. After that date, the strain became too great. In 1588, for instance, Sicily supplied more than half a million scudi in cash and provisions for the Armada. The good effects of administrative reform were nullified by the growing practice of selling offices. Philip II managed to keep the sale of the rights of jurisdiction to the nobles within bounds. His son had fewer compunctions. In 1621 the nobles finally obtained, as of right, the ability to buy jurisdictional powers over their fiefs. The instructions to the viceroys to protect the weak from the strong had become an empty formula.

The Sicilian parliament retained its privileges and powers because the crown was never required to attack them. It granted the king as much money as could reasonably be expected from a small country whose only economic assets were its production of grain and raw silk. At the same time, Sicily was preserved by her parliament from the degree of financial exploitation from which Naples and Milan suffered. Spanish rule did not cause the economic ruin of Sicily, as many Italian historians have supposed. It was rather that the crown's tacit support of the privileges of the predatory nobility and propertied classes rendered impossible the solution of the island's social problems. Sicily remained a country with great constitutional liberties but with an anarchical administration. Not surprisingly, the viceroyalty came to be regarded as the graveyard of the reputation of its holders. In Madrid they were judged mainly by the success or failure of their financial policy. They fought a losing battle against the privileges of the nobility and the lawlessness of the countryside. Their opponents could become familiars of the Inquisition and thus escape from the jurisdiction of the secular courts. The jurisdictional quarrels between the viceroys and the Inquisition sometimes came near to paralyzing the whole administration. Both sides would appeal to Madrid and both sides would find friends at court. Sooner or later, Philip would listen to the whispers against the viceroy's loyalty and recall him.[9]

In contrast to Sicily, Naples presented far fewer problems to the Spaniards. There was no effective counterbalance to the authority of the viceroys. The nobility remained divided, for, while the feuds between the Aragonese and Angevin factions had lost something of their former virulence, the Spaniards had encouraged the settlement of large numbers of Genoese in the kingdom, some two hundred of whom were nobles. Their position and their property depended on royal favor. The government, moreover, secretly fomented distrust between the noble and the popular *seggi* of the city of Naples. Government officials, from the viceroy downward, were notorious for their greed and corruption. The count of Miranda was reputed to have amassed a million ducats during his viceroyalty. The figure is, no doubt, exaggerated; but the count of Olivares used to say that one ought not to wish to be viceroy of Naples to avoid the pain of leaving the office.

In the virtual absence of constitutional safeguards against

9. H. G. Koenigsberger, *The Practice of Empire* (Ithaca, 1969).

the financial demands of the government, taxes and government revenues rose rapidly, probably more rapidly than prices, to the high figure of two million ducats in the 1570's and to almost four million by 1611. Most of these sums were spent on defense and on the Mediterranean fleet. But, as in the case of Sicily, after about 1580, increasingly large sums were spent in support of Spain's commitments in western Europe. The viceroys themselves had to reject royal demands for money, for no more could be wrung from the taxpayers. Naples, like Sicily, remained a poor, semicolonial country. Its trade was in the hands of Genoese merchants; its nobles tyrannized their vassals, despite all royal instructions to the viceroys to protect the weak against the strong; and its peasants and small traders were held to ransom by the bandits of the Abbruzzi. Yet the Spaniards, unpopular as they were, ruled in Naples because their rule was acceptable. The Venetian, Alvise Lando, marveled that "there has never been a kingdom, like this kingdom of Naples, which has fallen so often without having fallen and which, in perpetual bondage . . . should with the greatness of its foes have always boasted liberty and dominion."

The attitude of the Milanese was very similar. Lombardy had been the battleground of the great powers for sixty years. Against the background of burnt harvests and sacked cities, the Milanese were no longer willing to fight for the doubtful benefits of political independence. The Spaniards were unpopular. They continued to treat Milan as a military outpost of Spain and, now that there was peace, the exactions of the Spanish *tercios* were bitterly resented. But the towns retained both a great deal of their former autonomy and also some representation in the organs of central government. The last vestiges of medieval democracy had disappeared from the town governments, and their leading families who now monopolized all local power looked to the king of Spain to maintain them in their position. Only once was there a serious threat to Spanish power. In 1563 Philip decided to introduce the Spanish Inquisition into Milan. The Milanese reacted as violently as the Neapolitans had done to a similar attempt in 1547. Was not Milan one of the oldest Christian cities and never tainted by even the suspicion of heresy? they asked. There were riots. The archbishop, the Council of Trent, the pope himself supported the citizens. They feared for their own rights of ecclesiastical jurisdiction. And, as his father had done in Naples, Philip had to give way.

We have no detailed study of Milanese finances for this period. It does not seem as if the tax burden increased beyond what it had been in the later years of the emperor's reign. Milan was the fulcrum of Spanish power in Europe. From this position, the king dominated his Italian allies and maintained his contacts with the Austrian Habsburgs. From Milan he could throw his troops south against a Turkish threat or march north and west to intervene in the Netherlands or France. It would never do to antagonize the Milanese beyond endurance. Most of the revenues from the duchy, and large sums sent from Spain. had to be used for the regiments stationed in Lombardy. In spite of his theoretical power to impose taxes at will, the governor had to haggle with the individual towns over every extraordinary grant. The financial position of the government of Milan thus went from bad to worse, but the province itself was recovering from the disasters of the first half of the century. The population of its cities rose rapidly and with it their economic activity. Milan, with its one hundred thousand inhabitants, was one of the largest manufacturing centers of Europe, famous especially for its metal work and armament manufactures. Some smaller cities, like Pavia or the textile center of Como, expanded even more rapidly. Alone among Spain's Italian dominions, Lombardy was able to take advantage of the rising prices and expanding markets of Europe. Later, during the plague and war years of the seventeenth century, the Milanese came to look back on the reign of Philip II as almost a golden age.

While for the Milanese, Neapolitans, and Sicilians Spanish rule was never more than tolerable, a genuine feeling for Italian independence existed only in the still independent Italian states. Even there, it was usually little more than a literary sentiment. In the Italian comedies, as Boccalini remarked, the Spaniard had replaced the Neapolitan as the stock character representing absolute vanity. The Italian states were too jealous of each other to cooperate against Spain; but even their combined forces were puny compared with the overwhelming military power of the Catholic king. Renewed French intervention, hoped for by some and feared by others, was always talked about but was not a practical possibility until the end of the French Wars of Religion.

More than any other state, Genoa had staked her fortunes on those of the Spanish monarchy. Her bankers invested their money in Spanish loans and displaced the Germans as the principal creditors of the Spanish crown and farmers of Spanish revenues. Her merchants and nobles settled in Spain, Naples, and Sicily, intermarried with the local nobility, and cornered much of the trade between Spain and her dominions. Spinola commanded Philip III's armies in the Netherlands. The Doria family commanded the Spanish Mediterranean fleet while, at home, they maintained with an iron hand the rule of the Spanish faction of the Genoese nobility. As long as Peru sent silver to Seville, the Genoese plutocracy flourished. In the splendid painted palaces which Galeazzo Alessi built for them and in their portraits which Van Dyck painted in the 1620's, one can still catch something of the flavor of this elegant, civilized, and ruthless society.

In contrast to Spain's smooth relations with Genoa, those with the papacy were much more stormy. "There is no pope in Spain," said Figueroa, president of the Royal Council, and in this *bon mot* he epitomized the major cause of friction. Figueroa's claim, however, was true only up to a point. The king of Spain had the right of appointment to all ecclesiastical benefices, estimated by contemporaries at an aggregate value of over six million ducats. In consequence, the Spanish clergy looked to Madrid, rather than to Rome, for advancement. The enormous ecclesiastical patronage of the Spanish crown was one of its most powerful means of assuring itself the loyalty of the high nobility, the hidalgos, and the educated middle classes of the towns. Since the days of Ferdinand and Isabella, Spanish kings had pursued a deliberate policy of restricting papal influence on the Spanish Church. They claimed the right to prevent the publication in Spain of certain types of papal bulls and briefs. They tried to prevent appeals from Spanish ecclesiastical courts to Rome. The popes of the first half of the sixteenth century had been relatively complaisant in these matters. The popes of the Counter-Reformation, however, attempted to regain lost ground.

The first open clash arose out of the Spanish Inquisition's action against Archbishop Bartolomé de Carranza of Toledo. The case was a kind of ecclesiastical counterpart to that of Pérez. Carranza had made a name for himself by his reconciling and burning of heretics in England during the reign of Philip and Mary, and by his pious zeal in luring suspected heretics from the relative safety of Antwerp into territory where they could be seized by the Inquisition. But, after he had risen to the primateship of Spain, jealous emulators accused him before the Supreme Council of the Holy Inquisition, and he himself became a victim of the system of which he had been such an ardent and successful protagonist (1559). There were doubts in Spain itself about the justice of the accusations. The Council of Trent eventually declared his opinions to be orthodox. The case, however, hinged hardly at all on Carranza's opinions, but on the papal claim that a bishop could only be judged in Rome and the Spanish Inquisition's claim to complete autonomy in all cases involving heresy. The crown supported the Inquisition, for, as Cardinal Alessandrino wrote to Rome, "The most ardent defenders of justice here hold that it is better to condemn an innocent man than to let the Inquisition suffer any diminution of its powers." The case dragged on for seven years. Then Carranza was transferred to Rome. It was a substantial victory for the papacy, even though it was several more years before the pope dared to pronounce his sentence of virtual acquittal.

In Italy the quarrels over ecclesiastical jurisdiction were even more acrimonious. In Naples and Sicily the king's hold over the Church was even firmer than in Spain itself. By his right of *exequatur* he could deny the publication of all papal bulls, just as the kings of France could by their *droit de vérification.* In Sicily the king, moreover, exercised the *monarchia*, the rights and powers of a permanent apostolic legate. The claim was based on an alleged grant by Urban II to Count Roger of Sicily. The papacy, not unnaturally, disputed a claim which gave the king effectively as much power over the Sicilian Church as the English kings enjoyed over the English Church. The dispute was not resolved and remained alive until Pius IX formally revoked the *monarchia* in 1867. It was typical of Spanish institutions that the court of the *monarchia* developed a will of its own and came into conflict, not only with the Inquisition (like itself, claiming to be an ecclesiastical court recognizing no superior), but also with the royal power as represented by the viceroys.

It was in Milan that the most dramatic conflicts between church and state arose. Here they were the direct result of the counteroffensive of the reformed Roman Church after the Council of Trent. Its leading spirit was the young nephew of Pius IV, Carlo Borromeo, who arrived in Milan in 1566 to take up his duties as archbishop. In the words of Philip's confessor, he wanted "with excessive severity to impose on the masses that which was the end of the most sublime perfection." Like the Spanish Inquisition, Borromeo built up an impressive court and organized the city and the duchy into districts under his own officials. His armed guards clapped offenders against his spiritual decrees into the archiepiscopal prison. But when he proceeded to extend his authority from the supervision of the morals of the clergy to those of the laity, he began to fall foul of the civil courts. When he proclaimed the Tridentine decrees and the bull *In coena domini* (which forbade princes to levy further taxes on their subjects) despite the prohibition of the governor, the duke of Alburquerque, he challenged the royal power itself. Alburquerque arrested the archbishop's agents and sent troops to occupy the Borromeo estates. Borromeo answered with curse and interdict. He won great tactical victories. Alburquerque had to beg the pope for absolution. One of his successors, Don Luis de Requesens, obtained his absolution only because he left Milan to become governor general of the Netherlands. Borromeo's influence over the populace of Milan was enormous. His charity and fearlessness during the plague won the admiration of friends and opponents alike. But he was too much an aristocrat and authoritarian to wish to become the leader of a popular movement against established authority. Neither Rome nor Madrid could afford to push the quarrel to extremes. Philip depended on the pope for the grant of the *cruzada* and other ecclesiastical taxes in Spain. It was the price the Spanish crown paid for not having to argue about taxes with a clergy organized as an estate of the realm, as other European governments had to do. These clerical taxes could be as much as two million ducats a year. For such sums, Philip could afford to overlook the insults to his representatives in Milan.

Toward the end of Philip's reign, the quarrel broke out again. Federico Borromeo, cousin and successor of Carlo, attempting to imitate his great predecessor in the see of Milan, was ready to excommunicate the governor general. But Juan de Velasco was no Alburquerque; he refused to be browbeaten. Nor was Clement VIII a Pius V. The archbishop received no backing from Rome. But the disputes continued and even a compromise, in 1615, did not finally settle them. Fundamentally, however, relations between the papacy and the Spanish monarchy depended less on jurisdictional claims than on the policy of both toward their common enemies, the Turks and the Protestants.

Both the dukes of Florence and of Piedmont-Savoy owed their thrones to Spanish arms and diplomacy. Emmanuel Philibert of Savoy, indeed, argued that he had conquered his states in the battle of St. Quentin, where he had led Philip's armies to victory and forced the French to conclude the Treaty of Cateau-Cambrésis. Yet, in spite of this argument and of a French marriage, he never forgot his dependence on Spain. Savoy and Piedmont, freed from French and Spanish occupation, welcomed their duke with enthusiasm. Parliament granted him a huge tax and with the money Emmanuel Philibert could pay his troops. From then on, he no longer had any use for his parliament. The old ruling classes of the towns had been shattered by twenty-five years of foreign military occupation. The nobles were locked in private feuds, their estates were mortgaged, and many were receiving bribes from France or Spain, or from both at the same time. Morally and materially, they were incapable of defending their old political privileges. Emmanuel Philibert, with his own disheartening experience as governor general of the Netherlands in mind, established one of the most rigid systems of absolutist government in Europe. The administration of his country was carried on by middle-class functionaries who were completely dependent on the duke. The nobles were compensated for their loss of political power by titles and court positions and by the duke's renunciation of any effective interference in their estates, where serfdom often continued until the eighteenth century.

With the country thus firmly in his control, Emmanuel Philibert was able to increase taxation in a way no governor of Milan would have dared. Government revenues were pushed up from about ninety thousand ducats to half a million. All the duke's careful attention to the growth of industrial production in Piedmont could not make up for the stifling rate of taxation and the exactions of his standing army. Throughout his reign the Venetian ambassadors speak of deserted farm lands and almost universal poverty and apathy.

Emmanuel Philibert—he was nicknamed Iron Head—at least kept his country out of war and yet managed to make the French evacuate the towns they still garrisoned. His son, Charles Emmanuel I (1580–1630), added to internal despotism a romantic foreign policy. He dreamt of the crown of Portugal or of Bohemia, of Sicily or of Sardinia, even of the imperial crown. For the absurd hope of the French succession, after the death of Henry III, or of a kingdom in Provence, he gave up the possibility of conquering Geneva, his one aim which had both some historical justification and some chance of success. Charles Emmanuel has become famous as a practical exponent of reason of state who anticipated the role of the house of Savoy during the *risorgimento* in the nineteenth century. His contemporaries failed to see him in such a transcendental light. They only saw that he ruined his country economically and that, if Piedmont-Savoy survived as an independent state, it was due to luck and the interests of the great powers (just as was the survival of Geneva) and not to the policies of its dukes.

In 1530, the Medici, with the help of imperial arms, had overthrown the last Florentine republic. The Florentine aristocracy had suffered badly under the republic. Economically unable to stand on their own feet, and morally unwilling to co-operate with the republicans and *popolani*, they had now no choice but to lean on Medici support. First Alessandro and then Cosimo de Medici brilliantly exploited this situation. They transformed the "principate" into a dukedom, a police state no less despotic than that of the dukes of Savoy, but more efficiently run. The aristocracy was transformed from an urban patriciate into a service and court nobility. Most of them withdrew their capital from industry and trade, engaging only in banking or, much more frequently, developing their estates outside the city. Their social status remained unimpaired (though Cosimo enforced strict justice for all his subjects and abolished also the special privileges of the city of Florence) but, as a social group, they lost all political power. The institutions of the republic survived in form only, for the duke bypassed them by relying on his own functionaries. Significantly, the brilliant Florentine historians, from Machiavelli to Guicciardini and Varchi, found no successors after the deaths of those whose views had been formed under the republic. There was nothing more to write about but tedious court intrigues or the deeds of dukes who played but a very small part in the politics of the great European powers. The creative genius of the Florentines, so closely linked with the life of the city-state, wilted in the stifling atmosphere of the rigid court society of the dukes, even though the Medici did not give up their traditional patronage of the arts. But there occurred a shift in creative activity, from literature and the visual arts to natural science and music, activities which in Italy were not traditionally bound up with the artist's life in a city-state. In these, Florence became as famous as she had once been in painting and sculpture.[10]

The Medici dukes, true to their origins, were excellent financiers. Almost alone among contemporary princes they were always solvent. The financial resources of Cosimo I enabled him to conquer the republic of Siena (1557) and

10. Cf. H. G. Koenigsberger, *Estates and Revolutions*, chap. 11 (Ithaca, 1971).

Medallion of the emperor Charles V, by Hans Bolsterer, 1548. Kunsthistorisches Museum, Vienna.

Mary of Hungary, bronze bust by Leone Leoni. Kunsthistorisches Museum, Vienna.

Emperor Charles V, by Titian, 1548. Alte Pinakothek München.

Antoine Perrenot de Granvelle, by Titian, 1548. Nelson Gallery–Atkins Museum (Nelson Fund), Kansas City, Missouri.

Portrait of Philip II, by Titian, 1554. Courtesy of M and Mme Torsten Kreuger, Château de la Malvande, Chambésy-Genève.

Allegory of the Battle of Lepanto (1571), by Titian, 1571–1575. Museo del Prado, Madrid.

Ferdinand II, attributed to Frans Pourbus II, 1619.
Museo del Prado, Madrid.

The Surrender of Breda (1625), also known as *Las Lanzas*, by Velázquez, before 1635. Museo del Prado, Madrid.

The Count-Duke Olivares, by Velázquez, 1633. Museo del Prado, Madri[d]

to maintain a sufficient degree of independence from Spain to be treated as an ally, rather than a satellite. More than this was out of the question. The Spaniards held the *presidios*, five fortresses on the coast of Tuscany, from 1530, and kept a military stranglehold on the duchy. In 1570, Cosimo I obtained from the pope the title of grand duke of Tuscany. The need to have this title recognized by the emperor and Philip II made Francis I (1574–1587) even more dependent on Spain. Ferdinand I (1587–1609) was able to act more independently and, like Charles Emmanuel, he tried to fish in the troubled waters of Provence during the wars of the League. In the end he was lucky to withdraw without serious loss.

The price which Tuscany paid for the financial solvency of its rulers was, however, a heavy one. Taxation was crushing and nearly all industries were closely controlled by the state. The grain trade, the oil trade, shipbuilding, and shipping were government monopolies. Under Francis I they were exploited almost exclusively for the benefit of the grand duke's private purse. Under Ferdinand I the duchy recovered, to some extent, from a slump in the 1580's and from the misrule of his predecessor. Leghorn, virtually a free port, became the great entrepôt for the trade of northern and western Europe with the Mediterranean. But most of the great ships calling at Leghorn flew Dutch or English flags. The great days of Italian seafaring were over.

The only truly independent state in Italy was Venice. As Niccolò Contarini and other Venetian statesmen saw it, her continued independence was, in the long run, impossible without an independent Italy. The republic was therefore bound to be hostile to Spain, a fact which was appreciated as much in Madrid as on the Rialto. But there could be no question of an open breach. In the event of a Turkish attack, Venice needed papal and Spanish help. By the middle of the sixteenth century, Venice had at least partially recovered from the shock of losing the monopoly of the spice trade. Venetian merchants in Alexandria and Aleppo could still buy spices from Arab caravans and supply a large part of an expanding European market. They could also supply at least some of the cloth which the Arab and Levantine merchants wanted for their spices. For the first time in their history, the Venetians built up a major cloth manufacturing industry. Nevertheless, the brightly colored and cheaper English kerseys and French and Dutch says sold more readily in the eastern markets than the dull and expensive fabrics of traditional Italian manufacture. These products gave the western competitors of Venice an enormous advantage in the Levant trade. Moreover, this trade was precarious. The Cyprus war (1570–1573) and the activities of Moslem and Christian pirates interrupted commerce and caused the loss of valuable markets. The Turko-Persian war, following the Lepanto campaign, relieved Ottoman naval pressure in the Mediterranean and thus benefited Spain; but it interrupted the caravan trade with the East on which the supply of spices for Venice depended. In consequence, the Venetian patricians tended more and more to withdraw capital from trade and invest it in their estates on the Venetian mainland. Like the English country gentlemen of the eighteenth century, who rightly felt a close affinity to the Venetian patricians, they improved their estates and built their beautiful palladian villas and, when commercial prospects seemed good, reinvested in trade or industry. Venetian glass, ceramics, metal work, silk, and, not least, books were the finest in Europe. When Michelangelo had painted his last fresco and drawn his last plan for the dome of St. Peter's, there remained in the rest of Italy no painter of the stature of Titian, Tintoretto, and Veronese, nor any architect to rival Palladio. Unlike Florence, Venice could play her part in the new development of music without suffering a decline in the visual arts. Music had her very own home in Venice, wrote Francesco Sansovino in 1581. It could not truthfully have been said fifty years earlier. There is no clearer proof than this of the continued creative vitality of the Italian city-state. But the character of Venetian economic life was changing. In the early 1600's, the decline of Venetian trade was generally recognized. In 1610 a proposal was put before the senate to give foreign merchants extensive trading rights in the Venetian possessions and to allow them to acquire Venetian citizenship. But vested interest, conservatism, and the fear of opening the door to religious heresy defeated this proposal and with it, perhaps, the last chance of restoring the former commercial greatness of Venice.

Compared with the old Florentine republic, or with contemporary western Europe, Venetian politics remained in a minor key. The economic changes of the period did not disturb the social equilibrium. Given this fact, together with the superior military and naval power of Spain and the Porte, the Venetian ruling classes had little room for maneuver, either in internal or in external politics. The differences which divided the "old" and the "new" families, and the "young" and "old" patricians, were questions of attitude and tactics, of the length to which one could go in defying Spain or the pope, but not fundamental questions of government or religion. The Cyprus war discredited the ruling groups of the older patricians and the "new" families who had monopolized the office of doge for more than a hundred years. A loosely organized group of younger men, mainly from the "old" families, managed to reduce the power of the Council of Ten and its permanent executive committee, the Zonta, in 1582–1583. The leaders of this group, Leonardo Donato and Niccolò Contarini, spiritual descendants of the earlier Venetian religious reformers, Sadoleto and Gasparo Contarini, now began to steer the republic on a more anti-Spanish, antipapal, and pro-French course. They forced the rejection in 1585 of an attractive Spanish offer to Venice to take over the Portuguese spice trade. They feared, with justice, that the republic would become as much a satellite of Spain as Genoa had become. They recognized the succession of Henry IV and did much to persuade Sixtus V to alter his policy toward France. In 1605 they took up the challenge of the papal attack on the republic's control over its clergy. It was a quarrel over jurisdiction, like the many quarrels between Spain and the papacy. Unlike these latter, it led to a complete breach and a papal interdict over the republic (1606). The newly elected pope, Paul V (Borghese), thought he could, once for all, establish the maximum claims of the Holy See in the smaller Italian states. Spain did her best to goad him on, out of her traditional hostility toward Venice. The republic replied by electing Donato as its doge. The Jesuits, as the pope's most dangerous agents, were banished. Fra Paolo Sarpi, the friend of Donato and Contarini, brilliantly attacked the doctrinal justification of the papal action. It was the most serious crisis of Catholicism in Italy. But when Spain threatened war and Henry IV would give only diplomatic support, Venice accepted French mediation and a compromise on the immediate points at issue. In effect, however, Venice had won. The republic maintained the full independence of her secular government from clerical interference. In the following decade, Venice was to face one more attack by Spain, this time on the very existence of her political independence. This too the republic overcame. For the Italians of the early seventeenth century, it was the Republic of St. Mark, and not the princely houses of Savoy and Medici, which stood as the champion of what remained of Italian liberty.

The revolt of the Netherlands to 1585

When in 1520 Charles V left Spain after his first visit to his new kingdom, the towns of Castile rebelled against the Flemish domination of their country. In 1559 the roles were reversed. It was the Netherlands which had suffered a foreign succession and were alarmed by Spanish domination. Yet such a foreign domination did not exist, any more than it did in Spain in 1520.

Philip II's residence in the Netherlands, from his father's

abdication until 1559, was not a success. He appeared as foreign to the Netherlanders as his father had at first appeared to the Spaniards. His government's demands for money for the French wars led to prolonged and exasperating wrangles with the states general, the joint sessions of the provincial estates. The nobles and patricians in the assemblies of the estates blocked every attempt by the government to introduce new and fairer types of taxes which would no longer fall most heavily on the poorer people. In 1557–1558 the states general made a grant of eight hundred thousand florins per annum for nine years, but only on condition that their own commissioners should control the collection and expenditure of the money. Some of the provincial estates, notably Brabant, Flanders, and Holland, had done this before and had built up their own financial machinery. Now it was to be extended to all the thirteen provinces normally represented in the states general. The purpose was primarily the practical one of preventing money earmarked for the payment of troops from being used to pay the government's debts. Flanders and, later, Holland were opposed to the new system because they feared the predominance of Brabant in its administration. Nor did the new financial organization, headed by the Antwerp banker Anthony van Straelen, work particularly efficiently or honestly. The government was bound to regard it as a serious infringement of its rights and a dangerous advance in the power of the estates.

Just before Philip's departure for Spain, the states general demanded the withdrawal of the *tercio* of three thousand Spanish troops. The king had wanted to maintain them in the Netherlands, both as an effective defense force against France and as a reliable weapon against possible opposition in the country itself. All the opposition to Habsburg imperial policy, to the wars, the heavy taxation, the extension of government power at the expense of old privileges, was concentrated on this one issue. Philip had to give way, but he did so grudgingly and late. From then on, he determined that the states general could not be trusted.

The only sign of direct Spanish domination had now been removed. The government which the king provided on his departure was an almost purely Netherlands government in the Burgundian tradition. He appointed his half-sister, Margaret, wife of Ottavio Farnese, duke of Parma, as the new governor general. Margaret, an illegitimate daughter of Charles V, was herself born in the Netherlands, and her appointment seemed to continue the tradition created by the emperor with the appointment of his aunt, Margaret of Austria, and his sister, Mary of Hungary. The high nobility, members of the Order of the Golden Fleece, occupied the provincial governorships. Several of them, including the popular wartime hero the count of Egmont, the prince of Orange, and their friend, the count of Hoorn, became members of the Council of State. The high nobility had long since outgrown their purely provincial interests; they saw the best chance of advancement in the greatness of their prince. For more than half a century the Habsburgs had relied on them to further their policy of centralizing the government of the seventeen provinces. Philip thought he could count on their continued loyalty. At the same time, he did not fully trust them. In his secret instructions to Margaret of Parma, he commanded her to take all important decisions with the advice only of Granvelle, of the president of the privy council, Viglius, and of the ultraloyal Walloon, the count of Berlaymont. Ultimate authority resided, of course, in Madrid, and the king, as everyone knew, disliked taking decisions.

From the very beginning, Margaret's government was faced with a religious and a financial crisis. Heresy was spreading rapidly. There was nothing new in this. The established Church in the Netherlands had long been notorious for its worldliness and for its inadequacy in ministering to the religious needs of the population. Erasmus and his friends had sought to reform the Church from the inside and to instil into it the spirit of piety, enlightenment, and peace. They had great influence on the educated classes, and their spirit persisted even when, from the 1520's, more radical reformers began to appear. It was against these, the Lutherans, the Anabaptists, and, later, the Mennonites that the government of Charles V directed ever more rigorous placards. Hundreds paid for their faith at the stake; yet persecution remained sporadic and only very partially effective. Except for the Lutherans, the new sects had not usually touched the ruling classes of patricians and nobles. Yet many of these, and especially those influenced by Erasmian ideas, felt a growing revulsion against the practice of burning their fellow citizens for their religious beliefs. The placards were never executed systematically and the episcopal Inquisition remained highly unpopular.

But from about 1560 the situation changed. For the first time, Calvinist preachers began to appear in considerable numbers. Soon they could assure Calvin that the sale of his writings was increasing rapidly. The peace with France brought contact with the French Protestants. Calvin himself wrote, "I, too, am a Belgian." From Geneva, from Germany, and from England the propagation of his teaching in the Netherlands was organized almost as vigorously as in France. For the first time, too, the preachers began to make a large number of converts from among the patrician and noble classes. Socially, Calvinism was "respectable" in a way the Baptist sects could never be. As Catholic observers rightly saw, the preachers were particularly successful where there was unemployment and economic discontent among workers and artisans; but they mistook the nature of Calvinism when they argued that religion was only a pretense to cloak economic ambitions. It was precisely its religious appeal which enabled Calvinism to become a movement including all classes and then to draw to itself ambitious nobles or hungry weavers. It was this characteristic which made the Calvinist movement much more formidable and dangerous to the established order than the earlier heresies.

The development of Calvinist organization was much slower than in France. The dangers to the preachers and to the members of Protestant conventicles were real; nevertheless, they were coming more and more into the open. The mood of the country was such that the government dared not pursue a consistent policy of rigorous suppression of heresy. It seems that the Calvinists organized a definite propaganda campaign to make people believe that the king wanted to introduce the Spanish Inquisition. Philip had no such intention. He knew it would be far too dangerous. Besides, as he wrote to Margaret in 1562, the Netherlands Inquisition was less merciful than the Spanish, for it condemned to death even those heretics who were penitent. He never understood the peculiar terror and abhorrence which the Spanish Inquisition and its procedure inspired in the whole of Europe. But even before the Calvinist danger had become acute, he had determined to strengthen ecclesiastical authority and the fight against heresy by a complete reorganization of the Netherlands Church. In 1561 the pope published the bulls for the erection of fourteen new bishoprics. The right of election was taken away from the cathedral chapters and vested in the crown. Some of the oldest and richest monasteries, especially in Brabant, were to provide the newly appointed bishops with their episcopal revenues.

There was much to be said for the plan. It made the Church of the Netherlands independent of the archiepiscopal sees of Cologne and Rheims, both outside the king's jurisdiction, and it gave a better organization to a Church which was notoriously weak and badly staffed. But the plan proved to be exceedingly unpopular. The abbots of the monasteries clamored loudly against their loss of independence and income. The nobles saw rich prizes of patronage and careers for their younger sons slipping from their grasp and handed over to the hated lawyers and theologians. They joined the Calvinists in representing the scheme to the people as a first step toward the introduction of the Spanish Inquisition. Since the latter part of the emperor's reign, the high nobility had seen the control of the empire monopolized by Spaniards and Italians. All the more fiercely they now strove to assert their power in their own country. But Philip had allowed them only the shadow of power. Now the new primate of the Netherlands Church, the archbishop of Malines, would have the first voice in the assembly of the estates of Brabant, and this new archbishop was Cardinal Granvelle.

For William of Nassau, sovereign prince of the small state of Orange on the lower Rhone, and the richest of the Netherlands magnates, this was not just a matter of personalities. His family had served the Habsburgs for generations and he himself had been a great favorite with the emperor. His politics had been no different from those of other great lords in the Netherlands. Together with Egmont and Hoorn, he had for years quarreled with the estates of Holland over tax exemption of their properties in that province. As governor of Holland and Zeeland, he had always supported the authority of the central government against the estates. Later, he was to claim that his opposition to Philip II began when, during the negotiations for the Treaty of Cateau-Cambrésis, Henry II spoke to him of a plan of the two kings to join forces in putting down heresy in their dominions. But it seems probable that only gradually he came to see the full danger of Philip's policies for the Netherlands. The champion of narrow class interests developed into the defender of the liberties of all the king's subjects. William's religious convictions have been a matter of dispute. But there is no question that, like most of the educated nobility of the Netherlands, he detested all forms of religious persecution. More clearly, and earlier, than his noble friends he saw the implications of Philip's plan to reform the bishoprics: an enormous increase in the power of the crown. With complete control over the Netherlands Church, the king would be able not only to make religious persecution much more effective, but also to dispense more and more with the co-operation of the nobility and the estates. As yet, Orange was not prepared to co-operate with the Calvinists. Their intolerance repelled him. His upbringing and his marriage to Anna of Saxony, daughter of the famous elector Maurice, made him rather seek the support of the Lutheran princes of Germany. His opposition to royal absolutism was still largely that of the great lord whom his king would allow only the shadow and not the substance of power. It was Granvelle who seemed to personify the royal absolutism. From 1561, Orange, Egmont, and their friends tried to overthrow the cardinal.

For the government, this opposition was the more serious as the financial crisis left Margaret and Granvelle little room for maneuver. The servicing of the enormous government debt, the legacy of the French wars, swallowed up ordinary revenue and the eight hundred thousand florins a year of the nine-year grant by the states general. Troops and officials remained unpaid, and government authority in the country deteriorated dangerously. Margaret had to appeal to the estates for financial help and every appeal became a constitutional crisis, giving the estates and the high nobility a chance to attack Granvelle and the government's religious policy. Philip reacted, true to his character, by trying to stir up faction strife and by intriguing with one part of the high nobility against the other, even though Granvelle himself warned against the dangers of such a course of action. Not all the seigneurs had joined Orange's league against the cardinal. The duke of Aerschot, with the widespread family connection of his old Walloon house of Croy, and several others of the Walloon nobility resented the political leadership of Orange and Egmont and remained loyal to the government. As in France, the parties tended to crystallize around the personal rivalries of the great noble houses.

In 1564 the prince of Orange's league of the great lords, helped by a personal intrigue of Margaret of Parma against Granvelle, achieved their first political objective, the recall of the cardinal and his retirement to his estates in Franche-Comté. Granvelle never returned, though later he was still to serve his master faithfully in Italy and Spain; but for the nobles it was a hollow victory. The cardinal's party in the government accused the lords of incompetence and corruption, probably with some justice. Though Orange and his friends were now the government's spokesmen in the assemblies of the provincial estates, the deputies remained as intransigent to the lords' financial demands as they had been to the cardinal's. They insisted on a more liberal religious policy and on the summoning of the states general to deal with all the country's problems. The lords supported these demands. All sides sent complaints to Madrid and thus increased Philip's distrust of the Netherlanders. As early as 1563, the duke of Alva had recommended cutting off the heads of half a dozen great lords.

But as yet there was no alternative to government by consent. Philip had no means of carrying out Alva's suggestion, even if he had so desired. In the event, he tried honestly, though with his usual exasperating hesitations, to work with the nobles and meet at least some of their demands—all of them, so Egmont thought when he visited Madrid in 1565. Orange saw the situation more clearly. Philip would not really abdicate his control over the government to the nobility; nor would he make concessions on the religious question. In two letters to Margaret in October 1565, Philip put an end to all hopes of any Netherlands equivalent to an Edict of Amboise. The edicts against the heretics must be enforced, the king wrote, and the Netherlands Inquisition must continue to function. Margaret was not to summon the states general until the religious situation had improved. Finally, since the lords had wished for an increase in the membership of the Council of State, he now appointed the duke of Aerschot, Orange's most powerful opponent among the Netherlands nobility. It took Margaret a whole week to summon up enough courage to publish the king's orders. She was right in her apprehensions. Philip's letters were the signal for revolution.

The weakness of the Netherlands government, especially after the departure of Granvelle, had given the Calvinist preachers their chance to exploit the growing social tensions of Netherlands society. The lower nobility began to join the reform movement in large numbers and rapidly gave the religious conventicles the military character which had already made the Huguenots such a formidable power in France. Open mass meetings were held, with the women in the center and the men, armed with every conceivable weapon and commanded by a noble member of the congregation, standing guard. The court at Brussels, undoubtedly with events in France before their eyes, began to fear open rebellion or, at least, the seizure of some important towns by the Protestants. In November 1565 the members of the lower nobility formed a league, the Compromise, with the object of inducing the government to abolish the Inquisition and to moderate the edicts against the heretics. The leaders were men of almost the same social standing as the great lords of the Golden Fleece: Brederode, wild and hard-drinking, with Calivnist sympathies, and Louis of Nassau, brother of the prince of Orange, leaning rather toward the Lutherans. The Compromise, as its name indicated, was intended to, and did, include Catholics who disliked the government's religious policy. From the beginning, there was talk of using force, if the government should not agree to their demands. The two hundred noblemen who rode into Brussels on April 3, 1566, to present their petition with its four hundred signatures, did not, however, do much more than toast their new nickname of *gueux*, beggars, at numerous brave banquets. The majority of the lower nobility still stood aside, especially in the southern provinces.

The real revolution was started by the lower classes in the towns. Artisans' wages had caught up with rising prices, but those of unskilled workers had not. The textile and the shipping industries, depending on foreign supplies and on export markets, were subject to violent booms and depressions. The Seven Years War between Denmark and Sweden (1563–1570) and the temporary closing of the Sound to shipping had brought on one of these depressions. Anglo-Netherlands quarrels over mutual restrictions on each other's trade, English piracy in the Channel, and Granvelle's sensitivity to the English merchants' support for the Antwerpers in their resistance to the new bishoprics boiled up to a Netherlands embargo on the import of English cloth and the English removal of their staple from Antwerp to Emden (1564). In Antwerp there was heavy unemployment and a sharp fall in wages. The winter of 1565–1566 added famine, which the people blamed on the grain speculators and on the government. During the spring and summer of 1566, prices came down, but people remained afraid. In Antwerp and in the textile towns and villages of Walloon Flanders, they flocked in their thousands to the Calvinist preachers and their consoling and exciting sermons. Was it not intolerable that the Lord's elect should be excluded from the churches of their own towns and that these churches should be filled with idolatrous images and with the gold and silver which greedy prelates had wrung from the poor by a monstrous tithe? In July the radical wing of the Compromise agreed to co-operate with the Calvinist burgher communities. In August there was another, unexpected, rise in food prices. On August 10, rioting broke out. In Antwerp, and throughout Flanders and many other parts, crowds invaded the churches and monasteries and smashed pictures, statues, and altars. There is some evidence that it was an organized movement, but it is not conclusive. Where the municipal authorities stood firm, as in Amsterdam, they found it easy enough to maintain order and protect the churches. Elsewhere, as in Ghent, it seems that the city fathers preferred the spoiling of the churches to the threatened sacking of their own houses. The country was seething with rumors of vast hordes of armed Protestants marching on the cities and wreaking vengeance on priests and magistrates. The hordes never materialized.

The government in Brussels hesitated for two weeks. Margaret had no troops, and it was not immediately clear on whom she could rely to restore order. But the Catholics and moderates in the Compromise had been thoroughly frightened by the outbreaks and now hastened to assure the governor general of their loyalty. Margaret was able to persuade the leaders of the Compromise to dissolve their association in return for a promise to abolish the Netherlands Inquisition and moderate the edicts against heresy. Philip sent some money, and Margaret was now able to raise troops. In the autumn of 1566 and in the following winter, Brederode's armed bands were dispersed and the Catholic nobles defeated the popular Calvinist movements in Walloon Flanders. The majority of the high nobility, including Egmont, took a new oath of loyalty to the king. Only those most compromised fled abroad. Orange thought it safer to join them. He had tried to pursue a moderate policy by supporting the demands of the opposition but upholding the government's authority by foiling Brederode's attack on Antwerp. His policy had failed, and he was bitterly denounced by Catholics and Calvinists alike.

It was a commonplace of sixteenth-century statecraft that rebellions should be crushed in their infancy. The Scottish and French governments had failed to do this, and the disasters which followed were there for every sensible Catholic statesmen to see. In the summer of 1566, Philip II decided to send his best general, the duke of Alva, with a large force of Spanish and Italian troops to the Netherlands to reassert his authority. As always, it took time. Margaret, convinced that she had now broken the opposition, adjured her brother to leave well alone. There were doubts in Madrid about the wisdom of committing such a large part of the king's military resources so far from their base and from the main enemy, the Turk. The Netherlands nobility still had friends at court. But Philip had made up his mind, and the Gómez faction hoped to see Alva sink in the quicksands of Netherlands politics.

Alva arrived in Brussels on August 22, 1567, and effectively took over from Margaret of Parma. To the Iron Duke, the problem he was asked to solve appeared threefold. He must punish the leaders of the opposition for *lèse-majesté;* he must make the administration of the towns and provinces completely dependent on the central government; and he must secure a stable and permanent financial basis for his government and his army. The first aim was easily achieved. In September the duke arrested Egmont and Hoorn, all privileges of the Order of the Golden Fleece notwithstanding. The king himself followed suit by arresting Hoorn's brother, Montigny, in Madrid. A newly constituted court, the Council of Troubles, soon to be known as the Council of Blood, tried and condemned altogether some twelve thousand of those who had taken part in the movements of the previous year. As usually happens on such occasions, informers flourished. Mutual trust, the social cement of any society, began to break down. Alva's was a deliberate policy of terror and, in the short run, it worked. Not a single town rose to support the prince of Orange when he invaded the Netherlands from Germany in 1568. Alva took the opportunity to have Egmont, Hoorn, and several other nobles executed in the market square of Brussels. After that, he was able to deal at his leisure with Orange's ill-paid and undisciplined troops. As a general, the prince was no match for the duke.

Alva's second aim met with immediate opposition. Provincial governors and town councils resented the government's interference in their administration and its disregard of their privileges. Open resistance was out of the question; but the hostility of even the most loyal Catholics was unmistakable. Alva complained more and more bitterly to the king of the "satraps" Aerschot and Noircarmes, and even of the former yes men Berlaymont and Viglius. Alva's policy was producing an unexpected result: the birth of a new party, the *politiques*, who were Catholic and royalist but who put the independence of their country first and religion second. Alva was under no illusion about Philip's political practice. Sooner or later the king would listen to his opponents in the Netherlands and to their friends at court who were his enemies, just as he had listened to the duke himself against Margaret of Parma.

It was Alva's financial problem, however, which presented him with his most immediate difficulties. He demanded the payment of a once-for-all tax of a hundredth penny (i.e. 1 per cent) on real property. Secondly, he intended to introduce a 10 per cent import, export, and sales tax on all merchandise. This tax of the tenth penny, like the Spanish *alcabala*, was to be permanent and was to make the government independent of the estates. It is a sign of the extent to which sixteenth-century governments rested on consent and the co-operation of the governed that even Alva did not possess the power and the machinery simply to levy these taxes. He had to summon the states general in March 1569, but it was to meet for only one day, simply to approve the new measures.

The plan misfired badly. The estates agreed to the tax on property but refused the tenth penny. Alva threatened dire punishments and those estates which were constituted only of nobles and patricians gave in. The merchants could, after all, pass most of the taxes on to the consumer in the form of higher prices. But in Brabant, where the artisans were represented in the estates, the taxes were rejected. In the big towns of Flanders and the Walloon provinces, the deputies who had voted for the taxes began to fear for their lives, just as had happened in Castile in 1520. Caught between Alva's anger and the people's fury, the estates and town councils entered upon a policy of passive resistance. The governor general had, in the meantime, himself become convinced that the 10-per-cent sales tax would be disastrous to the trade of the country; or he may have been worried by the evident cooling of the king's enthusiasm for this plan to beggar his subjects. Alva therefore progressively modified the tax until it began to look more like the type of taxes which towns and provinces had themselves been imposing. But to the majority of Netherlanders it remained objectionable; it was still a perpetual tax and, above all, it was still appallingly heavy. Everywhere the resistance to the tax was hardening. Aldermen denounced it in the town halls, shopkeepers cursed it in the market squares, and priests fulminated against it from the pulpits. In the end, Alva's famous tenth penny, to which many historians have ascribed the economic ruin of the Netherlands, was levied even in its attenuated form only very sporadically in a few small towns, and in most provinces not at all.[11] The estates sent deputations to Madrid and offered Alva annual grants of two million florins on the basis of the traditional forms of parliamentary taxation. Alva agreed to negotiate on this basis, aware that he was losing the king's backing for his own proposals. Immediately, he was engulfed in all the exasperating parleys, bargains, and delays wihch had made the lives of previous governor generals such a misery. When, in 1572, Holland and Zeeland fell to the Sea Beggars and Ghent and Bruges were on the point of rebellion, Alva had to give up the tenth penny altogether and with it all hope of making the Netherlands pay for his military establishment. This burden now fell on Spain and the king's own treasury and this

11. J. Craeybeckx, "De Staten van Vlaanderen en de gewestelijke Financiën in de XVI eeuw," in *Handelingen der Maatschappij voor Geschiedenis en Oudheidkunde te Gent*, 1950; also "Alva's Tiende Penning, een Mythe?", in *Bijdragen en Mededelingen van het Historisch Genootschap te Utrecht*, vol. LXXVI, 1962.

at the very time when Spain was making her greatest efforts against the Turks.

Orange had organized the military and diplomatic offensive against Alva from his brother's principality of Nassau. He had become convinced that Philip's autocracy could be overthrown only by force. What he wanted to put in its place is far less certain at this point. Perhaps William was not entirely clear about it himself. But he was now committeed to a fight *à outrance*; whereas many on his side were willing to compromise with the king, he was convinced that Spanish power in the Netherlands must be completely destroyed. For the next sixteen years, until his death in 1584, he pursued this aim with complete singleness of purpose. Philip saw himself entrusted by God with the preservation of his subjects in the true Catholic religion. To accomplish this divine purpose he felt duty bound to use his royal powers, if need be, to the point of the most ruthless political tyranny. William, for his part, saw himself as the defender of his own aristocratic rights and liberties, of the rights and liberties of his order and, ultimately, of those of his country and of the individual conscience against political absolutism and religious persecution. There was no bridge between these two concepts. The court of Madrid misunderstood William's motives, attributing them to mere ambition; but it was right in seeing him as the driving force behind the revolt, without whose determination and political ability it might never have survived.

Louis of Nassau was in touch with Coligny and Walsingham, then English ambassador in Paris. There seemed to be no hope of success without French or English help. Louis, at least, did not hesitate to bribe potential allies with the promise of some of the seventeen provinces. The nobles who had fled from the Netherlands organized a naval force, the Sea Beggars. From Emden, La Rochelle, and England their ships preyed on Spanish and Netherlands commerce. Their activities, and the trade war between England and the Netherlands which followed Elizabeth's seizure of four ships with £85,000 Genoese money for Alva (December 1568), did much to increase the economic malaise of the Netherlands and the discontent of the lower classes. In April 1572 the Sea Beggars seized the small port of Brill in Holland. Then they set out systematically to capture the towns of Holland and Zeeland. In most cases the pattern of events was remarkably similar. The patrician councils of the towns had nearly all large Catholic majorities who were loyal to the government, even though they detested Alva's religious persecution and heavy taxation. The great mass of the burghers were with them in preferring peace and loyalty to war and revolution. Organized as *schutters* in the citizen guards, they proudly maintained that they were suffcient to protect their own towns, and they therefore opposed the entry of Spanish garrisons. Alva, short of money and troops, had no choice but to accept this position. In May 1572 Louis of Nassau captured Mons, near the French border. With the French government dominated by Coligny, Alva had to fear a full-scale French invasion. Orange was preparing to attack him from Germany. Alva turned south to deal first with the most dangerous threat.

He besieged Mons and annihilated a small Huguenot army sent to its relief. The massacre of St. Bartholomew (August 14, 1572) finally removed his fears from this front. Orange's offensive once more collapsed and Alva was now free to turn north.

It was already too late. The Beggars in Holland and Zeeland could rely on a small but determined minority of fanatical Calvinists in the town councils and on the sympathy of sections of the *schutters*. Calvinist preachers and organizers worked among the townspeople, making converts especially among the sailors, shipbuilders, and fishermen. When the Beggar forces approached a town, the Calvinist minorities would open the gates to them and force the authorities to treat. In most towns the Beggars entered by agreement. Where the strategic situation allowed, a determined council could prevent their entry. Thus Amsterdam maintained its loyalty to the king until 1578 and Middelburg resisted a Beggar siege for eighteen months. Its burghers showed no less heroism in their loyalty to Philip II than did those of Leiden in their famous resistance to him (1574). Once the Beggars were inside a town they rapidly broke their agreements with the authorities. Public preaching of the reformed faith was followed by the conversion of churches to Protestant use, by image-breaking, and by brutal attacks on monasteries and convents. Some of the *gueux* leaders used terror as a deliberate policy, just as Alva did, until Orange stopped them. Loyalist and moderate magistrates and officers of the citizen guards were replaced by Beggar officers and ardent Calvinists. The number of convinced Calvinists remained small for a long time. Only very gradually, through the work of schools, propaganda, and official pressure, was the majority of the population won over to the new faith. In July 1572 the estates of Holland met at Dordrecht and recognized the prince of Orange as their governor, nominally in the name of the king.[12]

The revolution now had a firm territorial basis. Holland and Zeeland were ruled by their estates in combination with their governor. Orange recognized that, effectively, his authority derived from the estates and no longer from the king. But the towns, and through them the estates, were still controlled by the patricians. On the religious side, Orange could not fully control the Beggar movement with its popular following and establish full toleration for Catholics, as he wished. Politically and militarily, he could still use the *gueux* for his wider plans of overthrowing the Spanish government in the whole Netherlands.

Alva's counteroffensive, in the winter months of 1572–1573, was formidable and ruthless. He gained notable victories and reconquered a number of towns. In the end he failed because he lacked sufficient sea power. The heart of Holland and Zeeland remained impregnable to land armies, protected as it was by the great rivers and by flooded marshes. In 1573 Philip acceded to Alva's repeated requests for recall. His policy had failed and his enemies in Madrid had undermined the king's confidence in him. He never

12. My interpretation of the revolution in Holland and Zeeland follows, roughly, the views of P. Geyl, *The Revolt of the Netherlands* (London, 1932), and of H. A. Enno van Gelder's many studies of the period.

regained it, even though he was to conquer Portugal for his master.

The new governor general, Don Luis de Requesens, immediately broke with Alva's policy of terror. He issued a general pardon and finally abolished the chimerical tenth penny. But Philip refused to make concessions on the religious issue, and so the struggle against Holland and Zeeland had to continue. Again the royalist armies, composed of Italians, Germans, and Walloons, as well as Spaniards, achieved striking successes in the field and again they failed against the Beggars' superior naval power. In the loyal provinces, Requesens was faced with the growing opposition of the old privileged classes who saw in the government's difficulties their opportunity to regain their lost power. More and more, he had to depend on Madrid for money to pay his troops.

Spain could not carry this increased burden. Philip had managed to double his revenues since his return, by increasing the *encabezamiento*,[13] by imposing new export taxes and by large subsidies from the clergy. Nevertheless, rising prices and the wars in the Mediterranean and Granada had pushed up government expenditure even more rapidly. In 1573 the government informed the cortes that its debts were close to fifty million ducats (they had been about twenty million at the abdication of Charles V). Perhaps one-third of all revenues was swallowed up by payments of interest on this sum. Philip now forced the protesting delegates of the cortes to raise the *encabezamiento* to more than double its previous amount (1574). But the

13. See Chap. I, p. 38, for the technical terms used here.

resources of the Castilian *pecheros* were exhausted. Several towns resorted to the imposition of the *alcabala* in place of the *encabezamiento,* and its yields fell far short of the government's expectations. On September 1, 1575, Philip's government had to suspend payment on its debts.

Spain's second bankruptcy caused a financial crisis in Genoa and Antwerp and threw out of gear the whole complicated credit structure on which the transfer of money from Spain and Italy to the Netherlands depended. The results were disastrous. The unpaid armies in the Netherlands mutinied. When the governor general died (March 5, 1576), the regiments got completely out of hand. The king's authority in the Netherlands collapsed with the collapse of his finances. When, later, Spanish finances partially recovered, owing to the vast increase of silver shipments from the New World, the king's authority was also partially recovered.

This was not, of course, the whole story. In the Council of State, the *politiques*, with the duke of Aerschot as their leader, seized the initiative. They outlawed the mutinous regiments, and the estates of Brabant raised troops of their own. On September 4, 1576, these troops, in conjunction with the citizen guard of Brussels, arrested the Council of State. Its *politique* members were released and gave their authority to a further revolutionary move, the summoning of the states general by the estates of Brabant. Its immediate tasks were to protect the country from the mutinous soldiers and to end the civil war with Holland and Zeeland. In the first of these objectives the states general signally failed. On November 4, 1576, Spanish troops entered

Antwerp, killed over seven thousand people, and subjected the town to several days of plunder and murder. Neither Antwerp nor Spain fully recovered from the material blow and the moral outrage. A few days earlier the representatives of the states general and of the prince of Orange had arrived at a compromise. The Pacification of Ghent (published November 8, 1576) stipulated the withdrawal of all foreign troops from the Netherlands, government only with the consent of the states general, the suspension of the edicts against heresy, and the settlement of the religious question by a future states general. The continued predominance of Calvinism in Holland and Zeeland, and of Catholicism in the other provinces, was thus tacitly acknowledged. The "Peace of the duke of Aerschot," like the "Peace of Monsieur" in France in the same year, was the high-water mark of the influence of the *politiques.*

Faced with the bankruptcy of his policy of the last ten years, Philip was as usual loath to take decisions. He appointed his brother as Requesens' successor, hoping that Don John's tremendous prestige would make a solution possible. But, from the spring to the autumn of 1576, he did nothing to intervene in the Netherlands nor even to support Gerónimo de Roda, his Spanish representative on the Council of State. Don John arrived in November without money or troops. It was clear that, at least on the political side, he and the king would have to make serious concessions. In February 1577 Don John signed the Eternal Edict with the states general. The Spanish troops were to be sent away, but the Catholic religion was to be restored in all provinces without reference to the states general. Holland and Zeeland immediately protested, recalled their delegates from the states general, and refused to recognize Don John as governor general.

For the next months, Don John tried to establish his authority. The states general and the great nobles, however, were unwilling to give up the power they had just gained. Don John was intelligent enough to know himself utterly unsuited to his exasperating task. "They fear me and regard me as choleric; I detest them and regard them as the greatest scoundrels," he wrote in February 1577. He knew now that neither the states general nor the king would sanction his plans for the liberation of Mary Queen of Scots. On July 24, 1577, he reverted to the more congenial role of soldier and captured Namur. The war had started again. For the moment, it seemed to be no longer a civil war but a national war against Spain.

Orange's ideal of the union of all the provinces against Spain had been achieved—but only at the cost of the homogeneity of his revolutionary movement. In Holland and Zeeland, the patricians of the towns had never had to share power with the gilds. The Beggar movement had made use of the artisans, but they were neither numerous nor politically experienced enough to act on their own. The patrician town councils, having accepted the reformed religion or replaced one group of patrician councilors by another, had remained in control of the towns and, through them, of the assembly of estates. In the large industrial towns of Flanders and Brabant, on the other hand, the artisans, through their gilds, had a constitutional voice in the government of their towns and a long tradition of upholding it by revolutionary action. Neither they nor the high nobility of the south were amenable to control by the Beggar movement, nor willing to accept Orange's policy of limited revolution and religious toleration. Here was a fundamental difference in the social and political structure of the northern and the southern provinces which foreshadowed the ultimate division of the Netherlands.

The towns of Flanders and Brabant had obtained the restoration of all privileges and these included much greater powers for the gilds. At the same time, the magistrates of the towns were still the old Catholic patricians, often appointed by Alva himself. From August 1577 social and religious revolutions broke out in Brussels, Antwerp, 's Hertogenbosch, and Ghent. In Brussels, the popular element in the city government chose a war council of eighteen which soon came to dominate it. Other towns followed this example and chose their own councils of eighteen. They were usually dominated by the Calvinists. The now familiar pattern of events repeated itself. The mobs were allowed, or incited, to sack churches and monasteries; Catholic magistrates were replaced by Calvinists; the councils of eighteen appointed their own creatures as captains of the citizen guards; and Catholic burghers were terrorized into silence.

Nowhere was the revolution carried so far as in Ghent. Fired by the demagogic preaching of Peter Dathenus, and organized by the able and ambitious lord of Rijhove and by the self-appointed popular tribune Jan van Hembyze, the Ghenters carried their revolution through the length and breadth of Flanders. With the help of native sympathizers, they set up revolutionary Calvinist governments in Bruges, Ypres, Oudenaarde, and other towns.

The political revolution of 1576 had become a social and religious revolution and this broke the common front against Spain. To the duke of Aerschot and his friends, it seemed that the towns had set up a political and religious tyranny even more odious than that of the Spaniards. The great lords had overthrown Spanish rule in the south, only to find themselves as powerless as before. In the autumn of 1577, they invited the emperor's brother, the archduke Matthias, to become governor general, but when they had installed him in Brussels, they found that he preferred to work with the prince of Orange, whom the states general had appointed as his lieutenant.

The old jealousy between the Croy and the Nassau flared up again. In January 1578, Don John inflicted a crushing defeat on the states general's troops, commanded by the nobility. In the mutual recriminations which followed the battle of Gembloux, the lords complained, with justice, that the states general failed to pay their troops. Singly, or in family groups, they began to make their peace with the king or assume an independent position, as "malcontents," looking to France and the duke of Anjou for support.

Orange did his utmost to prevent the breach and to moderate the revolutionary movements. In August 1579 he entered Ghent in force and, with the support of Rijhove and the moderates, disarmed the eighteen. Hembyze and Dathenus fled. But the harm was done. In January 1579 the Walloon nobles formed the Union of Arras, and in June this Union came to terms with the king.

Don John had died in October 1578, and Philip appointed his nephew, Margaret of Parma's son, Alexander Farnese, to succeed him. For the first time he had found a governor general who had all the qualities needed for this most difficult post. Farnese, at 33, had none of Don John's self-doubts nor any of his romantic visions of captive queens rescued and kingdoms conquered for himself. He was as convinced of the justice of the king's cause as Philip himself, although in temperament and religious beliefs he was nearer to his grandfather the emperor than to his uncle the king. Superbly confident in his own abilities, he rejected Philip's proposal to make him commander in chief while reappointing his mother, Margaret, as governor general. The king had to give way and, for once, delegated sufficient powers to his new governor general. Farnese had a free hand to make any concessions he saw fit, except in questions of the king's ultimate authority and in the maintenance of the old religion.

In the south the nobles were sufficiently powerful to carry the Walloon provinces with them into the Union of Arras, despite some resistance in the larger towns. Farnese had to agree, once again, to send all foreign troops away and to govern with the consent of the estates. The Walloon nobility seemed to have maintained all the gains of the Pacification of Ghent, which, indeed, they regarded as the basis of their Union. But the war continued and the king's foreign troops had to be recalled yet again. This inescapable necessity, and Farnese's skillful strategy, gradually weighted the balance of political power decisively in favor of the crown.

The northern provinces formed their union at the same

time (January 1579) and on the basis of their own interpretation of the Pacification of Ghent. It was a Calvinist and a constitutional interpretation, even though the union was formed against the opposition of the estates of Catholic Guelders. The Union of Utrecht (Holland, Zeeland, Utrecht, Friesland, Guelders, Drenthe, Overijssel and the province, but not the city, of Groningen) gave political power to the estates and to the house of Orange. The balance of power between them, however, remained the subject of conflict for more than a century.

Orange himself had originally favored a closer union of the northern provinces. The actual union was concluded against his wishes, for its uncompromising Calvinism made it virtually impossible to achieve his ideal of uniting all provinces on the basis of a religious peace. Farnese's military successes, moreover, induced the prince to look once more to France for help. To obtain this, he was prepared to offer the sovereignty of the Netherlands to Henry III's brother, the duke of Anjou, for the king himself declined it. Such plans were regarded as high treason in Madrid. Philip declared Orange an outlaw and put a price on his head. Orange answered with his *Apology*, the first consistent, and highly imaginative, statement of the "black legend" against Philip II and Spain. The pamphlet war now reached new heights, both in the level of argument and in shrillness of tone. The Calvinists and antiroyalists had the better of this propaganda warfare throughout the conflict. The royalist side was inhibited by its unwillingness to debase the king's authority by arguing about his policy with his subjects. In 1581 the states general renounced their allegiance to Philip II. "God did not create the people slaves to their prince," thus ran the Act of Abjuration, "to obey his commands whether right or wrong, but rather the prince for the sake of his subjects, to love and support them as a father his children or a shepherd his flock." Perhaps the wording was deliberately modeled on that of the instructions which Philip used to give to his viceroys, for it is strikingly similar.

The duke of Anjou, the new sovereign to whom the provinces now swore a reluctant allegiance, had been the leader of the *politiques* in France; but his ambitions were personal. All parties could therefore use him for their own ends. Henry III, fearing Anjou's influence in France, was glad to divert his energies abroad and, at the same time, make trouble for Spain without committing himself. Elizabeth had similar reasons in her enjoyable marriage negotiations with the duke; and if these also created trouble in France by raising Anjou's prestige, so much the better. Orange and the states general needed Anjou's name and troops, but would grant him no power in the government of the Union. More and more, the Netherlands became the focal point for all the political and religious struggles of western Europe—the only place where, as yet, France and England dared to challenge the hegemony of Spain. Flanders, Brabant, and the northeastern provinces became the battleground of international armies: Germans, Scots, English, and French on the side of the states general; Spaniards, Italians, and Germans on the royalist side. Only for the Netherlanders was it still a civil war.

Systematically Farnese set about his task of reconquest.

There were no more massacres to terrorize the population. If a town returned to obedience to the king and the old religion, the governor general promised the citizens their lives, property, and many of their local privileges. Town after town surrendered on these terms. Anjou's troops were both unsuccessful and unpopular. The duke himself found his relations with the states general as frustrating as had Don John. In France he was taunted with the concessions he had made to heretics and commoners. He reacted like Don John. In January 1583 he attempted to seize Antwerp. The coup failed miserably and Anjou lost what little prestige he still commanded.

As military reverse followed on military reverse, the extremists in Flanders once more gained the upper hand. Four years after their flight, Hembyze and Dathenus returned to Ghent (August 1583). The dictatorship was re-established. But, just as it was to happen in later revolutionary movements, the struggle for power inside the movement became more important than the struggle against the common enemy. Hembyze and Dathenus opened negotiations with Farnese and started replacing Calvinist officials with Catholics. This was too much for their own supporters. In March 1584 they arrested Hembyze, and on August 4 the old dictator was executed. But the revolution was lost; six weeks later Ghent surrendered to the Spaniards. In March 1585 Brussels fell, and in August Antwerp capitulated after a siege of thirteen months.

From then on, the issue between the rebels and the Spaniards became almost entirely a military one. The period of revolutions was over. In the south, Calvinists and

Catholics no longer intermingled in the former explosive mixture. Farnese expelled the Calvinist preachers and many thousands of laymen followed them to the northern provinces, or to England and Germany, for a variety of religious, political, and economic reasons. A reorganized and purified Church was able to win back to Catholicism the great majority of the population, and this without the use of the Inquisition. The contemporary penchant for burning the heterodox could be safely indulged against Baptists and witches without causing political repercussions. It was a practice in which, at least in the case of witches, the Protestant countries did not lag behind. At the same time, the idea of religious peace, of the co-existence of Catholics and Protestants in one political community and with equal rights, had died. Orange, its greatest protagonist, fell to the bullets of a fanatic (July 10, 1584). He had failed to preserve the unity of the Netherlands; but he had succeeded both in keeping alive the resistance to Philip II's political and religious absolutism and in co-operating, as head of a government, with an assembly of estates. It was a remarkable achievement for a conservative aristocrat turned revolutionary. No other revolutionary leader of the sixteenth century could rival him in his understanding of the political forces, both of his own country and of Europe, nor in the diplomatic skill with which he made them serve his own ends. He could not always control these forces; but, in the course of the struggle, he imposed his personality on his own side until, in the end, all the old distrusts were stilled and all parties accepted his leadership, however much they might quarrel with his tactics. Much of William's motivation and many of his aims remained obscure to his contemporaries, as they have also remained obscure to historians. In this sense, his posthumous sobriquet, the Silent, is apt. But it was always clear what he fought against: despotic government and religious persecution. His reputed dying words, "Oh God, have pity on my soul and on this poor country," were broadcast throughout the provinces. All parties could now claim him for their own. His actual achievement, and the power of the myth attached to his name after his death, created a political pattern which made the Union of Utrecht a viable political structure despite the medieval particularism of its constituent towns and provinces.

The French civil wars to 1585

In France the crisis following the end of the Habsburg-Valois wars had developed even more rapidly than in the Netherlands. Its causes were essentially similar. After the bankruptcy of 1557, Henry II squeezed another seven million livres in extraordinary taxes out of his unfortunate subjects. Nevertheless, the limit had been reached. There were peasant revolts in Normandy and Languedoc. The nobles, though exempt from taxation, had spent their incomes and mortgaged or sold their estates in the king's service or for the heavy ransoms demanded of noble prisoners after the disaster of St. Quentin (1557). Peace left many without income or employment. Unlike the English gentry, they or their younger sons could not make their fortunes in trade. Both tradition and a specific law of 1560 forbade such a course. The luckier ones could enter the

Church; for the French Church had become a part of the enormous patronage system of the crown and the high nobility, so that, as people said, "bishoprics were sold like cinnamon and pepper." But the unlucky ones swelled the growing number of those who were clamoring for Church reforms.

In the towns, the small artisans and shopkeepers had been hit by heavy taxation and by the periodic collapse of rural purchasing power which followed bad harvests such as that of 1557. The journeymen saw food prices rising faster than wages and found that the growing influence and rigidity of the gilds blocked the advance of the majority to mastership.

Such conditions provided a fertile field for the Calvinist preachers. Their sermons, their Bible readings, and their services with communal singing of psalms, attracted ever greater numbers. Too often, the local curés could not emulate the preachers' eloquence nor satisfy the spiritual longings of a people whose lives had become insecure. Yet, just as in the Netherlands, the appeal of the reformed religion cut across class divisions. Many of the richer bourgeois and professional men, and more especially their womenfolk, were drawn toward the new doctrines.

From 1555 Geneva sent an increasing number of preachers into France. They were all Frenchmen, and a considerable proportion were noblemen, for it was Calvin's deliberate policy to convert the nobility. Wherever a Protestant community was established, it elected its elders and deacons to assure the discipline of the faithful, administer its funds, and, in general, look after the physical and spiritual welfare of its members. The pastors of the larger communities, or groups of smaller ones, were appointed by Theodore Beza or by Calvin himself. Thus, spiritual control was centered in Geneva and the whole movement had the characteristics of an international, as well as of a national, party. After 1559 the nobility joined the movement in large numbers, especially in the south. By the beginning of 1562, the majority of the Calvinist communities had placed themselves under the protection of a local seigneur. His influence would bring new converts, especially from the country population which had been comparatively untouched by the new religion. More important still was the military element introduced by the nobility. The religious conventicles became military cadres. Mass meetings of armed men, protected by the local nobility and their retainers, began to invade the churches and to celebrate their services in open defiance of public authority and of the feelings of the majority of the Catholic population. Nor did this happen only in the south. In May 1560 their assemblies in Rouen were said to be twenty thousand strong. The figure may be exaggerated, but the royal commander, with five thousand troops, could not prevent the scaffolds and gibbets he had set up from being torn down.

The Huguenot cadres were now organized on a provincial and national basis on the pattern of the religious communities wth ther provincial and national synods. The synod of Clairac, in November 1560, divided the province of Guienne into seven *colloques*, each with its colonel. In 1561 the synod of Sainte Foy decided on the election of two "protectors" for the regions of Toulouse and Bordeaux. Under these, there was a whole hierarchy of communal leaders, each strictly responsible to his immediate superior. By 1562 this organization was more or less fully developed in Guienne, Languedoc, Provence, and Dauphiné, and it existed at least in outline in the rest of France. Inevitably, the control of the movement tended to shift from the preachers to the nobles, despite Calvin's misgivings and his efforts to prevent it.

This organization could not have been built up had it not been for the weakness of the government. Henry II had been determined to destroy the Protestants. Their growing success had been one of the reasons why he had negotiated the peace with Spain. The government in Paris, however, found it as difficult as the government in Brussels to persuade its local Catholic officials to execute the edicts against their Protestant neighbors and fellow countrymen. Many sympathized or frankly joined the movement; still more disliked persecution. Throughout the years 1560 and 1561, the vicomte de Joyeuse, acting governor of Languedoc, wrote to the government with increasing gloom about his waning authority, the unreliability of his officials, and the increasing power and influence of the Huguenots, who were insulting loyal Catholics by claiming to act in the king's name.

The situation might still have been restored if the government had vigorously backed its provincial governors in their struggle against the Huguenots. But this was precisely what the government could no longer do. Henry II died, on July 26, 1559, from an injury received in a tournament. Francis II was only 15—legally of age, but clearly too young to rule the kingdom. A political crisis was now added to the social, financial, and religious problems of France. Francis I and Henry II had governed with the aid of the high nobility. With the help of royal favor, the house of Guise had amassed huge estates in the east and the house of Montmorency in the north and in the Île-de-France. The Bourbons had managed to hang on to most of their property in the south and in Picardy, despite the misfortune of the treason committed by the constable Bourbon in the reign of Francis I. As ministers and provincial governors, these great lords had built up a vast network of clientage among the local nobility. Municipal and provincial officials looked to them for advancement in their careers. As long as Henry II lived, the inevitable rivalries of the great lords were fought out within the constitutional limits of court intrigue. Now Francis II threw himself unreservedly into the arms of the Guises, the uncles of his wife, Mary Queen of Scots. Duke Francis of Guise, the defender of Metz and conqueror of Calais, and his younger brother Charles, the cardinal of Lorraine, were a formidable team; but their ascendancy was bound to be challenged. As descendants of the house of Lorraine, they prided themselves on their foreign origin in order to emphasize their loyalty to the French crown and their equality of status with all French princes. Their rivals made it an effective propaganda point against them. The old constable, Anne de Montmorency, resented his exclusion from power. The Bourbons openly demanded power for themselves. They were the nearest relatives of the Valois, princes of the blood who could claim the constitutional right to govern during a royal minority. Anthony, the head of the family and, through his wife, king of Navarre, lacked the personality and willpower to become an effective party leader, and was both too vain and too vacillating to become the reliable tool of anyone else. His younger brother, Louis, prince of Condé, attempted to make up for his deficiencies. As early as 1555 he had visited Geneva and shown his interest in religious reform. Yet his motives and sincerity have remained controversial, not least because Calvin himself came deeply to distrust them. There is no doubt about his ambition for himself and his house nor about his appreciation of the political possibilities of the Huguenot movement. When he took the title of protector general of the churches of France, a great part of the enormous influence of the Bourbon connection was added to the Huguenot party. It was further strengthened when the constable's nephew, the admiral Gaspard de Coligny, brought to the Huguenots at least a part of the Montmorency clientage. Condé was thus the leader of a party formed by the union of aristocratic influence with the military organization of the Calvinist communities and financed by the backing of wealthy bankers and the voluntary contributions of the faithful. The members of this organization were fired by a religious faith kept alight by skillful propaganda, and organized in a strict communal discipline that held together in a common purpose nobles and artisans, soldiers and peaceful burghers. This was a political instrument such as no "overmighty subject" had ever commanded before. In Coligny, moreover, the Huguenots had a leader whose motives were never suspect. Like his uncle the constable, Coligny had spent his life in the service of his king, a brave soldier, an excellent organizer and a strict disciplinarian. His conversion had been slow and marked by strong internal conflicts. He had little of Orange's abhorrence of absolutist government. When he finally decided to take up arms, it was not to fight a political system, still less to fight his own king, but rather to obtain liberty of conscience and worship for his co-religionists and, if possible, to free the king from his evil advisers who were persecuting true religion. Coligny's singleness of purpose gave to the Huguenot movement in France a unity such as the Calvinist movement in the Netherlands never achieved.

Throughout the short reign of Francis II, political and religious passions rose alarmingly. There was much local violence, and the outrages committed by both parties led to bitter recriminations and further violence. The government was faced with a debt of over forty million livres; but the states general of 1560, summoned to give financial help, proved as difficult to handle as its counterpart in the Netherlands. Condé had many friends in the assembly. The third estate refused to vote taxes, but demanded that it should determine the country's religious policy and the composition of the government itself. From March 1560 the government gave up its official policy of imposing religious unity by force and issued a series of edicts, granting liberty of conscience, but prohibiting armed assemblies. Neither side was satisfied. No one, not even the chancellor, L'Hôpital, who opposed force in matters of religion, thought that a state could live with two religions. There had not yet been time for a party of *politiques* to develop. Those who held no strong religious views or disliked persecuting men for their opinions still hoped for a solution from a general or a national council of the Church.

In March 1560 the first big coup attempted by the Huguenots, the conspiracy of Amboise, misfired completely. Condé was arrested on the somewhat doubtful grounds of implication. But the government's weakness had become very obvious. "I never saw state more amased than this," the English ambassador reported from the court at Amboise; "they know not whome to mistruste, nor to truste." The Guises only maintained their position by giving much more power than before to the queen mother, Catherine de Medici.

Francis II died on December 5, 1560. Condé was immediately released, and the Bourbon claim to the regency for the ten-year-old Charles IX was now much harder to resist than in the case of Francis II, who had been nominally of age. The queen mother, however, was determined to control the regency herself. Catherine de Medici, half Florentine and half French, had long since identified her personal interests with those of the French monarchy. She was convinced that she must follow the example of Blanche of Castile, the mother of St. Louis, and preserve the authority of the French crown intact for her children. Only the monarchy could give France stability and preserve her independence from Spain. Every faction, however good its intentions, would necessarily work to the detriment of the monarchy. Hence, neither Guise nor Bourbon must dominate the government. Above all, she must win time for tempers to cool and for her sons to grow up. This was the aim which Catherine pursued consistently, though in a bewildering succession of tactical twists, during her sons' minorities, and even afterward. To achieve it, she was prepared to use every means to keep her own power. It is impossible to know how far this power became for her an end in itself. Catherine's field of maneuver, however, was dangerously narrow. She could no more rule without the high nobility than could Margaret of Parma. Like Margaret and Philip II before 1567, she could only play court politics, for her government had no money to raise an effective army of its own. For eighteen months Catherine tried to reconcile the princes or, when this did not work, to balance them against each other. All the time she had to look over her shoulder at Philip II, who threatened to intervene against the Huguenots.

On November 29, 1560, after much pressure from the cardinal of Lorraine, Pius IV finally published the bull reconvening the Council of Trent. But events in France moved too rapidly for Catherine to await its outcome. In the summer of 1561 she induced Protestant and Catholic theologians to meet at Poissy and attempt to arrive at an agreed position. The "colloquy" failed, not so much because Catherine regarded religion as a branch of politics and thought that theologians could be induced to maneuver and compromise like politicians, as because both sides wanted to secure the support of the monarchy but were quite unwilling to accept it as an arbiter between them. It was essentially the same difficulty that Charles V had faced, and Catherine understood it as little as the emperor had done.

In the autumn of 1561, the Guises and the Montmorencys, now in alliance, withdrew from the court. Catherine had mismanaged her relations with the irascible constable. When the old man was faced with the choice between the detested but orthodox Guises and his beloved but heretical nephew, he chose the Guises. Together, they won over Anthony of Bourbon with the promise of help for the recovery of the Spanish part of his kingdom of Navarre. Both Catholics and Huguenots were arming, and clashes were becoming more frequent. Catherine's maneuvers had left her powerless between two armed camps. She redoubled her efforts for peace. The Edict of January (1562) formalized her compromise agreement with the Huguenots; Protestant assemblies were allowed outside town walls and Protestant services in private houses. It was the greatest concession yet to the Huguenots, and it caused corresponding resentment in the Catholic camp. One more incident touched off civil war. On March 1, 1562, the duke of Guise's retainers surprised a Protestant service at Vassy and killed some thirty persons. At that point Catherine lost control over events. Condé's forces assembled at Orléans. He was able to count on the support of over two thousand Protestant churches. The Huguenots surprised Lyons, Tours, Blois, Rouen, and other towns. But Guise and Montmorency entered Paris at the head of their own armies. In May, there was open fighting.

There had not been a civil war in France for a hundred years, and many found it deeply shocking. The nobility on both sides were determined, so wrote La Noue, one of the Huguenot leaders, in his memoirs, to fight the war with the courtesies due to gentlemen. Negotiations never ceased, thanks mainly to the queen mother. When the war was over, all parties combined to expel the English from Le Havre, which Condé had handed to them in return for military and financial help. Yet both armies had committed atrocities and acts of deliberate terror, and the disillusionment was great. The Edict of Amboise (March 19, 1563) granted the Protestants liberty of conscience, but the celebration of services only to nobles and their households, and to the bourgeois only in one town in each *bailliage* and *sénéchaussée.* Calvin and Coligny bitterly reproached Condé for accepting conditions which favored his own class at the expense of the mass of the Protestant communities. The peace left more suspicion and fear than ever.

Only the queen mother had come out of the war with enhanced power and reputation. She had also been lucky. Navarre was killed at the siege of Rouen; both the constable and Condé had been taken prisoner by their opponents. The duke of Guise was assassinated by a Huguenot fanatic (February 18, 1563). Under torture, the assassin implicated Coligny. Coligny denied having instigated the murder, but rejoiced that the Lord had struck down this great enemy of his evangel. Nine years later, there were to be many who rejoiced at the murder of Coligny and his friends, though they, too, would not have commanded it.

With some of the great personalities out of the way, Catherine could now effectively assert her own authority in the name of the king. For four years she worked hard to maintain peace; but she could not allay the fears of both sides, nor prevent sporadic outbursts of local violence. The resolutions of the Council of Trent convinced many on both sides that a theological solution of the religious problem was no longer possible. A conference at Bayonne (1565), between Catherine on the one side and her daughter Elizabeth, wife of Philip II, and the duke of Alva on the other, was widely (and wrongly) regarded as the establishment of a Paris–Madrid axis for the express purpose of destroying the Protestants in France and in the Netherlands.

All the Huguenot fears seemed to be justified when in the summer of 1567 Alva marched his army from Milan to the Netherlands, along the eastern border of France. Personal rivalries at court played their part in increasing mutual suspicion. There is no evidence that the French Catholics planned an attack; but Condé and Coligny thought so and decided to strike first by capturing the king (September 1567). Once again, the Huguenot organization worked smoothly and the Protestants took over a number of towns. But the main coup against the court failed and open war broke out. More even than the first civil war, it became part of the European struggle between Protestants and Catholics. The government obtained help from Alva and introduced Swiss troops. The elector Palatine sent his son, John Casimir, with German *reîtres* (*Reiter* = horseman) to help the Huguenots. They were to become a regular feature of the civil wars and greatly added to their ferocity. The war ended with the Treaty of Longjumeau (March 23, 1568) and the re-establishment of the Edict of Amboise. The king agreed to pay off the *reîtres*.

It was no more than an armistice of a few months. At court, L'Hôpital and the moderates were discredited. The constable had fallen. The Guises were back in power and found a powerful ally for their aggressive policy in the king's younger brother, the duke of Anjou (later Henry III). Neither side was willing to abide by the terms of the treaty. The Huguenots were still on the offensive. When they could not dominate a region completely, they infiltrated into public offices, until there was a Huguenot hierarchy of officials intermingled with the royal administration, owing allegiance, not to the king, but to Condé and Coligny. "Thus they could, in one day, at one definite hour, and with all secrecy start a rising in every part of the kingdom," wrote the Venetian ambassador, with only slight exaggeration. It turned into the longest and most ferocious war yet fought. Anjou defeated the Huguenots at Jarnac and Montcontour (1569); but their organization held firm, and Condé's death at Jarnac gave them the added advantage of a unified command under Coligny. A brilliant strategist, though only a moderate tactician—he lost most of the pitched battles he fought—Coligny kept his army in being by a war of rapid movement which prevented the superior forces of the royalists from dealing the Huguenots a fatal blow. He had, moreover, the great advantage that he could recruit German *reîtres* even without money, for the Treaty of Longjumeau had shown that the king would eventually have to pay them off. By contrast, Catherine's generals bickered with each other and were all too often unwilling to pursue the war to a final victory, for fear of losing their profitable commands. The government's financial weakness made it impossible to keep large armies together for long enough to exploit tactical successes. The royalist nobility, moreover, had friends and relatives in the Huguenot army. Neither side wished for the total ruin of the other.

The Treaty of Pacification of St. Germain (August 8, 1570) once more restored the status quo; but, for the first time, the Huguenots were given the right to garrison four towns as security: La Rochelle, Montauban, La Charité, and Cognac. Catherine changed course once again. Philip II had snubbed her marriage proposals for her daughter Margaret and for Charles IX. The French ambassador in Spain reported how the Morisco revolt had shown up the military weakness of the Catholic king. He could be safely snubbed in turn. Catherine therefore arranged for the marriage of her daughter Margaret with the young Henry of Navarre, hoping, with characteristic optimism, that a Valois–Bourbon marriage alliance would settle the internal troubles of the kingdom. At the same time, she started negotiations for a marriage between Elizabeth I and Anjou. Nothing came of this; but the Anglo-French rapprochement led to the Treaty of Blois (April 19, 1572), a fully fledged defensive alliance. It included provision for the transfer of the English cloth staple from Antwerp to Rouen. Nothing came of this plan, but it was clear enough that the treaty was directed against Spain and the Netherlands, and Alva's government in Brussels was highly alarmed.

In the summer of 1571, Coligny appeared at court and rejoined the king's council. More consistently than Catherine, he had seen the solution of the kingdom's troubles in a vigorous anti-Spanish policy. If only all Frenchmen could combine against the old enemy of the kingdom, their more recent hatreds might be forgotten. Since 1568 Coligny had been in close touch with Louis of Nassau. The Sea Beggars had used La Rochelle as a base and combined their exploits with those of the Huguenot privateers. Coligny promised Nassau to support his attack on Alva. The Beggars' successes in Zeeland and Holland in the spring of 1572, and Nassau's capture of Mons and Valenciennes, seemed to present a golden chance. Best of all, Charles IX himself supported this policy enthusiastically. The melancholy and romantic young man had been captivated by Coligny's powerful personality. Jealous of his younger brother's military successes, he now dreamt of even greater exploits for himself.

But Coligny had misjudged both the internal and the international situation. The hatreds born of three civil wars could not be stilled by a simple display of jingoism. The Guises had never forgiven him for his alleged complicity in the murder of Duke Francis. Catherine and Anjou were increasingly jealous of his personal influence over the king. The Spanish ambassador and the papal nuncio worked feverishly against him. Catherine was becoming seriously alarmed at the prospect of open war with Spain. The battle of Lepanto had more than restored Spanish military prestige. Alva commanded a formidable army in the Netherlands and made short shrift of the small force which the Huguenots had sent for the relief of beleaguered

Mons. Little help was to be expected from England or the German princes. Elizabeth had balanced the Treaty of Blois by a gesture of goodwill to Alva. Early in March she had expelled the Sea Beggars from England—with the paradoxical, but to Elizabeth highly pleasing, result that they captured Brill and started the effective revolt of Zeeland and Holland. The council and its military experts agreed with Catherine; but Coligny, secure in the king's favor, persisted. The Huguenots began to talk of changing the king's council. They had fought three civil wars with the limited objective of security for themselves and their religious practices. Now, in peacetime, they seemed about to capture the government of France.

Catherine planned her stroke with all the economy of the experienced politician she was. The Guises were readily induced to have Coligny murdered. Once this dangerous man was dead and his fateful influence over the king had gone, the balance of political power would be restored, with the queen mother again having the decisive voice, and France could withdraw from disastrous adventures against Spain. On August 22, 1572, the assassins wounded Coligny, but failed to kill him. Immediately Paris was in an uproar. Thousands of Huguenot gentlemen had come to the capital for the wedding of Henry and Margaret—the marriage which was to have ended the civil strife. They now demanded revenge for the outrage committed on their leader. The king himself visited the wounded Coligny and promised punishment for the culprits. The plot had turned against Catherine. It was all too clear that she and the Guises would be implicated. Her reaction was the unpremeditated act of desperation.

On Saturday, August 23, she convinced the king that all Huguenot leaders must now be killed. All the Catholics in the council agreed. It seems likely that, even now, Catherine only thought of doing away with a comparatively small number of Huguenots. But at this point she once more lost control over the course of events. Anjou, the young duke Henry of Guise, and the provost of the Merchants of Paris organized the massacre for the same night. It was easy. The murderous proclivities of the Paris populace were well known; the Huguenots were unsuspecting. Who, indeed, could have suspected such a monstrous deed? Yet some such action had been discussed, though never planned, in Catholic circles for years. Neither Catholics nor Huguenots had clean hands in the matter of smaller massacres. On the night of August 23–24, St. Bartholomew's eve, and in the following days, several thousand Huguenot's were murdered. This time, Guise made sure of Coligny's death, waiting outside the admiral's house until the assassins had thrown his mangled body through the window. Of the leaders, only Navarre and the young prince of Condé were spared, both on abjuring their Protestant faith. The massacres spread to the provinces and several thousand more perished. The exact figures have always remained a matter of dispute.[14]

Even the duke of Alva was shocked, but certainly not displeased. Masses of thanksgiving were said in Madrid and Rome, and even the Venetian senate voted, by 162 to 2, to celebrate the joyful event by a procession. The Vene-

14. The best modern account is P. Erlanger, *Le Massacre de la Saint -Barthélemy* (Paris, 1960), trans. A. O'Brian, *St. Bartholomews' Night* (London, 1962).

tians had second thoughts fairly soon, and so had Catherine. The murder of Coligny had fitted into her plans; the massacres had not, for they destroyed the political balance in France and delivered her again into the hands of the Guise faction. She boasted of the deed to Philip II and the pope, rightly judging that it would be held to her credit. She excused it to Elizabeth I and to the German princes as self-defense and as a plot of the Guises. Almost immediately, she started negotiating once more with the Huguenots, not surprisingly, without success. The resumption of the civil war was therefore inevitable. The cardinal of Lorraine promoted the publication by the Italian Capilupi of *Lo stratagemma di Carlo IX* (Rome, 1572), a fanciful account of French royal policy, purporting to prove that the massacres were premeditated. Lorraine calculated, quite correctly, that the book would become a kind of devil's bible for the Protestants which would make their future co-operation with the monarchy much more difficult. As so often happens, the extremists on both sides were playing into each other's hands.

The fourth war of religion, mostly an unsuccessful siege of La Rochelle by the royalists, ended once more in a compromise when Anjou needed peace in order to take up the crown of Poland to which he had been elected (1573). It was only now that the Huguenot organization reached its full development, in a broad arc stretching from Dauphiné through Provence and Languedoc to Béarn and Guienne. As in the Netherlands, the successful revolution tended to become localized, both by an alliance with provincial feeling against an interfering central government and by the logic of the military situation. Again as in Holland and Zeeland, political authority came to reside in representative assemblies. They acted in conjunction with the princes, Condé and Navarre, after they had fled from court and returned to Protestantism (1574 and 1575 respectively). Huguenot propaganda now laid far greater stress than it had done formerly on constitutional theories against the absolutism of the French monarchy. But the Protestant movement had passed its peak. Outside the southern provinces it was declining.

It was able to survive owing to its alliance with the *politiques*. What Alva's Council of Troubles had done over a number of years, the massacres in France did in a few days; they persuaded many Catholics to seek a way out of the horrors of religious and civil strife by sacrificing the religious rather than the political unity of the state.[15] The *politiques*, or malcontents, like the other parties in France, were a mixed group and not nearly as well organized as the Huguenots or, later, the League. Among them were the Montmorency family with its clients, the moderates and Erasmians among lawyers and government officials, the bankers and merchants whose business had suffered from civil war, and all those among the Catholic nobility who hated the Guises. Their leaders were influential, but personally unattractive. The duke of Alençon, youngest of Catherine's sons and later, as duke of Anjou, notorious for his intervention in the Netherlands, saw in the *poli-*

15. H. A. Enno van Gelder, "De Nederlandse opstand en de Franse godsdienstoorlogen," in *Verslag van de Algemene Vergadering van het Historisch Genootschap te Utrecht* (1930), p. 29.

tiques a convenient instrument to further his political ambitions. The constable's son, Montmorency-Damville, was governor of Languedoc and interested more in his own authority in the south than in that of the crown. A Catholic without religious interests, he permitted effective toleration under his authority. Politically, he allied himself with the king against the Huguenots, or with the Huguenots against the king, as occasion arose. The only consistent part of his policy was his jealousy of the house of Guise.

The civil wars continued intermittently and with shifting alliances. As the Venetian ambassadors saw it, war had now come to be built into the social and political structure and habits of French society. The great princely houses, the Guises, the Bourbons, the Montmorencys, knew that war increased their hold over the central government or, at least, over the provinces which they governed. The lower nobility were impoverished by inflation and by the devastation of their estates. They could hope to recoup their fortunes only in war and in the service of one of the great lords. Now that every town and province had become a frontier in the civil war, the formerly pacific French population had been trained to warfare. As the marauding armies interrupted trade and made life insecure, an increasing number of young men came to prefer the life of the plunderer to that of the plundered.

In 1574 Charles IX died at the age of 24, haunted, so it was said, by the specters of the massacres. Anjou returned posthaste from Poland to wear the crown as Henry III. Intelligent, but without his mother's persistence and capacity for hard work, he was not the man to impose himself on the faction leaders. His extravagance made him unpopular with the taxpayers. His sexual proclivities and the favors which he bestowed on his *mignons*, brave and capable though some of them were, together with his growing distaste for warfare, made him despised by the aristocratic and military society of France. While the great lords went to war with their retainers and clients, the crown had to pay for most of the professional troops and was ruining itself. In 1576 Henry III and Catherine came to the conclusion that the Huguenots could not be crushed. Alençon negotiated a very favorable treaty for them: the exercise of their religion everywhere outside Paris and the residence of the court, eight places of security and mixed commissions in the *parlements* (*chambres mi-parties*) to deal with cases involving Protestants.

The "Peace of Monsieur" (i.e. Alençon) was the French counterpart to the Pacification of Ghent. In the Netherlands, Catholic extremism was represented by the monarchy. Its religious intransigence, together with the acceleration of the religious and social revolution in Flanders and Brabant, led to the breakdown of the compromise peace. In France, the monarchy had now become suspect to many Catholics. In consequence, an independent Catholic movement appeared which, in its turn, became revolutionary and antiroyalist. Local Catholic unions, or leagues, had been formed by local authorities, nobles, and prelates as early as 1560 and 1562. After the Peace of Monsieur, these local associations were organized into a nationwide Holy League or Holy Union. Where the Huguenot party had been built on the alliance of the militarized Calvinist communities with the Bourbon family connection, the League was built on the alliance of the military Catholic nobility in their local unions with the Guise family connection. Where the Huguenots looked to Geneva for spiritual guidance and to England and the Protestant princes of Germany for material help, the Leaguers looked to Rome and to the Catholic rulers of Spain and Savoy. Thus, all revolutionary movements of the period were linked to powers and interests outside their national boundaries. This added to their strength, but it also set up tensions within the movements that greatly increased the difficulties of unified leadership.

The League of 1576 was founded as a Catholic party of the nobility, with essentially conservative aims. Henry III and his successors were to be preserved in their authority, according to their coronation oaths; the provinces and estates were to have their ancient rights restored to them. This was not very different from similar feudal programs in the Middle Ages. The League's articles dealing with its organization, however, had a most unmedieval ring. All members were to be closely linked in mutual protection and obedience to their chief, without respect for any other authority. They were to contribute arms and men and hound down any defaulter, while the League would protect them from all reprisals. Every member had to take an oath to observe these articles, on pain of anathema and eternal damnation. In many parts of France, the League was broadened to include the clergy and the third estate and, just as in the Huguenot movement, the lower orders were enrolled to provide mass support.

The power of this new party became immediately apparent in the states general of Blois in 1576. It manipulated the elections and intimidated the voters. Leaguer *baillis* and *sénéchaux* tried to prevent the Huguenots from attending electoral meetings. Within the assembly, they organized an adroit attack on the king's powers in the name of the old privileges of the estates and provinces. Their inability to win direct control over the government had turned the extremist Catholics, like the Huguenots, into an antiabsolutist party.

Henry III was very conscious of the League's threats to his independence and he knew of its close links with Madrid. To draw its teeth and, if possible, to make it serve his own ends, he declared himself its chief in place of the duke of Guise (January 1577). But the Catholic nobility had no intention of exchanging their vague obligations to serve the king for the very precise and far-reaching obligations they would have to him as chief of the League. The organization which had been created to coerce the king disintegrated in his hands when he tried to use it for his own purposes. Henry got little help from the League and no financial support from the states general in his renewed war with the Protestants. If this was disappointing, it was still better than leaving such a weapon in the hands of Henry of Guise. Moreover, the inevitable divergence of aim between the Huguenots and the *politiques* allowed the royal armies considerable successes. In the Peace of Bergerac, the "King's Peace," the Huguenots lost many of their lately won concessions. The king declared all leagues dissolved.

A modus vivendi now seemed possible. Catherine worked

ceaselessly for it, traveling through the southern provinces and negotiating with *politique* governors and Huguenot chiefs. Local fighting never ceased completely; but the old queen mother managed to prevent all but one short open war (1579–1580). Since both Henry III and his brother, now duke of Anjou, were childless, Henry of Navarre was willing to bide his time in the hope of succeeding to the throne. Anjou found in the Netherlands a promising field for his ambitions, with the prospect of an English marriage and a crown on the further horizon. The French military nobility of all parties willingly followed his call to seek plunder abroad or, since they had long since ceased to be very particular in such matters, on their way through their own country. Guise, too, was looking abroad, dreaming romantically, like Don John of Austria, of liberating his cousin Mary Stuart. Philip II gave him good words, as he did the Scottish and English Catholics, but did nothing practical to help him. It could never be an object of Spanish policy to help the French establish themselves in the British Isles. Until he was strong enough to attack Elizabeth I without French help, Philip would plot against her life, but go to great lengths to prevent an open breach, for fear of an Anglo-French alliance against him. Henry III and Catherine, for their part, were mortally afraid of the power of Spain. They supported the prior of Crato in the Azores and Anjou in the Netherlands, though they officially disavowed him and constantly quarreled with him over his complaints of insufficient support. It is not really surprising that, in his irritation with French policy, Philip opened negotiations with Henry of Navarre to restart the civil wars in France. Navarre was too intelligent to fall into this trap.

The situation, however, remained tense. Nothing had really been settled. There was open warfare only in the Netherlands; but the great powers were maneuvering for position and building up their "fifth columns" inside their opponents' territories. In France none of the parties was satisfied nor had given up hope of bettering its position. With relative peace and a stable currency, after monetary reforms in 1577, economic life was beginning to recover, especially in the western seaports which handled most of the Spanish-Netherlands trade. But the tax burden increased, rather than diminished. Between 1576 and 1588, the *taille* was doubled and the *gabelle*, the hated tax on salt, was trebled. Peasants, artisans, and shopkeepers were ruined, while the great merchants and bankers (many of them Italians and Spaniards), the tax-farmers, and the king's favorites grew rich. The great political and social crisis of 1559 was only now reaching its climax.

The French succession and the war with England

The truce with the Porte and the conquest of Portugal marked a turning point in Spanish policy. The greatest danger to Spain was no longer in the Mediterranean but in the Atlantic. France and England were supporting her enemies in the Netherlands and in Portugal. Drake and the English pirates were wickedly and illegally disrupting Spanish trade with her colonies and robbing the king and his subjects. The pope, Cardinal Granvelle, and Philip's Spanish advisers were pressing for a more aggressive policy. Gradually, the king himself became convinced that the defense, both of his own interests and of the Church, demanded more active Spanish intervention in western Europe.

The immediate occasion for the change in Spanish policy was the death of the duke of Anjou and of the prince of Orange (1584). Even before Anjou's death, the United Provinces (i.e. the members of the Union of Utrecht) had once more approached both Henry III and Elizabeth I with offers of the sovereignty over the Netherlands. Henry III again refused. William's death and the fall of Antwerp made help urgent if the Union was to be saved. On August 20, 1585, Elizabeth therefore, while likewise refusing the sovereignty, agreed to send five thousand troops, under the command of the earl of Leicester, to the Netherlands. Leicester and two other Englishmen were to have seats in the Council of State. Brill and Flushing, commanding the estuaries of the Meuse and the Scheldt, were handed over to the English as bases and as security for the repayment of the English government's expenses. Elizabeth had driven a hard bargain and had still not yet broken completely with Spain. But, for the first time, she was committed to fight Philip II openly and, as it turned out, committed more heavily than she had bargained for.

In France, Anjou's death upset the precarious equilibrium of the previous years. Henry of Navarre was now the immediate heir to the throne. Faced with the specter of a heretic king, the Catholics resurrected the Holy League. It started as a secret society of a small number of fanatical Catholics among the Parisian bourgeoisie, mostly priests and professional men. Its discipline, dedication to the cause, and puritanical insistence on the personal virtue of its members were as severe as in any Calvinist community. When this society had built up a strong party among the artisans, gilds, and public officials of Paris, it entered into relations with Guise and the Catholic princes. Immediately, the old League of 1576 reappeared all over France. The signal was a declaration of the old cardinal of Bourbon, the cat's-paw of Guise, claiming the succession against the heretic Henry of Bourbon. In town after town, the Leaguers removed royalist commanders and governors and replaced them by their own men, on the pretext of insuring a firm anti-Huguenot policy. Not for the last time, a moderate government fighting a revolutionary movement found itself outbid by an extremist party on its own side.

On December 31, 1584, Philip II concluded the Treaty of Joinville with Guise and the Holy League. They agreed to recognize the succession of the cardinal of Bourbon and jointly to destroy heresy. Philip was to advance the League fifty thousand ducats a month and give military help, if necessary. In return, the League promised to help Philip recover French Navarre, Cambrai, and other towns to which he laid claim, and to continue the alliance after victory. Philip II had thus achieved what his father had always vainly striven for: alliance with a Catholic France under the leadership of Spain; but he had got it only from one party in France. The treaty itself remained secret, but the League's contacts with the Spanish ambassador, Bernardino de Mendoza, were evident. Henry III and Catherine were thoroughly frightened and once more veered toward the League. On July 7, 1585, Catherine and Guise concluded the Treaty of Nemours in which the king promised to abolish all previous edicts of pacification with the Huguenots. Navarre had now no choice but to start the civil war again.

Not only was Guise now financially dependent on Spain for his French policy; he also had to give up all his Scottish and English plans so as to be able to concentrate on the French succession question. This left Philip II free to pursue his own plans. Now that there was no longer any fear of French intervention, it seemed most logical to move against England. The English queen was under sentence of excommunication; she was oppressing her Catholic subjects; and she was keeping prisoner a queen whose title to the English throne was regarded by most Catholics as better than her own. It seemed, moreover, that only English help enabled Philip's rebellious subjects in the Netherlands to defy him. Religious, moral, and strategic reasons thus combined to lead Philip into the "enterprise of England," the invasion whose success must lead to the decisive defeat of Protestantism, to the restoration of the king's authority in the Netherlands, and to the strengthening of the Spanish leadership of Catholic Europe.

Philip's decision transformed the civil wars in France and the Netherlands into open European war. Since the French monarchy had surrendered its initiative to the League and since the League was dependent on Spain, the political opposition to Spain was now left entirely to the Protestants. For the first and last time, the lines of political and religious division coincided completely. To the whole of Europe it seemed that the decisive phase of the great struggle was now beginning.

The invasion of England was not a new idea. Philip's admiral, the marquis of Santa Cruz, had urged it already in 1583. From the spring of 1585, Philip began to plan it seriously. His financial position had improved since the bankruptcy of 1575. Shipments of silver from the New World had increased beyond all previous hopes. The Spanish government received the quint (a 20 per cent tax) and other dues directly. The rest was shipped to Spain on private account, and most of the money flowed into the hands of a comparatively small number of rich merchant and banking houses. They accumulated capital out of all proportion to their commercial needs. The Venetians and the Dutch merchants, in their heyday, carried on international trade with far less capital than the Ruiz, the Spinola, or the Fugger had accumulated. The siege of Antwerp and the Dutch blockade of the Scheldt, together with the Protestant privateers in the Channel and in the Atlantic, made trade routes precarious and reduced investment opportunities. Even mining did not usually call for the investment of hundreds of thousands of ducats. Thus, the great financial houses could employ their capital only in government loans—a very profitable, but very precarious, form of investment. The Spanish government, in particular, could therefore obtain relatively cheap loans of enormous sums in the international money markets. These formed the basis of the vastly increased military and naval activities of the period. In 1576 the Fleming Oudegherste had proposed to Philip II the establishment of banks in every part of his empire and the co-ordination of their activities by a council in Madrid. As in the case of most other proposals for the economic integration of the Spanish empire, nothing came of it. Philip II remained at the mercy of the bankers and their highly speculative bill-of-exchange transactions.[16]

When Leicester landed at Flushing (December 1585), the situation in the Netherlands was critical. Farnese—from 1586, he was duke of Parma—was advancing methodically against the Holland and Zeeland defenses in the south. In the northeast the royalists had held Groningen from 1580, when its governor, the count of Rennenberg, joined the malcontents and made his peace with the king. In the other eastern provinces the Catholics were still strong and the authority of the states general precarious. The Union of Utrecht itself was dangerously disunited. The revolt against the king had been, among other things, a revolt of the provinces against a centralizing government. Now the provinces were not minded to give up their newly won autonomy to another effective central government. Utrecht, Guelders, Overijssel, and Friesland were jealous of Holland and Zeeland and their dominating role in the Council of State and the states general. Holland was paying for about two-thirds of the whole war effort and was, in its turn, impatient of the susceptibilities of the poorer provinces. The victory of the reformed religion had left unsettled the relations between church and state.

16. H. Lapeyre, *Simon Ruiz et les "asientos" de Philippe II* (Paris, 1953), pp. 14 ff., 103 ff.

The regent class in Holland, the oligarchs who controlled the towns, had accepted Protestantism, but were, by upbringing and tradition, Erasmian and tolerant, just as they had been before the revolution. By contrast, the Calvinist preachers were intolerant and exclusive, claiming the right to supervise the religion and morals of people and magistrates alike. They were supported by the religious refugees from Flanders and Brabant and by precisely those classes, the petty bourgeoisie, the artisans, and the workers, whom the regents had successfully excluded from power after making use of them in the revolution of 1572. The clash between the state and the Calvinist Church therefore overlapped with a political and social struggle between oligarchic and popular groups.

Orange had lived and grown with these struggles. Through his personal prestige and the exercise of an astonishing political virtuosity, he had managed to remain above the party conflicts and prevent them from disrupting the Union. Leicester did not understand them and allowed himself to become the leader of one of the factions. At first there was much goodwill from nearly all parties. The states general made him governor general and gave him wider powers than they had allowed to Anjou or Don John (January 1586). But immediately it became apparent how equivocal his position was. His acceptance of the office went beyond his instructions. Elizabeth refused to accept it for a long time, and the earl's authority suffered in consequence. But there was worse to come. Elizabeth was still clinging to her policy of negotiating with Spain. She had sent Leicester to the Netherlands to bring pressure on Philip II, so as to obtain a reasonable settlement for herself and for the United Provinces. The Netherlanders, on the other hand, had lost all illusions about the possibility of such a settlement. They wanted to involve England in their war with the king. Between these divergent aims, Leicester's mission came to grief.

He quarreled with Holland and Zeeland when he attempted to prohibit their trade with Spain and with the southern provinces—the famous *handel op den vijand*, the trade with the enemy which, so the merchants argued, allowed them to finance the war. The preachers regarded it as treason, and Leicester agreed with them. In April 1586 he established himself in Utrecht, the center of the anti-Holland party. He helped to overthrow the oligarchy in the city itself and allied himself with the preachers and the popular party. With their help, and with the army, he hoped to bring the regents of Holland to heel. But he quarreled with the Netherlands army commanders; his actions against Parma were almost uniformly unsuccessful; his troops were unpaid and mutinous. Desperately, he begged Elizabeth to send him more money. But the queen had paid as much as, or more than, she had promised. Her financial resources were limited and she was more anxious for peace than for war. In December 1586 Leicester returned to England to obtain more money and to restore his shaken position at court.

By January 1587 Wilkes, the English representative at The Hague, reported that "we begin to grow as hatefull to the people as the Spaigniard himself who governeth his townes of conquest with a milder hand than we doe our frendes and allyes." When English commanders betrayed Deventer and the fortifications of Zutphen to Parma, the states general took action. Jan van Oldenbarnevelt, newly appointed pensionary of Holland, engineered a purge of Leicester's partisans in the Council of State and had Orange's young son, Maurice of Nassau, appointed commander in chief. But English help remained more necessary than ever, and Elizabeth was persuaded to send the reluctant Leicester once more on his "most perylous and most crooked voyage," as he called it (July 1587).

He continued to rely on the Calvinists, and his relations with the states general and the generals deteriorated still further. They accused him of negotiating with Parma. He denied it, but it was true. Elizabeth was willing to make concessions to Spain which the Netherlands could not accept. Leicester blamed Holland and Zeeland and threw English troops into a number of Dutch towns. For the third time, a governor general was attempting a coup against the states general and again it failed. Elizabeth's policy of negotiation had lost him the support of his own party, the Calvinists and the popular movement, even in Utrecht. At the end of 1587 he left the Netherlands, broken as much by the incompatibility of aim of the two countries he had tried to serve as by his personal insufficiency for the role he had been asked to fill.

Leicester's departure sealed the victory of the alliance of the urban oligarchies with the Netherlands military commanders. The popular movement was everywhere defeated. The states general was now convinced that the policy of offering the sovereignty to a foreign prince did not work. In the controversies of the Leicester period, the Dutch pamphleteers had developed the theory of the sovereignty of the states general. This body now decided to exercise it and to obtain foreign help only by way of alliances. In 1589 Oldenbarnevelt persuaded the estates of Utrecht, Guelders, and Overijssel to elect Maurice of Nassau as their governor. Since 1585 he had been governor of Holland and Zeeland. His cousin, William Louis, exercised the governorship in Friesland. The particularist tendencies of the provinces in the states general were therefore balanced by the unifying role of the house of Orange and of Maurice in particular. But the precise nature of their relation, as of that between church and state, was not settled and was to lead to renewed conflict once the immediate danger from Spain was past. For the moment, however, this danger still outweighed all other considerations, even the bitter feelings between the Dutch and the English, and kept alive the uneasy alliance.

It is generally held that Philip II should have concentrated all his resources on the reconquest of the northern provinces at this moment, and that he might well have succeeded. Philip, however, had decided to strike at England first. Mary Queen of Scots had written to Mendoza (May 20, 1586), making over her rights of succession to the English throne to Philip and asking him to take her under his protection. This gave the king the final moral justification which he craved for his plans. Parma agreed with him at first. From the early months of 1586, when both Parma and Santa Cruz presented detailed plans, preparations for the great expedition went ahead. The difficulties were enormous and Philip and his advisers were under no illusions about them, least of all about the superiority of English naval gunnery and the tactics the English were likely to pursue. Santa Cruz demanded 150 warships and 360 cargo and auxiliary ships, over 90,000 men and 2,200 pieces of artillery, all at an estimated cost of little less than four million ducats. These estimates could not possibly have been fulfilled and were drastically scaled down when it was decided that Parma's army in the Netherlands was to make the actual invasion. Yet it remained the greatest combined operation ever planned up to that time.

Inevitably, there were delays. The costs outran the estimates. Drake's raid on Cadiz (April 1587), pestilence, and bad weather held up the preparations, and every day's delay cost thirty thousand ducats for just the pay and maintenance of the troops. In the first five months of 1587 alone, Philip sent two and a half million ducats to Parma, and yet the duke owed his troops several months' back pay. The Spaniards resented having an Italian as commander in chief, and there was the usual ill feeling among Philip's ministers and generals. By the autumn of 1587, Parma had become convinced that the "enterprise of England" had no chance of success. Philip himself veered between hysterical commands for action and his more usual inability to take decisions. In February 1588 Santa Cruz died. Philip had many experienced captains, but none of them of a rank to command the obedience of the others. The experience of the Granada and Lepanto campaigns had shown that only a prince or a very great lord would be obeyed. He could be given technical advisers if, as Don

John had been, he was inexperienced himself. This, rather than his alleged preference for nonentities, was Philip's reason for appointing the duke of Medina Sidonia as commander in chief of the Armada.[17] The duke lacked Don John's spirit, but no Don John was available, and in courage and resolution he proved himself worthy of the finest Spanish traditions.

It was essential for the success of the expedition that France should be kept neutral. The renewed civil war therefore played into Philip's hands. From his point of view, it went excellently. Navarre defeated the royalists at Coutras (October 20, 1587), while Guise annihilated Navarre's German allies a month later. Only Henry III had lost further prestige. In January 1588 the Guises imposed even harder terms on him than before as the price for the continued alliance. Henry had promised aid to Elizabeth if she were attacked. He might not give it, but Philip had to make sure that he was not even in a position to do so. Nor did the League trust him. They later claimed that they had planned a coup in Paris as early as the spring of 1587 or even earlier. Its timing, however, was controlled from Madrid, through Mendoza's contacts with Guise and the League committees in Paris, to coincide with the sailing of the Armada. Guise was to gain control of the king, and Philip promised that he would then recognize the duke and the League as the provisional government of France, until the cardinal of Bourbon was crowned. He would help with money and troops, if necessary.

17. E. Herrera Oria, *Felipe II y el Marqués de Santa Cruz en la Empresa de Inglaterra* (Madrid, 1946), p. 87.

The Armada was expected to sail at the beginning of May 1588, though it did not, in fact, leave Lisbon until May 30. On May 9, Guise rode into Paris in defiance of Henry III's orders. Henry had a chance to arrest him but hesitated. In the capital, tension was at fever heat. The Leaguers had been rapidly gaining in strength and confidence. Their growing tyranny over the city has been brilliantly chronicled by Pierre de L'Estoile, their bitter enemy. The Paris mob, which had already proved its talent for murderous pogroms, was being systematically roused by the League preachers—for once the oratorical equals of the Calvinists—until every misfortune and every crime was attributed to the Calvinists and the *politiques.* There were rumors that Épernon, the king's favorite, was plotting with the Huguenots to set fire to the city. On May 11, Henry moved French and Swiss troops into Paris, but with orders not to take any action against the population. The next day, the Parisians threw up barricades and blockaded the isolated contingents of royal stroops. The action had been carefully planned by the League committees and was directed by Guise. The king had to appeal to him to prevent a massacre of his troops. On the following day, Henry fled from Paris and Guise remained in control of the capital. The main object had been achieved. Henry was no longer in a position to intervene in the Armada campaign. The coup drew Épernon and his forces away from Picardy, toward the king and Paris, and gave the League their chance to occupy the province and cover Parma's flank against a possible attack by the king.

This success did not save the Armada from disaster

(August–September 1588). For Spain it was not only a terrible moral and material blow; it also broke all hopes of an agreement with Elizabeth and ranged England irrevocably in the ranks of the Catholic king's enemies. He made plans for a renewed attack on England; but, more and more, his attention came to be focused on France. Here, it seemed, all Spain's failures might yet be triumphantly retrieved. Once more, Philip doubled the stakes. But Parma was convinced that he was only compounding his previous mistake.

During the summer and autumn of 1588, the League's power in France was constantly growing. Henry III had no choice but to maintain his alliance with Guise, and on the duke's terms. But the news of the defeat of the Armada restored his nerve. In September he dismissed eight of his closest advisers. They had been Catherine's creatures, and this palace revolution marked the end of the queen mother's influence. The states general met at Blois in October 1588, for the first time since 1576. The League had again a well organized majority in all three estates. They attacked Henry's administration on a wide front; they wanted decisions taken jointly by the three estates to have the force of law; they pressed the king to pursue the war against the Huguenots with more vigor and, at the same time, demanded sweeping reductions in taxation. Henry held Guise responsible for all his humiliations. The last straw was the duke of Savoy's attack on French-occupied Saluzzo. The king thought the attack was inspired by the League. He was wrong, for Charles Emmanuel was, as usual, only indulging his passion for power politics and nearly wrecked the Catholic alliance by causing a patriotic revulsion of feeling in favor of Henry III.

Guise had been warned not to trust Henry; but he was riding on the crest of popular favor and political success and despised the weak king. In his usual nonchalant way, he walked unarmed into Henry's trap, in the château of Blois, and was assassinated before the king's eyes (December 23, 1588). His brother, the cardinal of Guise, was arrested and murdered the next day. Catherine lay ill when Henry brought her the triumphant news. She remained sceptical about its effects. She died on January 5, 1589. The event "made no more stir than the death of a goat," said L'Estoile.

There was an immediate revulsion against the king. The Sorbonne declared him guilty of murder and tyranny and absolved all Frenchmen from their allegiance to him. The League became an openly revolutionary party. They recognized Guise's brother, Charles, duke of Mayenne, as lieutenant general of the realm for the cardinal of Bourbon, who was Henry III's prisoner. In Provence, the *parlement* declared for the League, and the towns renounced their allegiance to "the assassin Henry III." Elsewhere it needed the appearance of Leaguer troops to overawe the loyalist provincial *parlements*. The League had a strong party in the council of almost every town. With the help of Mayenne's troops, or with the force provided by the retainers of the local Leaguer nobility, revolutionary governments were set up in almost all the major towns of the kingdom. Secret or open League committees, composed of members of the three estates, supervised the councils and imprisoned nobles and officials suspected of royalist sympathies. In Toulouse, always fanatically Catholic, the *capitouls* (mayor and corporation) declared for the League and, when the *parlement* wanted to maintain the king's authority, the mob invaded the court and murdered the president and the advocate general.

In Toulouse, as in other towns, there had grown up a fierce rivalry between the *parlement* and the corporation. The civil wars and the general insecurity had induced many of the wealthier burghers to withdraw capital from trade. They sent their sons to study law and bought offices for them. But the members of the high courts had progressively closed their ranks to outsiders. Their offices had tended to become hereditary, and the growing number of lawyers found their careers blocked. They had to fall back either on royal offices in the provinces or on municipal offices. Where, before the civil wars, town councils had been controlled by wealthy merchants, they were now run by a class of professional lawyers with political ambitions to which the merchants had never aspired. Half the deputies of the third estate in the states general of 1588 were *avocats* who, with their friends, controlled the municipal governments of France. They became enthusiastic supporters of the League ideas of popular (i.e. nonaristocratic) government and of municipal and provincial autonomy.

It was in Paris that the revolution was carried to its furthest extremes. The League organization in each of the sixteen quarters of the city set up a committee charged with police functions and the supervision of the municipal officials. These committees, in turn, formed a central committee, called the Sixteen after the number of quarters in the capital, but with an actual membership of up to fifty. The Sixteen introduced the first revolutionary reign of terror that Paris was to experience. To co-ordinate the movement over the whole country, the Sixteen sent their agents to the provinces and received those of the provincial towns. The general council of the League thus controlled the whole network of autonomous Leaguer towns in France.

Henry III completely failed to follow up such advantage as he had gained from the murder of the duke of Guise. Within three months, his writ ran only in the towns of the Loire valley. In April 1589 he accepted the logic of the situation and allied himself with Henry of Navarre. With combined forces they moved on Paris and started the first siege of the capital. Paris seemed lost to the League, when a fanatical friar, Jacques Clément, struck down the king (August 1, 1589). As he was dying, Henry III recognized Navarre as his successor if he agreed to become a Catholic. The three persons mainly responsible for the massacre of St. Bartholomew had died within the space of eight months, two of them by assassination.

France now had two kings, the Huguenot king of Navarre, Henry IV of France, and his prisoner, the cardinal of Bourbon, whom the League and the Catholic powers recognized as Charles X. Henry had been a very different Huguenot leader from Coligny. His mother had brought him up as a Protestant, but he had none of Coligny's intense and compelling religious conviction. He made up for it by a grasp of political realities and a sense of opportunity which rivaled that of William of Orange. Where Coligny had imposed himself on his followers by his singleness of purpose and his severe integrity, Henry won men by a personal magnetism compounded of courage, military competence, and, not least, personal charm. His manner masked an authoritarian temperament as strong as that of Philip II. He kept it well under control until he could afford to indulge it. He sought even less than Coligny had done to overturn the political institutions of France or to weaken the crown to which he himself hoped to succeed. He had made his position clear, in March 1589, when he declared that he agreed to be instructed in the Catholic faith but refused to give up his beliefs simply to gain a crown, or thirty crowns. He would never impose his religion on Catholic France, he said, but his Huguenot co-religionists would equally not be converted by the sword. This declaration was insufficient for a large number of royalists who deserted him for the League or for an uneasy neutrality. Henry had to raise the siege of Paris.

There was now a good chance of preventing Henry's succession if all the Catholic parties could co-operate. But their interests were too divergent. Philip instructed Mendoza to put forward his own claims to the throne of France, or those of his daughter, Isabella Clara Eugenia, together with his claim to be recognized as protector of the Catholic religion in the kingdom of France. The pope, however, thought that this protectorate belonged to himself. The tense relations between Philip II and Sixtus V now deteriorated alarmingly. They had never been good, for Sixtus had tried throughout his pontificate (1585–1590) to keep some degree of independence for the papacy against the overwhelming power of Spain. He had confirmed Navarre's excommunication in 1585, when he thought that Henry III and the League were really cooperating against the Protestants. But Philip's open intervention in France, after the death of Henry III, made the pope afraid that the only Catholic power which could possibly counterbalance Spain would lose its independence. This was the argument put to him by the Venetians, who were the first Catholic power to recognize Henry IV, and he was impressed by it. Philip II, for his part, argued that he was offering all his resources for the defense of the Church. How feeble were the pope's own forces by contrast. As the weaker part, he should follow the stronger; it was the least the king could expect. Early in 1590 Spain and the papacy were nearer a complete breach than they had been since the time of Paul IV.

Sixtus V died on August 27, 1590, and the election of a more tractable pope now became a matter of vital importance for the success of Philip's plans. Up to this point, he had not directly interfered in papal elections. His representatives in Rome had simply been ordered to further the election of a pious pope and to exclude any candidate who was pro-French. This time, his ambassador, the count of Olivares, presented the conclave with a list of names from which alone they might choose. The majority of the cardinals received pensions or revenues from Spain or the Spanish dominions in Italy. Their families depended on

Spanish patronage for their advancement. To a greater or a lesser degree, they were sensitive to Spanish pressure. Olivares applied this pressure skillfully and ruthlessly, both in the election of Urban VII (Castagna), who died after twelve days, and in the long and bitter contest over the election of Gregory XIV (Sfondrato). Olivares went far beyond his instructions, but Philip did not disown him—a foretaste of the position under Philip III, when Spanish policy was made by ambitious and self-willed viceroys and ambassadors in Italy and Germany. Gregory XIV was an ardent supporter of the League. He sent money and troops to France, as well as backing the League with the moral authority of his office. His death, in October 1591, was a serious loss to Spain; but, once more, Olivares had his own candidate elected.

In the end, Spanish tactics were self-defeating. When Innocent IX died in December 1591, there had grown up a determined opposition in the college of cardinals against allowing the pope to become "the king of Spain's chaplain." In the most closely fought and dramatic of all recorded elections, Philip's preferred candidate was defeated (January 1592), and the conclave elected the young cardinal Albobrandini as a compromise candidate. Clement VIII was not anti-Spanish, but he was no longer dependent on Spain like his predecessors. His political views were formed under Sixtus V, who had bestowed the cardinal's hat on him. He could not immediately withdraw his help from the League, but he was not unwilling to listen to Henry IV's emissaries. The king would have to prove the sincerity of his return to the Church before the pope would absolve him. But the door to reconciliation was no longer closed.

Philip might temporarily control the papacy; he could not equally control his other allies. The death of the cardinal of Bourbon (May 1590) brought a host of claimants to the French crown into the field. Charles Emmanuel of Savoy and the duke of Lorraine soon withdrew from the race by modestly limiting their claims to kingdoms in Provence and Champagne, and they sent their troops into these provinces. Mayenne had his own designs on the French crown, but did not see eye to eye in this matter even with his own family. He distrusted the Spaniards, yet could not do without their help. In March 1590 Henry defeated him at Ivry and then began the siege of Paris for the second time. Supplies ran out and thirteen thousand were reckoned to have died of hunger. But the League preachers and the régime of terror of the Sixteen prevented a surrender. In September the duke of Parma with his Spanish veterans relieved the city. Spanish armies now operated in Brittany and Languedoc. It looked as if France would break up like the Netherlands. In 1592 Parma once more intervened to save Rouen from Henry.

Mayenne could not even control his own party, the League. More honest and less romantic than his brother had been, this fat and ambitious aristocrat lacked Duke Henry's personal magnetism and his ability of gaining both the confidence of his fellow noblemen and the enthusiastic admiration of the popular sections of the League. The aristocratic members of the general council of the League were becoming increasingly uneasy about the revolutionary and democratic policy of the Sixteen. L'Estoile was not alone in resenting the appointment of "small tradesmen and a bunch of Leaguer scoundrels" to the captaincies of the citizen guards and to high municipal offices. Already in February 1589 Mayenne had tried to counterbalance the popular wing in the general council by appointing to it fourteen members of the Parisian *haute bourgeoisie* and the *parlement.* The Sixteen answered by setting up a Committee of Public Safety, with ten members, selected by themselves. In November 1591 they struck against their most hated enemy in Paris, the *parlement.* Brisson, its president, and two councilors were arrested and executed for alleged treason. The act was justified, in a very modern fashion, both by the highly doubtful claim that the other members of the court had agreed with it and by the argument that treason against the public must be punished even by illegal means if legal ones were not sufficient.

This act made the breach between the nobles and the Sixteen irreconcilable. Mayenne arrested several of the Sixteen in December 1591; but he refused to act against the preachers or to destroy the Sixteen completely. Yet his attempt to hold together and balance the aristocratic and the revolutionary wings of the League was doomed to failure, just as was the similar attempt by the prince of Orange in the parallel situation in Flanders and Brabant ten years earlier.

The breakup of the Catholic front became most apparent in the states general of 1593. Mayenne had summoned it, with much reluctance, under pressure from Philip II. The Spanish ambassadors put forward the claims of the infanta, arguing that the need to prevent the succession of a heretic justified setting aside the Salic Law, which reserved the succession to males. But Mayenne was offended and the delegates were hostile. They preferred to negotiate with Henry. With superb timing, the king now announced his decision to return to the Catholic Church. The ceremony took place at St. Denis on July 25, 1593. The only effective bond between the different sections of the League, fear of a heretic king, had now disappeared. France threw herself into the arms of the king, as the Leaguer Jean de Tavannes said. Henry was liberal in his bribes of money, estates, and offices to the commanders and towns who accepted his authority. It was much cheaper than having to conquer them, he told the scandalized Sully. The lower nobility, lacking the bargaining counters of the princes and generals, had for some time begun to play for safety by placing a son in each of the opposing camps.

Paris was isolated. The interurban organization of the League was broken by Mayenne's intrigues and by Henry's renewed advance in 1594. Mayenne had undermined the position of the revolutionary leaders by his "Thermidor" of 1591. They were left with only one ally, the Catholic autocrat, Philip II of Spain. It was the *reductio ad absurdum* of revolution, and it was its end. Parma had died in December 1592, and the Spanish armies in the Netherlands were no longer in a position to come to the rescue when Henry marched on Paris for the third time. He entered his capital, almost unopposed, on March 22, 1594. As on every other occasion, he took no revenge on those who had opposed him so bitterly. Only a small number of the preachers and leaders of the League were banished for a short time.

It was the paradox of the revolutionary movements of the sixteenth century that they were led by men who were not revolutionaries. Condé and Navarre, Orange, Guise, and Mayenne did not create the organizations of their parties. Their aim, as that of many aristocratic rebels before them, was to capture the existing machinery of state, without overturning the social order or radically changing the political, or even religious, structure of their country. Yet they found themselves carried far along the path of political and social revolution by the parties of which they were the leaders. The lower nobility, who formed the most active elements in all the movements, together with the rich burghers and impoverished artisans of the citizen guards, were the real revolutionary forces. They were effectively revolutionary by virtue of their economic ambitions and their religious beliefs. Religion was the binding force that held together the divergent interests of the different classes and provided them with an organization and a propaganda machine capable of forming the first genuinely national and international parties in modern European history; for these parties never embraced more than a minority of each of their constituent classes. It was through religion that they could appeal to the lowest classes and the mob to vent the anger of their poverty and the despair of their unemployment in fanatical looting and in barbarous massacres. Social and economic discontent were fertile ground for recruitment by either side, and popular tyranny appeared both in Calvinist Ghent and in Catholic Paris.

In the long run, not even religion could reconcile the nobles with popular dictatorship, and one side or the other was driven into alliance with the former common enemy. The result was, in every case, the breakup of the revolutionary party and the defeat of the popular movement. Where the nobles and the patricians in the towns managed to maintain control over the revolutionary movement, they also managed to achieve a great part of their political and religious aims. But, once firmly in the saddle, they could afford to abandon the greater part of their revolutionary organization. Only in the field of religion did they carry their revolutions to the full conclusion. Yet neither with the Dutch Calvinists nor with the French Huguenots did the radical wing succeed in setting up a rigorous theocracy on the Geneva model. When the parties lost their revolutionary impetus and their preaching its social content, they rapidly lost the support of the lower classes. The devastations caused by the wars of the League and the increasing misery of the French peasants produced a growing number of peasant movements directed against the seigneurs and their rents, against the clergy and their tithes, and against the tax collectors and their *taille*; but they took no account of religion or the political parties. These *jacqueries* culminated in the movement of the Croquants in central and southern France in 1594–1595. They fought a pitched battle against a league of seigneurs, formed for the sole purpose of defeating them. This and many similar outbursts in the seventeenth century throw a somber light on the rural society and the tax system of France; but they remained without political effect until the revolution of 1789.

In January 1595 Henry IV declared war on Spain. He succeeded where Coligny had failed in unifying France against her external enemy. In September Clement VIII was finally induced to absolve Henry, after overcoming his anger at the Gallican Church which had claimed the power to do this without the pope. The papal absolution brought most of the remaining Leaguers onto the king's side. Mayenne made his peace in October, and only the duke of Mercœur in Brittany held out until 1598. In international relations, as in the internal affairs of France, the war with Spain was a victory for the *politique* idea of the primacy of the demands of the state over those of religion. The European state system was beginning to crystallize. Only ten years before, the Dutch had still been searching for a foreign sovereign. Now, the United Provinces of the Netherlands were accepted as equal partners in an alliance by the king of France and, with some reluctance, by the queen of England. Effectively, Spain was no longer engaged in putting down a rebellion and in intervening in a civil war, but in open warfare against the major powers of western Europe.

The strain of this war proved too much for Spain's financial resources. The cortes of Castile, powerless but outspoken, had as early as 1588 demanded to know whether France, Flanders, and England would really be better if Spain were poorer. Five years later their irony was even sharper when they petitioned the king to withdraw his armies from the Netherlands and France, for in this way the rebels who refused to accept the holy Catholic faith would be most effectively punished, "for if they wanted to be damned, let them be." [18] In 1596 Philip's government went bankrupt for the third time and once again the crisis spread through all the financial centers of Europe. Yet the effects were temporary. Silver imports from America were still rising and on this basis Philip could continue to borrow. Whenever the Spanish armies could be paid, they still proved their tactical superiority. They captured Calais, over the possession of which Henry IV and Elizabeth had bitterly quarreled (April 1596). A year later, they took Amiens. It took Henry six months of the most strenuous efforts to recapture the city. Honor was now satisfied on both sides, and the papal nuncio was able to negotiate the Treaty of Vervins (May 2, 1598). Spain gave up Calais, and, in most other respects, the conditions of Cateau-Cambrésis were restored. In 1559 the French had regarded that treaty as a major defeat; in 1598 they spoke of Vervins as "the most advantageous treaty that France had concluded for five hundred years." It was a sign of the dread which Spanish power had inspired in Europe during the reign of Philip II.

Elizabeth complained of Henry's breach of faith in concluding the treaty with Spain, just as the Dutch had complained about her negotiations with Philip in 1586–1588. With some justice, both England and France distrusted each other; but the nuncio's hope of a Franco-Spanish al-

18. C. Sánchez-Albornoz, *España un enigma histórico*, II (Buenos Aires, 1956), 346.

liance against England was much too optimistic. Henry maintained a benevolent neutrality toward England and continued underhand support to his Dutch allies.

Since the defeat of the Armada, the war between England and Spain had gone on without decisive advantage to either side. English attacks on the Iberian mainland in 1589 and 1596 (Essex's famous expedition against Cadiz) were spectacular but strategically ineffective. In between these dates, English commitments to Henry IV in Normandy and the attempt to hold Brittany against the Spaniards prevented attacks on Spain. Philip sent new and powerful armadas to invade England in 1596 and 1597; but they were wrecked by storms. English captains could maraud profitably in the Caribbean and off the Azores, or fight gallant actions against great odds like Grenville in the *Revenge*. But the Spaniards reorganized their navy and adapted their ships to English tactics. Their control of the ocean routes to the West Indies held. The English could capture isolated ships, but all the great treasure convoys got through safely.

In 1601 the Spaniards made one more attempt to attack England where they could expect local help. The idea of a Spanish landing in Ireland was not new; it had been seriously considered during the preparations for the Armada campaign. Tyrone's and O'Donnell's rebellion presented a splendid opportunity. The two Irish leaders were in contact with Spain. Already in 1596 they had asked the archduke Albert to become their sovereign. The Irish rebellions had become an increasingly serious problem for the English government. Money and troops which could have been used in the naval war against Spain were diverted, as they had earlier been diverted to help Henry IV. But, as usual, the Spaniards acted too late and with insufficient forces. The rebellions in Munster and Connaught had already been defeated. The Spaniards could not break out of the small port of Kinsale where they had landed in September 1601. Tyrone and O'Donnell marched south from Ulster to join them, but were crushingly defeated by the lord deputy, Mountjoy. On January 2, 1602, the Spaniards surrendered on honorable terms.

The Spaniards had not found co-operation with the Irish easy. Both sides now blamed each other for the defeat. For both it was the end of their hopes. O'Donnell fled to Spain and Tyrone submitted to the lord deputy. For the time being, at least, Ireland was pacified. When James I, shortly after his accession in 1603, offered to negotiate with Spain, Philip III grasped the opportunity to end a war he could no longer hope to win. The Treaty of London (August 19, 1604) marked the end of Spain's attempt to overthrow Protestantism in England. But she had successfully defended Portugal against all English efforts to upset Philip II's succession, and she had retained intact her monopoly of the West Indian colonies and their trade. As in the case of the Treaty of Vervins, honors were even.

Philip II had calculated that success in either his English or his French plans would mean certain success against the rebellious provinces of the Netherlands. Parma, in Brussels and nearer the scene of action, saw the same interconnection of the political problems but drew the opposite conclusion: Philip's English and French plans would fail, and with their failure would be lost all chance of conquering Holland and Zeeland. Only with the greatest reluctance he led his army to the relief of Paris and Rouen, knowing that he was disastrously weakening his northern front against the Dutch. He returned from Rouen a dying man. Parma had been Philip's best general and, to the end, he remained undefeated. By his firmness and moderation he had lifted the king's cause out of the moral bankruptcy into which Philip's intolerance, Alva's terror, and Don John's ambitions had plunged it. But Philip ignored his nephew's advice and in the end betrayed him, as he had betrayed so many of his best servants. Parma's enemies at court exploited his opposition to the king's policy. They blamed him for the defeat of the Armada. The Spanish captains in the Netherlands resented their Italian commander. He died just in time (December 2–3, 1592). Unknown to him, the count of Fuentes was already on his way to relieve him of his post and send him back to Spain. Philip would not even trust him to retire to Italy as the duke had pleaded, for some time, to be allowed to do.

Fuentes, the brother-in-law of the duke of Alva, dismissed Parma's Italian .and Flemish councilors and appointed Spaniards, in direct contravention of the Treaty of Arras, which had stipulated that the governor-general had to govern with the consent of the estates. Once more, the old duke of Aerschot and the Belgian nobility protested, but to no avail; nor did the short-lived governor-generalship of the archduke Ernest, the brother of Matthias, alter the situation. But the Spaniards could no longer wage a successful war on two fronts. The young Maurice of Nassau had reorganized the armies of the United Provinces. Methodically, he drove the Spaniards from Groningen, Overijssel, Guelders, and their bridgeheads north of the Rhine and the Meuse. Between 1590 and 1595, while the king's armies were fighting in France, he destroyed the favorable offensive position against Holland and Zeeland which Parma had built up with so much effort and skill.

The end of the wars

From then on, the strategic position remained stable. In 1600 Maurice invaded Flanders; but the Flemings did not rise to support him. In 1604 the Spaniards, once more led by an Italian, the Genoese Marquis Ambrogio Spinola, captured Ostend. After that they also could make no further progress. Both north and south had now achieved reasonably defensible fronts.

None of the protagonists in the long struggle in the Netherlands had foreseen that it would lead to the permanent division of the country. For all their jealous defense of their local rights, the provinces had felt themselves bound in a common destiny under their common ruler. Yet, by the end of Philip II's reign, thirty years of war had hardened differences in religion, in the social and economic structure of society, and in political customs until north and south were separated not only by the lines of soldiers and fortresses but by an unbridgeable gulf of incomprehension and indifference. Just before his death, Philip made over the Netherlands to his nephew, the archduke Albert, brother of the emperor Rudolf II and of the archdukes Matthias and Ernest, and betrothed him to his favorite daughter, the infanta Isabella Clara Eugenia. The sovereignty of the archdukes, as the couple came to be called, was severely limited by secret agreements; the king retained the ultimate authority. Yet, in practice, they enjoyed a great deal of independence, and the weak government of Philip III followed their lead more often than it led, just as it did in the case of its viceroys and ambassadors in Italy and Germany. The archdukes brought the Walloon nobility once more back into the government. Twice, in 1598 and 1600, they enlisted the help of the states general of the southern provinces to induce the northern provinces to return to their old allegiance, offering them complete autonomy and the exercise of their own religion. The attempts broke down over Madrid's unwillingness to let the southern exiles return and over the northern provinces' distrust of Spanish intentions. As Oldenbarnevelt saw it, it was ultimately a question of power. This became very clear when the archdukes overrode their states general's protests about increased taxes and ignored its demands to control government finances. The states general in the south was not summoned again until 1630. The provincial estates continued to meet. The nobility, the towns, and the corporations retained many of their old privileges—sufficient to make them content with the régime of the archdukes and unwilling to risk another rising for the sake of union with the north. Belgium, with its own traditions and loyalties, was beginning to emerge.

In the north, all was self-confidence and optimism now. Military successes were matched by economic expansion.

Amsterdam began to take over Antwerp's role of an international trading and financial center. The refugees from the south brought new industrial skills and commercial contacts. The economically most important trade of the United Provinces was in Europe. The most spectacular development, however, was the appearance of Dutch ships in the Indian Ocean. Despite the war, Spain had not been able to do without Dutch goods and shipping, even for the supplies of her armies in the Netherlands. This trade was fiercely attacked in both camps, but it was highly profitable. In 1595 Philip II placed an embargo on Dutch ships in Spanish and Portuguese ports and confiscated a number of them in Lisbon. But even before this blow fell, the Dutch had decided to bypass the Iberian ports and to fetch their spices directly from the Indies. A number of companies competing for the East India trade were formed in the last years of the sixteenth century. Mainly for political reasons, Oldenbarnevelt induced them to combine. In 1602 the fabulous United East India Company was launched—for nearly two hundred years one of the world's most successful trading ventures. The Dutch now began to build their own empire at the expense of Portugal and Spain. Once again, they were taking by force what Spain was not allowing to its own loyal subjects, for the Belgians remained strictly excluded from the trade of the Spanish empire. The advantages of political independence could not have been more strikingly demonstrated. The United Provinces were entering their "golden century."

But the war had to be brought to an end. The Anglo-Spanish treaty had left the United Provinces without an active ally. The Spanish government suffered yet another bankruptcy (1607). There was no means of raising the thirty thousand ducats per month which Spinola demanded if the war was to go on. The archdukes started to negotiate. After forty years of warfare, the difficulties were immense. In the northern Netherlands, Maurice and the merchants of Amsterdam who had grown rich in the war feared for their influence and profits. Philip III was reluctant to let down the Catholics in the United Provinces and to acknowledge the sovereignty of rebels. The inevitable court faction that was opposed to Spinola and the archdukes also opposed the peace. Dutch demands for the closing of the Scheldt and for free access to the Indies threatened the economic existence of the Spanish empire itself. Henry IV acted as mediator, but had his own designs on the sovereignty of the United Provinces. Thus it took two years of hard bargaining to reach a compromise. The Dutch gained most of their points, but only for the duration of a twelve-year truce (1609–1621). Before its expiration, Europe had plunged into another war that was to last for thirty years.

The three treaties, of 1598, 1604, and 1609, marked the failure of Philip II's grandiose plans of defeating Protestantism by establishing the political hegemony of Spain over western Europe. He had not started out with any such ambition. It was rather a policy which had crystallized in the last twenty years of his reign out of his reactions to a number of more limited problems and opportunities. To its achievement, he had sacrificed the treasures of the Indies and the blood and property of his Spanish subjects. When he died on September 13, 1598, Spanish government debts were estimated at one hundred million ducats. Interest payment on this sum amounted to about two-thirds of all revenues. The finances of the Spanish government never fully recovered and, in the seventeenth century, staggered from inflation to deflation of the coinage and thence to renewed bankruptcies. The fundamental weakness of the Spanish economy could not be remedied. The crushing tax burden on the *pecheros* inhibited investment and economic growth. The social prestige of soldiers, ecclesiastics, and civil servants drew the most enterprising elements of the population away from agricultural and industrial production. The success of a handful of merchants and financiers could not counterbalance this tendency. "These kingdoms seem to have wanted to become a republic of enchanted men living outside the natural order of things," wrote the economist and moralist Cellorigo in 1600. Since the Spaniards could not themselves supply their colonies with the textiles, arms, and other manufactured goods which they wanted and were willing to pay for in good silver, they had to import these things from their allies, rivals, and even enemies. The Spaniards' zealously guarded monopoly of trade with their colonial empire did not prevent the rest of Europe from sharing in its profits.

Philip II had no eyes for these problems. He lived from crisis to crisis and gambled on the increasing yields from the silver mines of Potosí, always hoping for the great political success which would allow his treasury and his subjects a long respite for recovery. Yet the sacrifices had not been wholly in vain. He had defeated and contained the great Ottoman offensive in the Mediterranean. He had preserved Italy from attack and had given her a long period of peace. In the Iberian peninsula, he had continued the work of unification, begun by the Catholic kings, by adding the crown of Portugal to those he had inherited and by curbing the excessive liberties of Aragon. Most important of all in his own eyes, he had won great victories for the Catholic Church. England and Scotland, indeed, were lost and so were the seven northern provinces of the Netherlands although, he hoped, not yet irretrievably. But he had saved Brabant and Flanders when they too had seemed lost. He had prevented the spread of heresy in Spain and Italy. Perhaps, he had also saved France; for had not his interventions forced Henry IV to buy Paris with a Mass? Everywhere in Europe, he had stiffened the resistance of the Church against Protestant attack and helped it to win back lost ground. The Spain of the "golden century," with its wonderful achievements in painting, in literature, and in religious and moral thought, was a self-confident society, a society which saw itself as the moral leader of Catholic Christianity, proud in the knowledge that its kings were the arbiters of Europe, that its soldiers defended Christendom from Turks and heretics, and that its sailors and missionaries were conquering conquering continents for Spain and Christ.

Unlike the Netherlands, France had maintained her political unity, but only just. The Huguenots were disappointed and alarmed by their leader's conversion. They tightened their political and military organization. There was talk of renewing the civil war; the thirty-five hundred Huguenot gentlemen could still put twenty-five thousand fighting men into the field. Henry IV may not have been sorry to see their threatening attitude. It made it easier for him to convince the Catholics of the need for a settlement. He had made incompatible promises to both sides, but he had publicly and often admitted his obligations to his old party and his determination not to impose either religion by force. The Edict of Nantes (April–May 1598), formulated after much bargaining, was in the tradition of the previous edicts granting limited toleration. The Protestants were granted freedom of conscience and the right to worship where they had worshiped before, except in and around Paris. They were also given the right to hold all public offices, and in the *parlement* of Paris a special chamber was constituted in which ten Catholic and six Protestant councilors judged all cases involving Protestants. To guarantee the observance of the edict, they were allowed to garrison some hundred places of security at the expense of the royal treasury. In return for these concessions, Catholic worship was to be allowed where the Protestants had prevented it before.

It was a compromise which did not satisfy either side. The *parlements* refused to ratify the edict. The king had to make some concessions, to persuade, to cajole, and to threaten, before they finally agreed. He showed himself at his most brilliant in this crisis. Clement VIII thundered his disapproval. The "leap across the ditch" which he had taken with Henry's absolution could also be made in reverse, he threatened. But he needed French backing in the acquisition of Ferrara for the Papal States, and, like the French Catholics, he finally gave in with bad grace.

The Huguenots had failed to convert France. Their two thousand congregations of 1562 had sunk to less than eight hundred. The northern and eastern provinces were almost wholly lost to them—one of the League's definite achievements. In the south, however, from Guienne through Languedoc to Dauphiné, they remained strong, a state within the state, and this in an age when few men believed in toleration as anything but a regrettable necessity and when nearly everyone was convinced that a healthy state must have no rivals within its boundaries. *Sub specie aeternitatis*, the Edict of Nantes may be regarded as a milestone in the history of toleration. To most contemporaries, it was a temporary shelving of the problem of coexistence of two religious faiths in one body politic.

The most urgent task facing Henry IV in 1598 was the economic and political reconstruction of France.[19] Most contemporary observers agreed that France recovered remarkably quickly from the terrible devastations of the last stages of the civil wars. The country's greatest wealth, her fertile soil, had not been destroyed. Hard work restored the abandoned fields and rebuilt the burnt houses. By 1609 France exported so much grain that it "robbeth all Spain of their silver and gold that is brought thither out of their Indies," as the English ambassador reported. Sully, the king's old Huguenot comrade-in-arms, reorganized the administration of the royal finances. It became

19. Cf. J. H. Mariéjol, *Henri IV et Louis XIII (1598–1643)*, vol. VI, part II, in E. Lavisse's series *Histoire de France* (Paris, 1905).

more efficient and a little more honest, but taxation was only a little less heavy than it had been during the civil wars. Sully made no fundamental changes in the French system of taxation. The *taille*, a personal tax, became more and more a peasants' tax. The nobles did not pay it and an increasing number of bourgeois obtained exemption by office-holding, by buying letters of nobility, or simply by usurpation. Sully managed to have a surplus of as much as one million livres a year in budgets of perhaps thirty million, and Henry boasted of his accumulated treasure. But the hoard deprived the country of much-needed capital, and the heavy rates of taxation, as the estates of Normandy complained, weighed in peacetime on the country as if it were still at war. The sums which the government spent with much boasting on the rebuilding of roads and bridges and on the navy were a fraction of the king's household expenses. For the majority of the French peasants, there were few of the "chickens in the pot" which Henry wished for them.

Henry's heavy household expenses were not, indeed, all frivolous. He had to spend large sums in pensions to the nobility to attract them to his court and to assure himself of their loyalty. The civil wars had been only a temporary solution of the economic and social crisis of the French nobility. Many had spent their fortunes in the service of one or other of the parties. Prices were still rising and it was difficult to adjust rents to keep up with them. Younger sons could rarely be provided for. There were still careers in the Church. But the Church, too, had lost much property during the civil wars, and Catholic opinion was now beginning to demand a higher standard from its clergy than many semiliterate country gentlemen could attain to. Their honorable habits of violence and plunder were now frustrated by the king's peace. They found some compensation in duels fought in contravention of royal edicts and often organized as pitched street battles, in which they could kill each other by the hundred every year.

The high nobility, the towns, and great corporations like the *parlements* presented even greater problems. Henry had no difficulty in dispensing with the states general. At its last meeting, in 1593, it had fought not so much for a permanent political order as for the victory of an ecclesiastical policy in conjunction with a foreign state. Henry's victory therefore left it without power or support in the country to oppose his absolutism. The revived power of the crown appeared less as a suppression of ancient rights than as a victory over a foreign state. Contemporary political thought, especially as expressed by the lawyers, was now almost unanimous in its support of royal absolutism. In the Netherlands, the anti-Catholic party had necessarily been antiroyalist. Its victory therefore led to the establishment of constitutional government in the United Provinces. In France both extremist parties had been, to some extent, antiroyalist and therefore constitutionalist. The royalist *politique* party was, in consequence, anticonstitutionalist, and this was true especially during the League's attack on the monarchy. The victory of the *politiques* was therefore a victory for absolutism and the divine right of kings. "The finest privilege which a people may have is to be in the good graces of its king," Henry said to the provincial estates of Burgundy.

But, in practice, it was not so simple. The last Valois kings had lost many crown rights through grants or simple usurpation. Henry IV himself had been prodigal with them when he bought the support of the Leaguer nobles and towns. There were towns, and not only Huguenot ones, where his troops might not enter and where his writ ran only by favor of the local magistrates. The governors of provinces had usurped the appointment of crown officials. Henry's old allies, Montmorency-Damville in Languedoc and Lesdiguières in Dauphiné, ruled their provinces like princes. There was no short cut to the restoration of royal authority. Henry won it back piecemeal, by constant pressure and by skillful exploitation of favorable circumstances in individual cases. The great seigneurs were rigorously excluded from his council. Sully, though created a peer, came from a minor noble family and was a Huguenot and therefore without following among the Catholics. In any case, he was very unpopular. Henry's other councilors came from the nobility of the robe, the "penne and inkhorne gentlemen," as the English ambassador said. They had been formerly servants of Henry III or of the League and were now devoted to the new king's service. The high nobility were dissatisfied with their exclusion from power, and especially the royalists and *politiques*, who felt, with some justice, that the king was more generous to his former enemies than to the friends who had stood by him in his adversity. The two most dangerous conspiracies of the reign were headed by Henry's old allies, Marshal Biron and the duke of Bouillon.

The crown did not even have full control over its own officials. No other country had as many as France, from the councilors of the *parlements* at the top to the officers of the *sénéchaussées* and the *bailliages* and down to the humble guild and market officials. The crown sold these offices for their revenues and for the status they gave their holders, and constantly created new ones. It was estimated that there were more than fifty thousand. During the civil wars, sales of and appointments to offices had become part of the aristocratic patronage system and the princes of the League had used it skillfully to win supporters in the towns. When the succession of Henry IV became certain, officeholders appointed by the League began to fear for the legality of their position and deserted the League for the king. This movement explains much of the political landslide of 1593–1595. In 1604 Sully introduced the *paulette*, an annual tax of four pence in the pound on the value of offices, payment of which made the offices hereditary. The original purpose of the tax was probably financial; but it had the effect of making officials less dependent on the patronage of the high nobility and, for this reason, it was later defended by Richelieu. It also associated a large section of the propertied classes with the monarchy and the government of the country. As the English ambassador wrote in 1609, the king was "sharing the booty gotten from the common people . . . with the clergy, nobility, gentry, and officers of justice. . . . At least in time of peace they go jollily with it; but yet not without danger, if the times should change."[20]

20. Sir G. Carew, "A Relation of the State of France," in T. Birch, *An Historical View of the Negotiations between the Courts of England, France, and Brussels* (London, 1749), p. 462.

War-weariness and Henry's intelligence and determination, coupled with his great personal charm, allowed the monarchy to regain many lost positions. But the political situation remained unstable. The king's death and a renewed minority, as many observers had forseen, threw the fate of the French monarchy once more into the balance.

Henry IV had concluded the peace with Spain because he needed it for his work of reconstruction and because he had achieved his immediate object, the restoration of the frontiers of France. The old hostility, however, remained, for the ultimate problem of power in western Europe had not yet been settled. Since neither side could afford open war, both now directed their policies toward the small states on the borders of France: Savoy, the Swiss cantons, Lorraine, and the German principalities on the Rhine. Here was the strategic route, the famous Spanish Road by which Spain kept open her communications between Italy and the Netherlands. When the Dutch and the English blocked the Channel, there was no other route, except much farther east, through the Valtelline; but this route was considered neither politically safe nor topographically convenient. Both sides therefore used every diplomatic trick to retain or gain control over the Spanish Road and, from time to time, also over the Valtelline. Only once did they slide into open warfare. When Charles Emmanuel failed to return Saluzzo, which he had occupied in 1588, Henry invaded Savoy. The threatening attitude of Spain induced him to conclude a rapid but not unfavorable peace. He gave up Saluzzo in return for Bresse, Bugey, and Gex, French-speaking Savoyard territories west of the Rhone (Treaty of Lyons, January 17, 1601). It meant at least a temporary French withdrawal from Italy and left Charles Emmanuel free for his last, unsuccessful, attempt on Geneva (1602). But the Spanish Road had now, at one important point, been reduced to a narrow tongue of Savoyard territory, the Pont de Grésin in the Val de Chézery, which preserved the link between Savoy and Spanish Franche-Comté. The French could, and on occasion did, quite easily cut this link.

The Spanish peace with England and the truce with the United Provinces did nothing to diminish Franco-Spanish tension. When a dispute arose over the succession of the duchies of Juliers, Berg, and Cleves, and involved the emperor with the military alliance of Protestant German princes, the Union, Henry IV decided to intervene, to prevent an extension of Habsburg power on the lower Rhine. The diplomatic situation was not favorable. England and the United Provinces would not break with Spain. The Protestant princes of Germany did not look with enthusiasm on French intervention in Germany. Charles Emmanuel, with his eyes on Milan, urged Henry on, but his previous career did not inspire confidence either in his strength or in his reliability. Yet Henry seemed determined on a showdown. New and highly unpopular taxes were imposed; the army was put on a war footing. His attitude toward Brussels and Madrid became increasingly threatening. With the archdukes, he had a personal quarrel. He had pursued the beautiful wife of the young prince of Condé. Condé had fled to Brussels taking his rather unwilling lady with him. The archdukes saw their honor engaged and refused to send them back to France. Another of Henry's lighthearted love affairs had suddenly taken a grave political turn. Condé, whose name evoked great Huguenot memories, was nearest in succession to the throne after Henry's children by Marie de Medici, and grounds might always be found for impugning their legitimacy. Even then, war was not yet certain. It would not have been the first time that Henry had used his love affairs to cover more subtle political designs. His real intentions have remained a mystery. He was about to leave Paris to join his army, when he was struck down by the dagger of Ravaillac (May 14, 1610). Like the assassin of Henry III, Ravaillac was convinced that he was performing a pious deed. Henry's eldest son, Louis XIII, was not yet nine. The regency government of his mother, Marie de Medici, immediately came to terms with Madrid.

Henry IV's death postponed but did not prevent the outbreak of renewed European war. Many issues had been settled in the fifty years since the Treaty of Cateau-Cambrésis. France had remained Catholic. England had maintained her independence and her own brand of Protestantism. The northern Netherlanders had won theirs, at least provisionally. But the great political crisis of the mid-sixteenth century had not yet been resolved, neither in the internal structures of the states of western Europe nor in their relations with each other. It was not to be fully resolved for another fifty years.

☙ III

The European Civil War

They came marching, this day then that, one from sunrise the other from sunset, he from south and they from north, and have wanted to contain and assuage the fire, but only increased its fury.

Pastor Johann Georg Dorsch, of Bad Peterstal, Black Forest, preaching on the occasion of the Peace of Westphalia.

IN THE SPRING of 1618 Europe was at peace. There was nothing usual about this. War was endemic in European society. Men deplored it and would blame those responsible for breaking the peace, although they rarely agreed on the identity of the culprit. A particular war, men agreed, might have been avoided; but war as such seemed to be part of the natural order. Princes and their juristically schooled advisers, happily confirmed in their own feelings by the dazzling logic of Bodin's theory of sovereignty, argued that all sovereign states had the right to wage war by virtue of this very sovereignty. It seemed, moreover, that warfare had many moral and practical virtues. The duke of Rohan voiced a common opinion when he wrote that external wars occupied ambitious and unquiet spirits, banished luxury, made a people warlike, increased its reputation among its neighbors and was the best means of preventing civil wars.

Rohan, the leader of the Huguenots in a succession of civil wars, knew what he was talking about. But civil wars had their own justification: the right of resistance to tyranny. This classical concept, which had never completely died in European thought, had received a new and sharp edge in the religious wars of the sixteenth century. The rulers of that century had done their best to maintain the religious unity of their countries; but, outside Spain and Italy, they had been singularly unsuccessful. In England and France, in the United Provinces and the Swiss Confederation, in the Empire, in Poland and in Hungary, heterodoxy had obstinately persisted and was constantly threatening to turn political and constitutional disputes into civil wars, fought for the very best of Christian reasons.

Not all those who took up arms felt that they needed a Bodinian or a Christian justification. Oppression by the local nobility or royal officials, or just sheer misery, were sufficient reasons for repeated armed uprisings by French, Austrian, and Swedish peasants, even though, on occasion, they too were not averse from quoting the Bible to justify themselves. Armed robbery on land and piracy at sea were ubiquitous and often organized under the most august auspices. Dutch and English pirates, encouraged by their governments, systematically preyed on Spanish and Portuguese shipping. The king of Spain retaliated by licensing the Dunkirk privateers. Both this ruler and the emperor set the Uskoks, a piratical frontier community on the coast of Dalmatia, to attack Venetian shipping. The Barbary pirates of North Africa hunted Christian ships from the eastern Mediterranean to the shores of Iceland and forced the European maritime powers to conclude ignominious, and far from effective, treaties to safeguard their shipping. Out on the oceans and in the overseas colonies, the peace treaties of the European powers were all but completely disregarded, and practically every one thought it perfectly proper to hunt for Negro slaves in West Africa or to pay local chieftains for doing so. The ethos of the European upper classes was essentially military. The majority of young noblemen received a military education, either privately or in one of the military academies which were just beginning to be popular. The more enterprising would learn the art of war in the service of a well-known general. A large proportion of the high officers of the first half of the Thirty Years' War had been trained in the "schools" of Spinola or Maurice of Nassau.

Nevertheless, for two decades the forces of peace had been in the ascendant. One after another the great wars had been settled: between Spain and France in 1598; between Spain and England in 1604; the emperor and the sultan concluded a truce in 1606, and Spain and the United Provinces another, for twelve years, in 1609; Denmark and Sweden made peace in 1613; Sweden and Russia in 1617. By the spring of 1618 the Swedes and the Poles were on the point of arranging a truce and so were the Poles and the Russians. Men were aware that these treaties did not settle all the disputes which had previously led their signatories into war; but they were to look back with regret to the good years before 1618. All the evils which followed seemed to arise directly from the Bohemian revolt. Contemporaries did not think that this event was a sufficient explanation for the great war, but most of them were agreed that this was when it started.

The Bohemian revolt

The Defenestration of Prague, when two royal governors of Bohemia and their secretary were thrown out of a seventy-foot-high window of the Hradčany Palace on May 23, 1618, was the result of a genuine conspiracy and confirmed those who viewed all history and politics in terms of conspiracies. Count Thurn and his friends who were responsible for the act wanted to prevent any possible reconciliation between the king and the Bohemian estates. It was, however, an ominous sign that the affair was half bungled from the start. The three victims unaccountably escaped with their lives. Tradition has it that they fell on a refuse or dung heap. The secretary was compensated for his harrowing experience with the title of Freiherr von Hohenfall—Lord of the High Jump. An element of the grotesque was to remain a characteristic of the Bohemian rebellion until it finally turned to tragedy.

But from the beginning it was more than a conspiracy. Kepler had predicted in his prognostic calendar for 1618—hackwork with which he tried to earn money for his serious astronomical and astrological studies—that in May there would be much trouble in places where there was great political liberty. The likelihood of trouble, though not of course the date, was not difficult to prognosticate. Ferdinand, the nephew of the old Habsburg emperor Matthias, who had recently been "elected" king of Bohemia, had shown his intentions twenty years earlier, as duke of Styria. A former student at the Jesuit university of Ingolstadt, this amiable, music-loving, spendthrift and indolent mediocrity was as determined to fulfil his duty to God, as a prince and a true Catholic, as ever his elder cousin, Philip II of Spain, had been. He had taken his coronation oath to observe the liberties of his subjects; but these liberties, he said, had nothing to do with religion. He had simply banished the Protestant leaders of the Styrian estates and had replaced them with his own officials. Counter-Reformation and political absolutism could clearly be made to work hand in hand. When they encountered the alliance of Protestantism and anti-absolutist estates no compromise was likely to last for long. Nor was it possible to isolate the Bohemian conflict, as Ferdinand had successfully done in Styria. Some of the Calvinist Bohemian magnates had for years been in touch with other Calvinist leaders: with Erasmus von Tschernembl, the leader of the Upper Austrian estates; with Charles Žerotin, the governor of Moravia; with Gábor Bethlen, the Calvinist prince of Transylvania who, with encouragement from his overlord, the sultan, was maneuvering for the crown of Hungary; above all with Christian of Anhalt, the ambitious minister of the elector Frederick V of the Palatinate. It seemed a formidable combination. Frederick was the nephew of Maurice of Nassau and the son-in-law of James I. No one knew how far family and religious sentiment might not commit the two great Protestant powers. If Frederick could be substituted for Ferdinand as king of Bohemia, there would be a Protestant majority in the electoral college, perhaps a Protestant emperor. The Austrian Habsburgs would be left powerless, petty princes of three or four Alpine duchies whose estates would prescribe their policies. Spain might then well find it impossible to hold northern Italy and the Netherlands.

Such seemed to be the potential escalation of disasters as it presented itself to Ferdinand and to Oñate, the Spanish ambassador in Vienna. In July 1618 they carried through a coup d'état by arresting Cardinal Khlesl, the leader of the old emperor Matthias' peace party. All compromise was now ruled out.

The pamphleteers were first in the field. Scioppius (Kaspar Schoppe) admonished the emperor to exercise vengeance against heretic and rebellious princes and to exterminate the inhabitants of cities that had changed their religion, "even the very children and infants," so that they should not lose their eternal life. The Protestants, with as yet comfortable shudders, quoted Scioppius' Latin in German translation and then replied in kind, urging the Christian duty to resist tyranny. In the autumn of 1618, fighting started in Bohemia. But as yet there were few soldiers; the government in Vienna had not prepared for war. The Bohemians had their chance. But this was no repetition of the Hussite wars of two hundred years before, when the fight for religious and political freedom had found an echo in all classes. Now, the German-Czech nobility had no use for the peasants as allies and very little for the towns, except to get money from them. Even Tschernembl, the friend of the Huguenot intellectuals, Hotman and Duplessis-Mornay, and the one leader of the rebellion with a grasp of the political realities of the situation, was a prisoner of his aristocratic preconceptions and his rigid Calvinist thinking about the role of the lower magistrates in resistance to tyranny. Thus the social basis of the rebellion remained disastrously narrow, and its leaders never managed to shake off the deadly flavor of mere conspiracy. Anhalt dangled election to the Bohemian throne before the romantic eyes of Charles Emmanuel of Savoy and persuaded that inveterate old hunter of elusive crowns to pay for an army for the Bohemians to be led by the Catholic mercenary leader, Count Ernest of Mansfeld. Anhalt then double-crossed Savoy and persuaded the Bohemians to elect his master, Frederick V. This happened on August 27, 1619. A day later the electors at Frankfurt, ignorant of events at Prague, made their choice of a new emperor (Matthias having died earlier in the year). The Protestants, including Frederick, unable to reach agreement among themselves, voted for Ferdinand. Ferdinand, still acting as king of Bohemia, voted for himself. Only later did Frederick learn of the Bohemian offer and, after a period of hesitation, accept it.

The Catholic counterstroke

During the following year, Anhalt's lighthearted cleverness and the Bohemian nobility's political and military incompetence frittered away their remaining opportunities. Only in the summer of 1620 was the Catholic party ready for its counterstroke. Maximilian of Bavaria had reorganized the League of the Catholic Princes of Germany. Ferdinand had to pledge him Upper Austria for his campaign expenses and, secretly, promise to transfer to him the Upper Palatinate and Frederick's electoral dignity. Spain mobilized its army in the Netherlands to attack the Rhine Palatinate. Sigismund III of Poland, worried by the prospect of a Hungarian-Bohemian Protestant alliance, sent a corps of Cossacks. Even Pope Paul V, though rarely inclined to look beyond Italy, sent money to Munich and Vienna. John George of Saxony was promised Lusatia for preferring loyalty to the emperor to loyalty to his Bohemian neighbors and co-religionists. The government of Louis XIII, hoping to preserve peace in Germany and prevent Spanish intervention, arranged a truce between the armies of the League and of the Protestant Union and thus inadvertently freed Maximilian from fear of a Protestant countermove against Bavaria. On November 8, 1620, Maximilian's Belgian general, Tilly, annihilated Frederick's and Anhalt's army in the battle of the White Mountain, outside Prague.

Twenty-seven noblemen and burghers were executed in Prague; the Protestant preachers were banished; the estates lost all effective power. A new Bohemian nobility, of German, Italian, Spanish, Flemish, even Scottish origins, joined the few remaining German-Czechs who had chosen the imperial side and, like these latter, did well out of wholesale confiscations of the estates of the rebels. Their loyalty was not to the Bohemian tradition but only to the house of Austria in whose service they had made their fortunes.

It should now have been possible to make peace. If the fate of Bohemia terrified Protestant Europe, it was still only the fate of rebels within the emperor's own dominions. But the Palatinate was a different matter. Here was a major principality of the Empire, in a strategically sensitive area, straddling the middle Rhine, in which none of the great western European powers could afford to disinterest themselves. That it should now have become the connecting link between the power struggles of western Europe and the complex religious and political struggles of the Empire and of northern and eastern Europe was due not so much to the frivolous scheming of Anhalt and Frederick V as to the ambitions of the Wittelsbachs of Bavaria. Maximilian was now officially also elector Palatine. His brother was archbishop-elector of Cologne. Several of his cousins held smaller principalities, both secular and ecclesiastical. It seemed natural that Maximilian should be the leader of the Catholic German estates, pursuing the double objective of preventing any further losses to the Protestants and of preventing the house of Austria from infringing the German liberties, i.e. the power of the princes. The foolishness of his distant cousin, Frederick V, opened up the further prospect of acquiring his lands and titles for the Bavarian line of the Wittelsbachs. In Bavaria, Maximilian had a centrally situated state of some one million inhabitants in which both Protestantism and the opposition of the estates had been eliminated two generations earlier. Almost absolute powers of taxation and a regime of careful economy gave him a substantial income. As head of the Catholic League he had a fine army, commanded by Tilly, one of the best generals of the age.

To Maximilian his ambitions appeared both just and realistic in their limitations. But almost immediately the inherent contradictions of his aims became apparent. By obtaining from Ferdinand the transfer of the Upper Palatinate and the electoral dignity, he set a most dangerous precedent for the extension of imperial power in Germany. The Protestant princes of the Empire, and especially the electors of Saxony and Brandenburg, did not accept the transfer. From the beginning, the self-proclaimed champion of the estates had raised half of them against himself. The marauding campaigns of Frederick V's generals, Mansfeld, Baden-Durlach, and Christian of Brunswick, gave Tilly the excuse to move into the Rhine Palatinate; but so did a Spanish army from the Netherlands. From this moment the course of events escaped from Maximilian's control, and not all of Tilly's victories could ever restore it to him.

Spain's role

In the spring of 1621 the twelve-year truce between Spain and the United Provinces of the Netherlands ran out and was not renewed. In Spain the quest for a *monarchia universal*, a world empire, had died with Charles V; the universal championship of an aggressive Counter-Reformation had died with Philip II. But the idea of a Spanish empire (now sometimes actually referred to by this name) which should play some not very clearly defined, but certainly Catholic-Christian and politically preeminent, role in Europe and the world—this was an idea which still filled the minds of many of the Castilian grandees. As viceroys of Naples and governors of Milan, as amabssadors in Rome, Venice, Prague, and Brussels, they had chafed under the inactivity imposed on Spanish policy by Philip III's favorite, the duke of Lerma. In 1618 they won control of the Council of State in Madrid. When the young Philip IV succeeded his father in 1621, their victory was complete. The most intelligent, ambitious, and determined of their number, the count-duke of Olivares, now enjoyed the unshakable favor of the king.

There was much discussion, in Brussels and Madrid, over the wisdom of renewing the war with the Dutch "rebels." They had made use of the truce to capture the carrying trade from western Europe and the Baltic to Spain. Worse still, they had never ceased their piracy on the oceans and their attacks on the Spanish and Portuguese overseas colonies. In these twelve years, said Don Carlos Coloma, they had gained as much reputation in the Indies as the Spaniards had in a hundred and twenty. If they were allowed to continue, said Don Balthazar de Zúñiga, first the Indies would be lost, then the rest of Flanders, the Spanish dominions in Italy, and finally Spain itself would be in danger, for it would have lost that which had made it great. Once again, the argument from the potential escalation of disasters confirmed those who were temperamentally inclined toward an aggressive policy. The contrary arguments from the Council of Finance were overruled. The young king understood only this, that he was not responsible for the debts left by his predecessors. Neither he nor anyone else could know that the recent reduction in the silver shipments from America was not due to temporary difficulties but heralded a permanent decline. It seemed enough to Philip IV to declare his pious intention not to burden his subjects any further. Velázquez' portraits of the king show, with incomparable insight, the pathos of a man who is half aware of his personal inadequacy for the role he is called upon to play. But Philip never wavered. With the enthusiastic support of the nobility and clergy of Castile, but of few others, he led his country for forty-four years from disaster to disaster.

Once war had been decided, Spanish policy remained perfectly consistent. All hope of success must depend on keeping open the road between Spain and the Spanish Netherlands. There were three alternative routes: (1) by sea; (2) the old "Spanish Road," via Genoa, Savoy, Franche-Comté, and Lorraine; and (3) via Genoa, Milan, the Valtelline, the upper Rhine, and Alsace. To safeguard the first, the Catholic king was willing to contemplate marrying his sister to the heretic prince of Wales (later Charles I), perhaps even, to please the English, to agree to the restoration of Frederick V to the Palatinate. There was some feeling of relief in Madrid when neither possibility materialized; but, clearly, Spain was not engaged in a Catholic crusade. The two overland routes both presupposed Spanish domination of northern Italy and the co-operation of the emperor. When, in 1624, the abortive negotiations for the English marriage were followed by a desultory naval war, Madrid proposed to Vienna a Habsburg league which the pope and other Catholic powers would be invited to join, specifically to safeguard the road to the Netherlands and to co-operate against common enemies. These included France, as well as the Protestant powers; for in October 1624, Richelieu had sent French troops into the Valtelline.

This league was never formally concluded, but co-operation between Madrid and Vienna became very close. The Valtelline became one of the focal points of the war. Its Catholic inhabitants were under the political authority of the Protestant Grisons League, allied to, but not part of, the Swiss Confederation. Spanish, French, and Venetian attempts to control the Valtelline passes became entangled in the religious and family feuds of the Grisons. Francophile Salis and hispanophile Plantas murdered each other and invited, or helped to expel, the troops of one or other of the great powers. A former Protestant pastor, George Jenatsch, made himself virtual dictator of the Grisons, maneuvering with ferocious virtuosity and at least one change of religion, until he himself was finally assassinated (1639). In the end the Grisons kept the Valtelline but granted Spain the right of free passage.

"*A Calvinist international*"

If Spain had made a deliberate choice to restart the Netherlands war, so had the United Provinces. Their decision had become virtually certain when Maurice of Nassau had won his long duel with Oldenbarnevelt and the regents' party. The opportunities seemed splendid and the risks not too great. At sea the Dutch were supreme. A chain of modern fortresses and the most professional and best-paid army in Europe guarded the provinces on their land frontiers. Behind these, life could continue peacefully and placidly, with perhaps more personal freedom than anywhere else in Europe. For some years, there were hopes of inducing the southern Netherlands to overthrow their Spanish government. But the Belgians, though anxious for peace, were loyal to the king of Spain. Until the later stages of the French war, they, too, suffered relatively little from the frontier war.

Both friend and foe recognized that the United Provinces were the center of all resistance to the house of Austria. In Maurice's words, they were fighting for their own and for universal liberty. Dutch ambassadors and agents worked in London and in Constantinople, in Stockholm and Moscow. With Venice, there was a regular alliance; later, there was to be another with France and—a great dynastic coup for the house of Nassau—a marriage alliance with the Stuarts. The greater part of Europe's trade with the Baltic was carried in Dutch ships. Netherlanders, many of them religious or political refugees from the south, formed important settlements in the German North Sea and Baltic ports. From there they spread their activities to Scandinavia and Russia. The Marcelis mined Norwegian copper, exported Russian grain, and helped to organize the Russian armaments industry at Tula. Later, they became the king of Denmark's economic advisers and organizers of his war effort. The De Geer and the Trip combined interests in Swedish copper, brass, and iron with the armaments industry of the lower Rhine and Belgium. In Paris, the Hoeufft supplied Baltic naval stores to the growing French navy and arms for the French troops. These firms had capital resources, commercial and industrial expertise, and, above all, family connections. They intermarried and formed partnerships. Their brothers or cousins sat in Amsterdam and had access to the world's richest money market and the best commercial information. Belgian and Portuguese-Jewish connections gave them entry to the Ibero-Indies trade, and the Spanish government's elaborate system of licensing ships and cargoes could not prevent this commercial penetration.

Here was a "Calvinist international" that was much better organized, and potentially much more powerful, than Christian of Anhalt's correspondence club of incompetent aristocrats. But it was not a conspiracy against Spain nor against the Catholic religion. While others fought for religion and politics, these Calvinist capitalists were out to make money. One of them, the Antwerpner Jan de Witte, financed Wallenstein's armies. In 1645 the Amsterdam money market was perfectly happy to equip naval squadrons for both the Swedes and Danes to fight each other. Most of these firms probably preferred to finance the war efforts of the Protestant powers; all of them were willing to trade with Spain, even in war materials. Maurice of Naussau cheerfully maintained that the Dutch would bring provisions to the devil if they were not afraid that hell-fire might burn up their ships. Spain could not carry on the war without the provisions which the Netherlanders or their agents alone could provide. The United Provinces could not pay for its soldiers and warships without the wealth which this trade with the enemy helped to bring into the country.

Both sides were fully aware of the baleful implications

of this sordid symbiosis. But, even after the long stalemate that followed the Spanish capture of Breda (1625)—Veláquez deliberately painted the scene as the beginning of a reconciliation—both sides always found good reasons for continuing the war. Olivares still believed in victory. His creatures in the Council of State—the praetorian buccaneers of the 1610's had been pushed out or had died—took their cue and added unwarranted innuendos against Spinola's loyalty when that most brilliant and faithful of the king's generals pleaded for peace. In that year, 1628, the Dutch admiral, Piet Hein, captured the Spanish silver fleet in the West Indies. The balance of the war was beginning to tilt against Spain. From the Caribbean to the South Atlantic and the Indian Ocean, the Dutch pressed their attacks. For the first time, a European war was becoming a world war. The Gold Coast, Cape Verde, parts of Angola, and half of Brazil, all of them Portuguese possessions, fell into Dutch hands during the 1630's and early 40's.

The war, however, imposed heavy strains on the United Provinces. Taxes were high; the Dunkirk privateers continued to take a heavy toll of Dutch shipping; and as long as powerful imperial armies fought in Germany, the military position remained precarious. The war with Spain seemed to be fought more and more for the benefit of the house of Nassau and its hangers-on, for the shareholders of the West India Company which was conquering Brazil, for a handful of millionaire firms with interests in the war economies of the different European states, and for the spiritual satisfaction of the orthodox Calvinist preachers.

The regents' party, gradually edging back into key positions, and the East India Company, jealous of the southerners who directed the West India Company and more worried about English than about Spanish trade rivalry, all these would have liked to end the war on any reasonable terms. But many were also afraid of renewed civil and religious strife, once the country was at peace again. For a long time Prince Frederick Henry's military successes, his virtual toleration of the Remonstrants and his moderation toward the regents' party seemed preferable to anything that might happen if he were seriously opposed.

The rise of Wallenstein

The Dutch had always been sensitive to the military situation in northwestern Germany. When Tilly smashed Frederick's supporters on the middle Rhine, during the early 1620's, their situation became critical. They needed a new ally and they found him in Christian IV of Denmark. Christian, in his capacity of duke of Holstein, had for a long time indulged in that favorite Protestant pastime, the secularization of ecclestical lands. His brother was bishop of Schwerin, his son of Verden, and he himself now had his eyes on Bremen, Osnabrück, and Halberstadt. Any further advance by Tilly into northwestern Germany would put an end to all these ambitions. In 1625 the United Provinces and England offered him an alliance and money to intervene in Germany. To Christian it seemed a splendid opportunity to act as the leader and savior of the Protestant princes of the Empire and to balance the recent victories of his great rival, Gustavus Adolphus, over Poland.

It was a sad miscalculation. The Danish Council of State washed its hands of the affair. The Dutch were themselves hard pressed and had little money to spare. English help in money and troops, though not negligible, was quite inadequate for the ends pursued. Nevertheless, Maximilian was sufficiently alarmed by Christian's plans to urge the emperor to raise an army of his own in support of that of the Catholic League.

Ferdinand entrusted the organization of this new army to a Bohemian country nobleman, Albrecht von Wallenstein. Wallenstein had remained loyal during the Bohemian rebellion and had received princely rewards out of confiscated estates. Together with Prince Liechtenstein, the imperial governor of Bohemia, several of Ferdinand's ministers in Vienna, and the financier De Witte, Wallenstein had formed a consortium which farmed the Bohemian mint and issued a depreciated currency (1622). Many of the north German princes had been systematically depreciating their coinages since 1620; but the Bohemian inflation topped them all. Liechtenstein may have made up to ten million guilders profit; De Witte certainly over thirty million. Wallenstein used his profits to buy himself the duchy of Friedland in northern Bohemia and, altogether, more than fifty noble estates.

From the beginning, Wallenstein treated his army command as a big business operation. Through De Witte he raised loans in all important financial centers, from Venice to Lyons, and from Antwerp to Nuremberg and Hamburg. He made contracts with rich noblemen and businessmen to raise regiments. Systematically and deliberately he outbid Maximilian, so that Tilly found whole regiments disappearing from Bavarian into imperial service. Wallenstein's Bohemian estates supplied much of the grain and fodder this army needed. Iron founders, gunsmiths, powder grinders, brought from Germany and Italy to Friedland, started a minor industrial revolution in the duchy and made it into one of the principal centers of the European armaments industry. The army itself, however, flooded into north Germany and forced the German princes, provinces, and cities to pay for its upkeep. This was the famous system of contributions, huge taxes in money, and provisions, imposed on friend, neutral, or foe at the point of the gun and the halberd, for the upkeep of the army and the profit of its colonels and generals. The system was not new, except in detail; but never before had it been used so ruthlessly and on such an immense scale. Wallenstein demonstrated that it was possible to raise mercenary armies of over one hundred thousand men and build up a most formidable military machine on a quite narrow territorial and industrial basis, provided one's financial and administrative organization was really good, and provided also that one was willing to spread both recruitment and the maintenance of the army over large areas of a relatively rich country. The lesson was not lost on the kings of Sweden and, later, Prussia, who found that independent princes, with the help of conscription and the backing of a regular civil service, could do even better than an upstart adventurer with a genius for organization.

This pattern was not really broken until the appearance of the national mass armies of the French revolutionary wars and the advance of military technology in the nineteenth century, which completely changed the scale of the demographic and industrial basis that a country would need if it wanted to be a great military power.

The war in Germany was very different from that waged by Spinola and the princes of Nassau in the Netherlands, where the siege and capture of a relatively small city, like Breda or Bois-le-Duc, was glory enough for several years' campaigning. In Germany there were no chains of fortresses. Few cities had modern defenses, for fortification was an expensive business, neglected during the half century of peace before 1618, and difficult to make good once the war had started. Most cities, therefore, could not hold up a determined assailant for more than a few days or weeks. From 1620 onward, when Mansfield had marched his unpaid army from Bohemia to the Palatinate, Alsace, and East Friesland, the character of campaigning remained similar: relatively small armies, with all their impedimenta of baggage and munitions trains, soldiers' wives, prostitutes and children, and a host of hangers-on turning their dishonest pennies at the expense of soldiers and civilians alike—such armies would crawl slowly in pursuit of each other over vast distances, engulfing villages and small towns on their way, picking up every local disease and spreading it in their tracks. The wastage rates were enormous. In 1626 Wallenstein chased Mansfeld from Dessau, on the Elbe, through Silesia to Hungary where Bethlen had promised support against the emperor. Mansfeld's army practically disappeared during this march.

Wallenstein's survived only just sufficiently to frighten Bethlen into making peace.

During the winter Wallenstein again recruited a huge army. Tilly had won one of his brilliant victories, the battle of Lutter, against Christian IV (August 27, 1626). But in the campaigns of 1627 and 1628, it was Wallenstein's much larger army which carried the imperial standards on a broad front through Brandenburg, Pomerania, Mecklenburg and Holstein, right into Jutland. On July 7, 1629, the emperor and Christian IV concluded the Peace of Lübeck, by which Christian was allowed to keep Denmark and Holstein but had to leave his unfortunate German allies to face Ferdinand's revenge.

Vistas of possibility

No emperor since Frederick Barbarossa, in the twelfth century, had been as powerful in Germany as Ferdinand II was in 1629. With half of Germany occupied and the other half open to blackmail by Wallenstein's armies, there might well have been a chance to set up a strong central monarchy in Germany, or even to set course for the universal monarchy of the house of Austria which its enemies always accused it of pursuing. Wallenstein may have toyed with such ideas. He spoke of plans to drive the Turks from Constantinople, to set up a huge new empire in eastern Europe. But no one in Vienna had any such plans. The objectives of the house of Austria remained limited and tactical; yet they were such that they could not help but confirm all current suspicions of the overmighty power of the house of Habsburg.

It was Madrid, rather than Vienna, which grasped the

potentialities of Wallenstein's control of the German Baltic ports. If a Spanish imperial fleet were built in the Baltic, perhaps with Danish and Hanseatic help, the United Provinces could be struck in their Achilles' heel, their vital Baltic trade. Olivares wanted no more than that. But could any outside power believe, or afford to believe, that Spanish imperial seapower in the Baltic would not be permanent and overwhelming? Even though the plan did not prove immediately feasible—neither Habsburg resources nor the available ports were adequate for such an ambitious scheme—the mere project was bound to bring in a new and powerful enemy: Sweden.

The plans of the court of Vienna were rather different. Ferdinand and his clerical advisers saw their chance to restore the Empire to the state it had been in at the time of the Peace of Augsburg in 1555. This meant that the Protestants would have to restore all the ecclesiastical property which they had acquired since then. It might even mean that imperial cities, such as Augsburg, would have to accept a Catholic government. John George of Saxony and the other Lutheran princes of the Empire who had hitherto faithfully and not unprofitably supported the emperor, would never willingly accept such a reversal. But Ferdinand published the Edict of Restitution on March 6, 1629. Very soon it became clear that it was not an altruistic act, designed simply to right the wrongs which the Catholic Church had undoubtedly suffered since 1555. Germany was treated to the unedifying spectacle of a race between Habsburg and Wittelsbach to capture the reconstituted prince-bishoprics. The Habsburgs won, with the splendid prizes of Magdeburg, Bremen, and Halberstadt for Archduke Leopold William (already bishop of Passau and Strasbourg), against the less important Osnabrück, Minden, and Verden for the Wittelsbachs. No other house had a chance; but the lesser pickings of this feast, the monasteries, prebends, and schools, were disputed loudly and embarrassingly by the different monastic orders.

There is no evidence that Ferdinand wanted to destroy German Protestantism or to transform the Empire into an absolute monarchy. But it looked like that to the German princes. His general, Wallenstein, openly showed his contempt for them. The electors should depend on the emperor, he said, not the emperor on the electors, as hitherto. Or, less ominous but even more wounding: "Herr Tilly is a slave to the Bavarian commissars. . . . The good old chap will gain a martyr's crown for the patience he has to show to these varmints." And this upstart had been created a prince of the Holy Roman Empire, enfeoffed with the ancient duchy of Mecklenburg whose dukes the emperor had deposed for rebellion (1628). It was becoming only too clear what a dangerous weapon Maximilian had pressed into the emperor's reluctant hands when he had insisted on the destitution of his cousin Frederick.

France intervenes

In the meantime the war had flared up in Italy. This was inevitable once France began to play an active role in European politics again. Throughout the 1620's, France had been preoccupied with her internal problems and with her unsatisfactory relations with England. In 1627 a number of relatively minor irritations brought the two countries into open war. The duke of Buckingham, then all-powerful in England, thought that he could carry off a brilliant coup: the occupation of the island of Ré. This would help La Rochelle and the Huguenots if they rebelled again, bring commercial and piratical profits to England, inhibit French naval building before it became really dangerous and, above all, present Buckingham as a champion of Protestantism to parliament. Richelieu took the threat very seriously. But the English just failed to capture the island and, by 1629, Richelieu had, once and for all, broken the military power of the Huguenots.

"Princes command peoples and interest commands princes," wrote Richelieu's great antagonist, the duke of Rohan. The decision which Richelieu now took to intervene in Italy was, in his own view, dictated by interest and was duly admired by Rohan himself. Yet was this the real interest of France? Richelieu's rival, Michel de Marillac, and his circle did not agree. France was not menaced, they argued, and it was wrong to fight other Catholic powers when these were engaged in a life-and-death struggle with Protestant powers. The French people was poverty-stricken, overburdened by taxes, and rebellious. The power of the crown was still shaky and must first be strengthened. Richelieu did not altogether deny these arguments. The deliberate choice which he made was partly based on a different appreciation of the danger to France arising from the startling victories of the house of Austria. But the cardinal stressed equally the glory and reputation which the king would gain from the war. In the course of the

1630's, Richelieu was to develop realistic and moderate war aims, based on the idea of interlocking guarantees for future peace as a system of collective security against aggression. This certainly was reason of state actively applied to the true interests of France, perhaps of Europe. But the decisions of 1629–1630 were mixed with a good deal of that traditional military pride of the European aristocracy which made warfare almost an end in itself. As to the cost, "War is one of the scourges with which it has pleased God to afflict men," Richelieu wrote to Marillac; and with this solace the French peasants had to be content.

The occasion for French intervention was provided by a Spanish-imperial act of aggression in Italy. The last Gonzaga duke of Mantua died in 1627. His heir was a French subject, Charles, duke of Nevers. Fearing that the French might obtain a foothold on the Lombard plain, Madrid and Vienna decided on preventive military action against Mantua. Many contemporaries were, later, to regard this war, with its unsatisfactory outcome, as the turning point in the history of Spanish power and of the emperor's position in Germany which, it was argued, was fatally weakened by the diversion of troops to Italy. Yet the evidence is all the other way. The Spanish-imperialist armies were highly successful against the French. If Richelieu was able to conclude the favorable Peace of Cherasco (June 19, 1631) which gave France Pinerolo, and Nevers the imperial investiture with Mantua, this was only because the imperial position had meanwhile suffered a disastrous setback in Germany.

This setback had very little to do with the Mantuan war

and almost everything with the inability of Ferdinand's corrupt and incapable council to develop a rational imperial policy on the basis of Wallenstein's victories. In the summer of 1630 the emperor traveled to Regensburg to persuade the Catholic electors—Protestant Saxony and Brandenburg refused to participate in the meeting—to elect his son, Ferdinand, as king of the Romans, and to participate in the Spanish war against the Dutch. The family interests of the house of Habsburg could not have been more blatantly preferred to those of the Empire. The electors countered with the demand for Wallenstein's dismissal and for a large reduction of the imperial armies. Wallenstein had many enemies at court. They persuaded Ferdinand that the Catholic and Protestant princes of the Empire might make common cause against him, or even join the king of Sweden who had just landed in Pomerania (June 26, 1630). Ferdinand should prove that he did not wish to change the Empire into an absolutist monrachy. On August 13 the emperor gave in and dismissed his general. Wallenstein's financial organization, shaky during the previous year, now collapsed altogether. De Witte jumped into a well in his own garden.

Having thrown away his ace, the emperor quickly lost the other tricks. The electors refused to join the war against the United Provinces, they pressed for peace with France, and they did not elect young Ferdinand king of the Romans. Maximilian forced the emperor to accept Tilly as the new commander in chief of the greatly reduced imperial, as well as the League, armies. At the same time Maximilian negotiated an alliance with France which was formally concluded, in the Treaty of Fontainebleau, on May 30, 1631. Richelieu's armies had been defeated and his diplomats bungled their part of the negotiations at Regensburg; but thanks to Bavaria he had won a major victory over the house of Austria. He followed it up by an alliance with Sweden (Treaty of Bärwalde, January 23, 1631).

Sweden: a leader of genius

In the twenty years before this treaty the young Gustavus Adolphus of Sweden had modernized and centralized the administration of his country. He had done this in alliance with the high nobility, more especially the Oxenstierna family. He had encouraged Louis de Geer and other Netherlanders to build him the most modern armaments industry in Europe and to develop the old copper mines of Falun until Swedish copper came to enjoy a virtual monopoly of the European copper market. When the Swedes conquered Riga and other Livonian ports from Poland-Lithuania, another Netherlander, Pieter Spierinck, organized for the king the systematic exploitation of the export tolls on grain. The social cost of Gustavus' policies was high, and there were some economic setbacks. The peasants, burdened by high taxation, plagued by recruiting for the army, and often handed over, willy-nilly, to suffer further exploitation by the aristocratic recipients or usurpers of crown land, were almost annually goaded into local riots and rebellions. In 1626 the Spanish government alternated its habitual *vellón* inflation with one of its periodic attempts at deflation, and the bottom fell out of the copper market. Nevertheless, Sweden maintained its predominant position in copper. By foisting copper coins on conquered territories, and by De Geer's astute manipulations of the markets in Hamburg and Amsterdam, the Swedish crown still extracted large sums from this export.

Gustavus Adolphus had already had to fight for his crown, and for Swedish independence, first against Christian IV who would have liked to revive the Union of Kalmar (the late-medieval union of the three Scandinavian kingdoms under the Danish crown), then against Sigismund III of Poland, his cousin, whom Gustavus' father had deprived of the Swedish crown. The claims of the Polish Vasas were the more serious as they involved a threat to Swedish Protestantism, for Sigismund was an enthusiastic champion of the Counter-Reformation. The motivation of these wars seems to have contained strong economic elements. Both Denmark and Sweden claimed the *dominium maris Baltici* which meant, in practice, that they would levy tolls on each other's and everyone else's shipping wherever they could: the Danes in the Sound, and the Swedes at the entrance to the Neva and in any Baltic port they managed to control. Both countries, no doubt, wished in this way to protect and encourage their own shipping and commerce; but this was only a small fraction of the total Baltic trade. Ultimately, Denmark and Sweden, unlike the United Provinces, fought for economic and financial advantages because these were the tools of power.

The Swedish-Danish war had ended, with some Danish advantage, in 1613. The Swedish-Polish war, however, continued intermittently, partly because Sigismund would not give up his claims to the Swedish crown and partly because Gustavus was doing well out of it. By 1622, Livonia was in Swedish hands. In 1626, Gustavus invaded Prussia and began to speak airily of attacking the emperor, once he had finished with Poland. The confrontation began when Wallenstein, nervous for his right flank, sent troops to help Sigismund. The collapse of Denmark precipitated the crisis. Once again, the argument of the potential escalation of disasters justified a war of aggression. As early as the beginning of 1628, the Swedish *riksdag* accepted Gustavus' analysis of the dangers threatening Sweden, "the open conspiracy (by the emperor and the king of Poland) to deprive us of all trade and navigation, and . . . of the sovereignty of the Baltic." In September 1629 France mediated the truce of Altmark between Sweden and Poland. The Polish problem was now isolated from Germany, and Sweden was free to intervene in the general war. Sweden retained the right to collect the export tolls of the Prussian ports. As much as the copper exports, and more than the French subsidies promised in the Treaty of Bärwalde, these tolls were to be the financial basis of Gustavus Adolphus' campaigns in Germany.

No one in 1630 thought that Swedish intervention should be taken lightly; few realized just how formidable it was to be. The Swedish army, hardened in the long years of war on the Livonian and Prussian marches against the redoubtable Polish horsemen, knew all about the most modern Spanish and Dutch tactics and it added some new ideas of its own, notably the close co-operation of musketeers with cavalry and the greatly increased use of field artillery. This army was backed by a country more thoroughly organized for war than any other in Europe, and it was commanded by a leader of genius. By all contemporary accounts Gustavus Adolphus was the most charismatic personality to appear on the European scene since the death of Henry IV. This big blonde "Goth" from the barbarian north who spoke most European languages fluently and with éclat, who liked good literature, music, food, and drink, whose Protestant convictions were sincere but not intolerant, who was immensely sure of the justice of his cause and of his ability to lead it, who used his personal charm to balance his quick and terrifying temper and his bouts of repulsive self-righteousness—this man could inspire enthusiasm where the other two outstanding leaders of the age, Richelieu and Wallenstein, could inspire only cold admiration and awed hatred. He was served by men of exceptional ability: Axel Oxenstierna, his chancellor; the Netherlanders who ran the Swedish economy; and his generals, Horn, Banér, and Torstensson. It was more than luck; it was intelligent and unprejudiced selection, as well as loyal support of those once chosen (a point whose importance Richelieu never tired of stressing to Louis XIII). It was Gustavus Adolphus who made the reluctant Swedish nobility open their ranks to foreigners, Netherlanders and Germans, Balts and Scots, and even more unwillingly, to men of lower birth, administrators and diplomats, financiers and professional men.

"The lion of the north"

Gustavus unfolded his German campaign carefully and ruthlessly, advancing from one strategic conquest to the next, and meanwhile first persuading, then blackmailing the unenthusiastic Protestant princes of northern Germany into increasingly dependent alliances with him. At the same time he expanded his armies by much the same methods that Wallenstein had used. By March 1632, he had some one hundred and forty thousand men under his command, of whom only thirteen thousand were Swedes.

The king's shattering victory over Tilly, at Breitenfeld near Leipzig (September 7, 1631) stilled for the moment all Protestant misgivings over Swedish reason of state and over the king's role in the catastrophe of Magdeburg—the city whose smoking ruins showed the result of trusting Gustavus' promises of relief from Tilly's besieging army. After Breitenfeld, even John George of Saxony spoke for a moment of electing Gustavus emperor. The king wanted nothing so quixotic; but he was certainly not averse to rearranging the map of the Empire to suit his own interests. Once again, ecclesiastical lands became the most convenient prize with which to reward German allies and Swedish generals. The famous liberty of the German princes soon appeared to be in greater danger from the "Macedonian domination" of Sweden than from the autocratic but legalistically minded emperor.

Richelieu had hoped that Gustavus Adolphus would strike directly south, through Bohemia to Vienna. It was on this presupposition that he had signed his alliance with Bavaria; and this alliance was necessary to him, not only because it gave him a counterbalance to the house of Austria in Germany, but also because it was meant to prove to the pope, and even perhaps to himself, that the war in Europe had nothing to do with religion. But for Gustavus a direct attack on Vienna appeared both tactically difficult and strategically unrewarding, for it would not necessarily break the main sources of imperial power. A move southwestward, on the other hand, to the Rhine and the Alps, would bring him control of the still undevastated, rich states of southern Germany, would isolate the emperor from Spanish help from Italy and the Netherlands, and would finally allow a decisive campaign eastward down the Danube. At Christmas 1631 the king held court at Mainz. There he informed the French ambassadors that he would "devastate Bavaria by pillage, fire and blood," unless Maximilian laid down his arms. Richelieu, placed before the choice of a victorious Sweden and a crumbling Bavaria, threw Maximilian to the wolves. For France it was a diplomatic defeat. For Bavaria it was disaster. Maximilian, the triumphant leader of the Catholic estates of Germany had, after all, only played sorcerer's apprentice, unleashing forces he could not control. On May 5, 1632, Gustavus Adolphus and Frederick V entered Munich.

This was the high-water mark of Swedish power. In January 1632 Wallenstein had once more taken command of the imperial armies, with more extensive powers even than during his first command. With Spanish money and with the credit which his name still carried he managed to finance a new army. From Bohemia he invaded Saxony. Gustavus, to save his most important and most unreliable German ally, John George, had to turn north. Throughout the summer the two armies faced each other and fought without decision. The king continued to make grandiose plans: a firm league of Protestant German princes under Swedish leadership; then one more great campaign, and his "knee on their neck and a dagger at their throat" would force his enemies to accept the peace he would dictate. After that he would turn to Poland and partition that kingdom with Russia.

On November 6, 1632, at Lützen, once again on the plains of Leipzig, Gustavus attacked Wallenstein. A decisive victory seemed within his grasp, for Wallenstein had already dispersed half his army into winter quarters and many of his units only arrived on the field of battle in the course of the day. But Gustavus himself fell while leading the charge of one of the Swedish regiments. His army fought on until, at dusk, Wallenstein was forced to retreat But the victory meant little, for Gustavus Adolphus was irreplaceable.

Axel Oxenstierna who now took over the direction of Swedish affairs for Gustavus' six-year-old daughter, Christina, shed the more fantastical of the king's plans, notably those concerning Poland, and brought the rest down to earth. In January 1633 he defined Swedish war aims as security for Sweden and some "satisfaction," i.e. compensation for her efforts on behalf of the German Protestants. These remained Sweden's basic terms until the final peace treaty, though views changed as to what exactly was meant by them. For these terms the Swedish nobility was willing to continue to fight; there were still many splendid personal prizes to be won by successful generals, and the cost to Sweden itself was relatively slight. *Bellum se ipse aleat*, let war feed itself, Mansfeld's and Wallenstein's old maxim, was being practiced with ever more brutal efficiency by the Swedish commanders.

Wallenstein falls

Wallenstein is reported to have remarked that Gustavus Adolphus' death was well and good, "for two cocks on one dung heap could not get on." But what did he now crow about? Was he a Bohemian or Czech patriot, wishing to make himself king of an independent Bohemia? or a German patriot, struggling to free Germany from Swedes, Spaniards, and other foreigners? Was he a traitor to the emperor, aiming only at self-aggrandizement, or did he intend to impose peace on a war-weary Europe? These and other interpretations have all been learnedly, and often passionately, canvassed in the historiographical treatment of the "Wallenstein problem." Seen in such terms of motive, with or without elaborate psychological underpinning, the solution to the problem is likely to remain speculative even if, as now seems possible, much hitherto unused material may become available. There is little doubt that Wallenstein's rapidly deteriorating health, throughout the year 1633, impaired his powers of making clear decisions. But much more important was his complete failure to understand the role which the commander of even the

The Murder of Wallenstein and His Officers, anonymous copper-plate engraving, 1634. Propyläen Verlag Berlin.

largest, most successful, and most personal army could play in a seventeenth-century state. He could sell his army to another war lord, the Swedes or the French, as Bernard of Weimar was to do a few years later. That would have simply meant exchanging one master for another. Yet, by themselves, Wallenstein and his army could never impose any political settlement. Unlike the New Model Army, fifteen years later, Wallenstein's army stood for nothing; it could command no political or religious loyalty. The very aims of its commander were bound to be secret. Only if Wallenstein had first used his power to impose his will on the imperial government could he then have hoped to carry through whatever plans he may have had. Julius Caesar is said to have remarked that Sulla did not know the ABC of political power when he retired from the dictatorship of Rome. In Caesarian terms, Wallenstein was a child-in-arms. He did not even see that there was a Rubicon to be crossed.

Without decisive leadership, Wallenstein's party at court disintegrated during the summer and autumn of 1633. After that, his enemies had little difficulty in winning over his senior officers. Having made their choice, these officers improved their case by freely inventing such evidence of treason as might still be lacking against their commander. At last, Ferdinand was convinced; but his conscience had still to be put at rest by a formal trial accorded to his general. His confessor assured him that it did not matter that the accused knew nothing of this event. The death sentence was executed against Wallenstein and three of his loyal followers at Eger, on the night of February 25, 1634, in a manner highly reminiscent of Machiavelli's admiring account of the more lurid deeds of Cesare Borgia. The double-crossing generals, the treacherous colonels, and the murderous soldiers who committed the deed, were all richly rewarded by a grateful emperor.

The year 1634 was a good one for Ferdinand II. In September his son, Ferdinand of Hungary, together with Philip IV's brother, the cardinal infante Ferdinand of Spain, annihilated the Swedish-Protestant army at Nördlingen. The Swedes had to evacuate southern Germany altogether. In the north, most of their German allies, led by Saxony, made peace with the emperor. In the Peace of Prague (May 1635) the emperor only gave way on the Edict of Restitution—not indeed revoking it, but shelving it for forty years. But all alliances between the German princes were forbidden and their troops were to form an imperial army which was to take an oath to the emperor. It was a brilliant victory for the emperor and, secondarily, for Saxony which kept Lusatia and obtained Magdeburg in addition. The peace-loving, beer-drinking Lutheran prevaricator, John George, had done rather better than the austere Catholic power politician, Maximilian of Bavaria.

But the war was not over. The very extent of the Spanish-imperial victory forced Richelieu's hand; for the specter of a Habsburg domination of Europe seemed now more threatening than ever. On May 5, 1635, France formally declared war on Spain.

The first all-European war

The ring of alliances was now complete. The Bohemian rebellion had become the first all-European war in which, of the greater powers, only England, Poland, Russia, and the Ottoman empire remained relatively uninvolved. No bilateral treaty, nor even a treaty between two groups of states, could now end the war. Most of the treaties of alliance contained specific clauses prohibiting separate peace treaties. In any case, how could any government be certain that the enemy with whom it treated would not lead it into a trap, isolating it from its friends and joining forces with its betrayed allies? Only a general peace could now give security, and this could be achieved only through a general peace conference. It took time before the combatants fully understood this, and then it took more time to organize such a conference, to decide its form, and to agree on who had a right to be represented and in what capacity; for the question with whom one was prepared to treat raised some of the fundamental issues of the war. What rights, if any, were to be allowed to the Bohemian exiles, to the heirs of Frederick V, to the Catalans and Portuguese, both in rebellion against their lawful king since 1640, or to the Swiss cantons who had not fought at all but were an interested party in the future constitution of the Empire?

In the meantime the war continued. Central Europe could no longer maintain the huge numbers of soldiers that Wallenstein and Gustavus Adolphus had had at their command. Small armies, rarely more than fifteen thousand of whom often half were cavalry, would now march rapidly over long distances, moving from one undevastated area to the next until this too was burnt out or until supply lines became too long and the enemy could temporarily concentrate superior forces. Grand strategy in the manner of Gustavus Adolphus, aiming at the annihilation of the enemies' forces and total conquest, was no longer possible. Three times the Swedes swept through Bohemia. Vienna, even Paris, had moments of panic when enemy armies approached. But storming or besieging such great cities was not to be thought of. In the long run, the resources of the anti-Habsburg forces and their fighting ability proved to be superior. In 1638 Bernard of Weimar's German army, in French pay, captured Breisach and with it the control of the upper Rhine valley and Alsace. The Spanish Road was now all but blocked. In the following year the Dutch admiral, Tromp, sank a great Spanish armada in the battle of the Downs, in neutral English waters. In 1640 the Dutch followed this up by a brilliant victory over a Spanish-Portuguese fleet off Bahía, which confirmed the Dutch hold on Brazil.

Spain's weakness

The Spanish monarchy could make no riposte. Its fundamental weakness was now revealed: the narrowness of its base. Castile and the silver from its American colonies financed and defended the empire; the other dominions were, to a greater or lesser degree, onlookers. In 1624 Olivares had suggested that these dominions could be induced to play a full part in the burdens of empire if they could be allowed to share in its fruits: the honors, commands, and control over policy that had been all but monopolized by the Castilian ruling classes. It might just have worked. In the 1560's Cardinal Granvelle had made very similar proposals to Philip II. It is not clear whether Olivares knew of these or not; but both sets of proposals suffered a similar fate. Castilian vested interests would not even allow their serious discussion. The results were disastrous in both cases. Philip II fell back on the duke of Alva's policy of repression and lost the northern Netherlands. Olivares had to fall back on a policy that drove him, slowly but inexorably, into a similar policy of repression which lost him Catalonia and Portugal. This alternative policy was the "Union of Arms," a scheme for the creation of a common imperial reserve of one hundred and forty thousand men to whose maintenance all the states of the empire were to contribute in fixed proportions. But without the *quid pro quo* of the original proposal, the "Union of Arms" was inevitably disliked and distrusted by the non-Castilian dominions. Catalonia was the state with the greatest surviving autonomy and with an archaic and inefficient government that could do little to pacify its feud-riven and bandit-infested countryside. It made practically no contribution to the Spanish war effort. Having for fifteen years failed to get voluntary help, Olivares determined to pitchfork the province into war by attacking France from the Catalan border (1639). The need to defend their country should force the Catalans to support the army, regardless of their liberties. But the Catalans, led by their clergy, did not see it this way, High-handed actions by the Castilian troops were met by riots and these turned into rebellion. By July 1640 the viceroy had been murdered and the authority of the Madrid government in Catalonia had collapsed.

The last available troops in Spain were now sent against the Catalans. This gave the Portuguese their chance. Increasing financial demands for a war effort which had signally failed to protect the Portuguese colonies in Africa and Brazil turned the commercial classes and the nobility against Madrid. The lower classes, vociferously supported by the clergy, had always hated the Castilians. On December 1, 1640, Portuguese conspirators, probably with French backing, seized power in Lisbon and proclaimed the greatest nobleman of the country, the duke of Braganza, as King John IV of Portugal.

In January 1641 the Catalans transferred their allegiance to the king of France, "as in the time of Charlemagne." Peace with France was now impossible, for Philip IV would never consent to the loss of Catalonia and the king of France's honor was engaged to his new subjects. But it was the end of Olivares. In 1643 the Castilian grandees forced his dismissal and exile. Two years later he died, broken and insane—a classically tragic figure whose grandiose vision of an international Catholic-Spanish empire was flawed by the aggressive militarism that was central to the Castilian aristocratic tradition and whose personal character was flawed by the *hybris* that was the indelible mark of this tradition.

The disasters continued. In 1643 the prince of Condé broke the Spanish infantry's century-old reputation for invincibility in the battle of Rocroi. In 1647, revolts broke out in Naples and Palermo. After Castile, Naples was probably the most heavily taxed dominion of the Spanish crown. But the millions which the Spanish viceroys had to press out of that kingdom forced them into two contradictory policies: they had to increase viceregal authority at the expense of the liberties of the country but, at the same time, they had to grant or sell new liberties and privileges to the Neapolitan nobility without whose support the taxes could not be collected. It amounted to a virtual abdication by the monarchy of authority over the countryside. The nobles, exercising ever-widening powers of jurisdiction, buying up or usurping whole towns, and terrorizing anyone still outside their direct power through gangs of bandits whom they protected from royal justice, were progressively reducing the kingdom to anarchy. On July 7, 1647, a popular revolt broke out in the city of Naples and spread immediately to the provinces. It was led by a gifted but unstable fisherman, Masaniello, but was stage-managed by an octogenarian lawyer, Antonio Genoino. Within five weeks very much the same pattern, though without the Neapolitan bloodshed, was repeated in Palermo and western Sicily. These revolts were directed both against the Spanish viceregal governments and against the nobility. Both in Naples and Palermo the original leaders disappeared within a week, after setting up their popular dictatorships. But effective control over the two capital cities remained with the revolutionaries for many months. Only step by step and, finally, with the help of a Spanish fleet, did the two viceregal governments and their noble allies re-establish their authority (spring 1648).

Peacemakers

The position of the Austrian branch of the house of Habsburg, if not quite as critical, had also deteriorated decisively. The loss of Alsace allowed French armies to invade southern Germany at will. In 1641 the young elector Frederick William of Brandenburg broke the Peace of Prague and declared his neutrality. Bavaria did the same in 1647. The German princes had recaptured the right to an independent foreign policy, and the emperor implicitly recognized this when he agreed that they were to be represented at the peace conference. Imperial hopes revived in 1643, when Christian IV of Denmark, old now but still incurably optimistic, broke with Sweden. But the Swedish riposte was devastating. Torstensson overran Jutland and then turned south to crush an imperial army sent to help the Danes. When Christian was also defeated at sea he had to accept the Treaty of Brömsebro (1645), by which he had to give up to Sweden the islands of Gotland and Ösel and the province of Halland for thirty years. Denmark thus lost her strategic strong points in the eastern Baltic and only just managed to keep her most important strategic and financial asset, the control of the Sound.

This was also the end of Danish attempts to mediate at the two peace conferences of Münster and Osnabrück, which had begun meeting in 1643. The role of peacemaker was now taken up by Venice and the papacy. Neither power had been completely neutral. Venice, the ally of France and the United Provinces, had disputed the Valtelline with Spain and, for short periods, had actually been at war with the house of Austria; but from 1630 onward she had withdrawn from the European struggle, and from 1645 she had to fight a bitter war against the Turks for the defense of Crete. The Venetian senate was therefore most anxious that the Christian powers should stop fighting each other and become aware of the renewed danger to Christendom from the Turks.

The position of the papacy was more complex. Paul V (1605–1621), Gregory XV (1621–1623), and Urban VIII (1623–1644) had all supported the Catholic cause. But, right from the beginning of the war, Rome had found it difficult to decide which of the powers most truly fought for this cause, and this problem was complicated by the pope's purely political interests as a territorial prince in Italy. Not unnaturally, successive popes had tended to prefer Bavaria to Austria and, with more serious consequences, France to Spain. Most of this support was diplomatic—welcome, no doubt, but as Maximilian remarked about one of the papal diplomats at his court: "Father Giacinto demands great faith and patience, but we and the soldiers a great sum of money." And money Rome gave only very sparingly. To the scandal of contemporary Catholics, but to the undoubted enrichment of the Church and of the world, far larger sums went to the papal nephews. Instead of adding to the slaughter in Germany, the popes and their families paid for the Baroque Age of Rome, the squares, palazzi, and churches of Bernini and Borromini, the paintings of Pietro da Cortona and Poussin. Paris, Madrid, Amsterdam, and London all had their patrons and artists, some of them—Rembrandt and Velázquez—the greatest of the age. But it was Rome which became, for the last time in its long and splendid history, the greatest single center of art and architecture in Europe.

All this did not interfere with papal mediation at the

peace congress. But when Rome would not sanction any Catholic concessions to the Protestants, or even to accord them diplomatic recognition, the powers found that they could do without papal services. The curia was aware of this dilemma, but was bound by its most venerable traditions. The final, and unheeded, protest by Innocent X against the peace treaties was, however, a diplomatic blunder, for it showed starkly the gulf between the political-religious claims of the papacy and the realities of European political life.

While the delegates negotiated, the Catholics at Münster and the Protestants at Osnabrück, there was no truce and the parties still tried to improve their bargaining position in successive campaigns. The wonder is therefore not that it took five years to make peace, but that it was made at all. The almost universal corruption of the delegates of the smaller states and of Sweden helped to smooth away many minor difficulties. They invented a special word for it, *Realdankbarkeit* (practical gratitude). The decisive move was made by Ferdinand III and his principal adviser, Trauttmansdorf. Pressed by Maximilian, who threatened to make a separate peace, and against the violent protests of Spain, they accepted French claims to Lorraine, Alsace, and the bridgeheads of Breisach and Philippsburg. This meant the irrevocable end the Spanish Road and, effectively, the end of the close alliance between the two branches of the house of Austria. Philip IV drew the logical conclusion from this situation and came to terms with the United Provinces. Spanish recognition of the complete independence of the United Provinces and the closing of the Scheldt were hard to swallow but did not call for any change in the position as it had existed for many years. The Orange party and the French did their best to wreck the negotiations; but Frederick Henry had died in 1647, his son William II was still very young, and the province of Holland was determined to have peace. It was signed in January 1648.

After this, it was relatively easy to persuade Brandenburg and Sweden to divide Pomerania between them. Sweden also obtained the bishoprics of Bremen and Verden and was thus firmly established on the estuaries of three great German rivers, the Oder, the Elbe, and the Weser. Brandenburg was given Magdeburg and Halberstadt, in compensation for western Pomerania—this time at the expense of Saxon claims. Maximilian had to be content with the Upper Palatinate and the electoral dignity. Charles Louis, son of the unfortunate Frederick V, was allowed to return to the Rhine Palatinate, with an eighth electorate especially created for him.

Postwar settlement

More important than these details was the final settlement of the relations between the emperor and the princes. Although still fighting on the imperial side, they were effectively supported by France and Sweden. Step by step, Trauttmansdorf had to retreat before their combined pressure. In the end, the sellout of Spain proved to have achieved practically nothing. The princes and imperial cities were confirmed in their absolute right to determine the religion of their subjects. Only a few concessions were made to the heterodox, but at least they were again granted the right to emigrate which they had first obtained in the Peace of Augsburg, in 1555. The Calvinists were now included with the Lutherans in the peace. The "normal" year for the ownership of ecclesiastical property was to be 1624—a more favorable date for the Protestants than 1627, the date set in the Peace of Prague. Finally, the imperial estates retained, as of right, the ancient and disastrous practice of making alliances and waging war.

What was left of the medieval universalist ideals, as represented by the pope and the emperor, had now completely disappeared. The pope was ignored. Ferdinand III had virtually to write off the Empire. From now on his house concentrated its efforts on a very different political structure, a multiracial but Catholic Danubian empire in which the emperor was a virtually absolute ruler. At the same time, the statesmen of the age had become acutely aware of the danger of a protracted general war. Something had to be found to replace the old universalist ideal, and this turned out to be the idea of a universal guarantee of peace. It was the merit of Richelieu and his circle that they worked out this idea systematically and made it the basis of French war aims. Originally, Richelieu claimed only such territorial acquisitions for France as would enable her to fulfil her obligations in such a system of collective security; but even during his lifetime, the very successes of French arms led to an expansion of French territorial claims. Mazarin compromised the original plans still further until, to the rest of Europe, French war aims did not appear to differ in essentials from those of all the other powers.

Nevertheless, in a modified form, Richelieu's system was

written into the peace treaties. The signatories guaranteed the treaties, if need be by force of arms, against any disturber. The new constitution of the Empire was thus made part of the public law of Europe and guaranteed by non-German powers. To later generations of Germans it seemed that these powers were deliberately trying to keep Germany weak. There is some truth in this. Yet the division, and the consequent political impotence, of Germany was primarily the fault of the German estates; for it was the inevitable result of their "liberties" for which, in a sense, they had fought the Thirty Years' War—even when, like Maximilian, they had fought as the emperor's allies. But in any case, the politicians of 1648 really did want a secure and reasonably permanent peace, and no other way of obtaining it was remotely feasible.

It was not really the fault of the peace makers that the treaties, signed on October 24, 1648, did not after all turn out to be either secure or permanent; nor did this prove that their basic ideas were wrong. It was rather that they had not gone far enough in settling all specific disputes and that they were not able to eradicate the tradition of the quest for military honor and the spirit of aggression. France and Spain did not make peace in 1648. Mazarin was riding on the crest of the wave of military success and hoped for even better things; Philip IV and his new adviser, Don Luis de Haro, imagined that, with the Dutch war off their hands, they could hold France and reconquer Catalonia and Portugal. Despite the desperate exhaustion of Castile they were almost right. The Fronde neutralized France for five years—time enough for Madrid to settle the revolts of southern Italy (1648) and to reconquer Catalonia (1652). The Catalans received back all their old liberties. The Spanish monarchy thus reverted to its old policy of alliance with the local ruling classes of its various dominions—the policy that had kept the Spanish empire in Europe alive for two hundred years and was to do so for another fifty.

Spain should now have concluded peace with France, but Philip IV, aging and obstinate, still found his honor engaged over Portugal and over the person of the prince of Condé who had fled from France and become the commander of Philip's armies in the Netherlands. It was, however, not really Philip's fault that he became involved in another war, with England.

In 1652 the old and exasperating rivalry between the English and the Dutch had escalated, through the Navigation Act of 1651 (an attempt to cut out the Dutch carrying trade from foreign countries to England) and royalist privateering from Dutch ports, into open naval war (1652–1654). The English, with considerable strategic and technical-naval advantages, came well out of this war, and this success perhaps helps to explain English enthusiasm for the almost purely aggressive war against Spain, in 1656. Mazarin offered Dunkirk to Cromwell for an offensive alliance. It would be useful against the Dutch. Perhaps it may have seemed useful also against the French if, as now seemed likely, they captured the whole of the Spanish Netherlands. The rest was pure imperialism: conquest in the West Indies for the sake of both religion and trade.

The English naval war was not a complete success. The

capture of part of a Spanish silver fleet and the still undeveloped island of Jamaica were balanced by heavy shipping losses. But Dunkirk was captured by an Anglo-French army, after its victory over Condé in the battle of the Dunes. In 1659 France and Spain finally concluded the Peace of the Pyrenees: France received Artois, Roussillon, and Cerdagne, and Philip IV's daughter, Maria Theresa, married Louis XIV. In 1662 Charles II sold Dunkirk to France—a striking demonstration of the basic futility of Cromwell's war with Spain.

Once again Philip IV had concluded a peace treaty to have his hands free against another enemy: the last and the most unforgivable of all, the Portuguese. But it was now too late. The Portuguese had reconquered Brazil from the Dutch. It did not matter that this was possible largely because of the hostility of the old Amsterdam patriciate to the West India Company whom they starved of financial and naval support to resist the Portuguese attack. For the Portuguese it was a notable victory, bringing with it new financial resources and much-needed self-confidence. In 1665 they routed the last Spanish army at Villaviciosa. A few weeks later Philip IV died and in 1668 Spain officially recognized Portuguese independence, just as Louis XIV was marching into the Spanish Netherlands. But that war belonged to a different age when the Spanish monarchy had become an object of the ambitions of other powers.

Sweden at war again

Over half of Europe, groups of disbanded soldiers were roaming, useless, unwanted and destructive. Discharged officers sat bored and discontented on impoverished estates, nostalgic for the gay life of the camps. In Sweden they controlled the government, and the king was one of them. Christina's minority and reign had witnessed an unprecedented rise in the numbers and wealth of a now partly international and very militarist Swedish nobility. They had come to own some two-thirds of all the farms in the country, mainly at the expense of the crown. At a *riksdag* in 1650, the estates of the clergy, towns, and peasants combined against the nobles, and the country was on the verge of civil war. Christina took advantage of this crisis to secure the right of succession for her cousin, Charles Gustavus. In 1654 she abdicated, partly because she had become a Catholic in a Lutheran country, partly because she preferred a quiet life among artists and philosophers in Rome to the political struggles which were looming so menacingly on the Swedish political horizon. Charles X Gustavus did indeed make a start with the partial resumption of crown lands (*reduktionen*). But he had been Swedish commander in chief before 1648, and, with the enthusiastic support of the nobility, he sidestepped the internal problem and threw Sweden into a new war against Poland (1655).

Poland seemed on the point of dissolution. A Cossack revolt, in 1648, had brought the Russians on the scene as allies of the Cossacks. City after city in Lithuania and eastern Poland fell to their massive attacks. The Swedish action therefore seemed to promise the double advantage of forestalling a likely Russian penetration to the Baltic and of securing for Sweden Poland's Baltic coastline, perhaps even the Polish crown.

Three times Charles X reached Kraków. He won brilliant battles and, at times, the Polish nobility was willing to accept him as their king. But the Swedes could not control the vast areas of the Polish plains. The Poles turned back to their old king, John Casimir; the emperor sent support. In 1657 Denmark declared war on Sweden. It seemed a unique opportunity to reverse the Treaty of Brömsebro, and the United Provinces, fearful of a Swedish monopoly of the Baltic grain ports, urged the Danes on. The result was unexpected. Charles X turned north and, like his master Torstensson in 1643, overran Jutland. Then, in January and February of 1658, he marched his army over the ice of the Little Belt and then, from island to island, to Zealand. Denmark had no choice but to accept the Treaty of Roskilde, ceding Bornholm and her remaining provinces in southern Sweden. A few months later Charles re-started the war by attacking Copenhagen. There had been some Danish provocation, but essentially it was an act of aggression. Charles now wanted to re-create the Union of Kalmar, but under Swedish leadership. But in October 1658 a Dutch fleet sailed into the Sound and forced the Swedes to lift the siege of Copenhagen. It was a most impressive demonstration of the uses of sea-power. The Dutch effectively dictated the peace they wanted, which was to keep the two sides of the Sound under different political control. The old Danish blackmail of the Sound tolls was finished for good, and the Swedish attempt to keep all foreign warships out of the Baltic was frustrated.

It was probably lucky for Sweden that her brilliant but

irresponsible king died in 1660. The regency government for his young son, Charles XI, concluded the Peace of Copenhagen with Denmark (1660) which confirmed the Treaty of Roskilde, except that Sweden gave Bornholm and Trondheim back to Denmark. By the Peace of Oliva with Poland, also concluded in 1660, Sweden kept Livonia but not Polish (West) Prussia and Danzig, and the Polish Vasas finally gave up their claims to Sweden. Frederick William of Brandenburg who had maneuvered unscrupulously between the parties had the possession of East Prussia confirmed in full sovereignty. In 1667 Poland made peace with Russia, at the cost of most of her territories east of the Dniepr.

The cost counted

The treaties of the Pyrenees, of Copenhagen, and Oliva formed the necessary supplements to the Peace of Westphalia. The period that followed was concerned with new and different problems, its leaders filled with different ambitions. Yet there is much to be said for the old interpretation of the Thirty Years' War, as a single process from 1618 to 1648. People spoke of it in this way and by this name as early as the 1650's. They saw this unity in the central importance of the imperial and of the religious problems, even though the war ranged far beyond the frontiers of the Empire, and even though religion was only one, rarely the most important and certainly a diminishing motive force for the combatants. But the religious motivation was there, however Richelieu might deny it, and it was deliberately taken into account in the terms of the

Peace of Westphalia. After 1648 there was a real change. Religion might still produce sympathy or antipathy between states, but it no longer determined alliances nor did it lead countries into war. From 1648 until the French Revolution the European states were engaged in pure power struggles only diaphanously veiled by the laws of inheritance and quotations from Grotius' *De jure belli et pacis.*

All this is clear enough and has been generally accepted; but the immediate effects of the Thirty Years' War on the economic, social, and political structure of European society, and on its cultural life, are more difficult to interpret and have remained highly controversial. Only quite recently has it been recognized that the beginning of the war coincided with an economic crisis that affected most of Europe and some parts of the rest of the world, and that this crisis was followed by an economic depression that lasted, in varying degrees of severity, until at least the middle of the seventeenth century. The causes of the crisis and the depression are not yet fully understood. Almost certainly they were complex, compounded of such phenomena as the German currency inflation which made Dutch and English cloth temporarily unsaleable in central Europe, the vagaries of Spanish monetary policy, the dislocation and unemployment produced by the victory of the "new draperies" over the traditional cloth industries of England, Holland, and northern Italy, a decline of population with a consequent slump in agricultural prices (but why did population decline even in countries unaffected by war?) and the quite dramatic collapse of the Spanish-

American trade after 1620—a collapse due, in its turn, primarily to the catastrophic decline of the native population in the Spanish-American colonies during the previous hundred years. It seems inconceivable that the Thirty Years' War, with its destruction of life and property, its dislocation of trade routes, and its distortion of investment and production for military purposes should not have added to the economic malaise. But exactly how this happened is far from clear; and the reverse effect—that of the depression on the course of the war—has hardly begun to be studied. The United Provinces, with their near-monopoly of the European carrying trade, with their profitable commerce with all the combatants, and with their successful break into the Portuguese colonial trade, suffered least of all. The Swiss made neutrality pay very well. The English economy was sufficiently flexible to adjust itself, in the long run very successfully, to the changing economic circumstances. The French did not do nearly so well, and both the Spanish and the Italian economies continued to decline until the end of the century. The anti-economic ethos of a clerical and courtly society, which showed itself in the massive shift of capital investment from trade and manufacture to land purchase and building, caused the relative economic decline of southern Europe compared with the economically dynamic northwest.

The direct effects of the war on central Europe are better known, but their extent is still a matter for debate. The peasant revolt in Upper Austria (1626), with its strongly Lutheran tinge, still followed traditions that went back to the previous century. But another peasant revolt, in Bavaria in 1634, was quite free from religious motivation. The peasants rebelled against the elector who, they said, had delivered the country over to the detested soldiery. The scenes of soldiers' cruelties and the peasants' brutal retaliations, described in Grimmelshausen's *Simplicissimus* and etched in Callot's *Les Misères de la guerre*, are not exaggerated even if, for literary and artistic effect, different incidents may well have been brought together. It is not for nothing that in Germany the horrors of the Thirty Years' War have lived on in popular memory as those of no other war. Of the bigger cities, only Magdeburg suffered complete destruction; but scores of smaller towns, and thousands of villages and hamlets, were plundered or burnt or left deserted by their inhabitants. The high mortality rates, however, were due mainly to local famines and to the contagious diseases spread by the soldiers and the refugees in the towns. Northwestern Germany, Prussia, and most of Austria got off lightly. But in Brandenburg, Mecklenburg, Pomerania, in the Palatinate, in Württemberg, and in parts of Bavaria, population losses were up to 50 per cent or even more. The price paid by the common people for the ambitions of the princes and the arrogance of the Churches was high indeed.

It does not seem, however, as if the war changed the secular trends of social development in central Europe. The imposition of a new serfdom on the peasantry of the Baltic littoral, from Denmark to Prussia and Poland and inland in Bohemia and Hungary, had started in the sixteenth century, or even earlier, and was only accelerated by the population losses of the Thirty Years' War. By contrast, in many areas of western and southern Germany, the dissolution of the old manorial system, well advanced in 1618, was all but completed, and depopulation provided better opportunities for the surviving peasant families. Nor is it possible to see the war as a great cultural turning point in the history of Germany. While it lasted there was, naturally, very little money or opportunity for great building programs or for the patronage of painting and sculpture. But the greatest period of German art had ended as early as the middle of the sixteenth century, and a revival, the South German Baroque, began not so long after the end of the war. The Bavarian monasteries, which had bought up cheaply the estates of the impoverished Bavarian nobility, proved to be among the most imaginative patrons of this art. If German literature produced no great dramatist or poet like Corneille or Calderón, Milton or Vondel, neither had it done so in the previous century. But it was precisely the emotional impact of the war which has left us the moving poetry of Gryphius and the devastating satires of Grimmelshausen and Moscherosch: a corpus of antiwar literature as powerful as any before Voltaire. In the middle of the war the Jesuit Spee had the courage to defy the traditions of the Church and of his order and publish the first systematic attack on witch hunts and witch trials, the *Cautio criminalis* (1631–1632). But it was in music that German creative gifts survived the war most triumphantly. Throughout its course, and often under tremendous difficulties and strain, Heinrich Schütz composed his motets and passions at Dresden, and so did many lesser musicians in courts, cities, and village churches throughout the country. It seems as if people fled to music, perhaps even more than to religion, as a refuge and consolation from the almost unbearable ills of the times.

Power struggles within the Empire

The Thirty Years War started with a revolution in central Europe; it ended amid revolutions and coups all over western, southern, and northern Europe. This was not fortuitous. The aim of all European monarchies was the imposition of effective central control over their countries. This brought them into conflict with forces that still retained, from the Middle Ages, autonomous powers within the country: estates and parliaments, provinces and cities, cathedral chapters, monasteries and universities, and above all the great nobles. Their powers and their respective importance varied from country to country. Often, some of them found their best interest in alliance with the monarchy. The lines were never sharply drawn, not least because the monarchies' own agents, law courts and royal officials, tended to imitate the autonomous corporations, claiming special privileges and immunities and often acting in opposition to royal commands and interests. Nevertheless, the conflict over ultimate power was perfectly clear. It might be temporarily compromised or postponed; it could not be permanently ignored. It was likely to flare up over questions of money and taxation, for here the wishes of the prince and of his subjects were diametrically opposed: the princes needed money and their subjects did not want to pay. It was, moreover, always possible for these political and constitutional conflicts to become entangled with social movements that had, in themselves, very little to do with political power. From the latter part of the sixteenth century, religious differences became involved and these tended both to intensify and to internationalize the social and political conflicts in any particular country. Religious motivation and religious organization could become the basis of revolutionary movements spanning, at least temporarily, all classes, from the artisans of the cities to the highest nobility. Such was the case with the Huguenots, the Holy League, and the Sea Beggars during the French and Netherlands civil wars in the sixteenth century. In Austria and Bohemia, however, where the cities were small, only the peasants could form a popular wing of a revolutionary movement; but the peasants here had their own, terrifying, revolutionary traditions, and the nobles, fearful of extending the revolution to their own estates, refused to accept the peasants as allies. In every case, however, in which religion was involved, the contestants tended to take up rigid attitudes, compounded of the self-righteous conviction of the justice of their own cause and intense distrust of the sincerity of their opponents. As a result, old and almost traditional struggles for a different balance of power within a state tended to turn into civil wars, fought *à outrance* for complete victory. Such civil wars inevitably forced both sides to look for allies outside their own country and to merge their private quarrels with the current international power struggles.

To many Germans this seemed to be precisely what was

happening in the Holy Roman Empire during the Thirty Years' War, and this on two different levels. The first, the Bohemian revolt, was the classic case of an aristocratic-religious rebellion against a centralizing monarchy which turned into a deadly struggle for ultimate power during which both sides called on outsiders for help. The second —precipitated by the first—that of the struggle between the emperor and the estates of the Empire, was much more complex since the estates were, in fact, semi-independent princes and since the religious issue cut across the constitutional question. On the other hand, popular movements could not possibly become involved in this struggle, since no prince could put himself at the head of a movement which (as Maximilian of Bavaria found in 1634) must threaten him as much as the emperor. The outcome of the power struggle in the Empire was not a foregone conclusion. Indeed, it was only the intervention of Sweden and France which led to the decisive defeat of imperial power in Germany. Within the majority of the German states the power struggle between the monarchies (princes) and the autonomous forces (estates, parliaments, nobility) had yet to be decided. But the middle of the seventeenth century was not the time for this. Until 1650, when the great armies were finally disbanded, there could be no question of resistance to authority, and for another generation, at least, the Germans seem to have had enough of political struggles and wars. Characteristically, the stiffest resistance opposed to any German prince during this period came from the city of Königsberg in East Prussia, a province all but untouched by the great war (1662).

The limits of absolute monarchy

In the states of western and southern Europe, however, it was precisely their involvement in the war which precipitated open conflicts for ultimate power. The war, coinciding as it did with the long years of economic depression, made demands on the financial resources and administrative machinery of these states which forced their governments both to extend their administrative competence and to increase taxation. But while these two policies were logically complementary, they proved to be politically incompatible. The bureaucratic machinery for the extension of royal power either did not exist at all or, where it did, was inefficient and ill-controlled. The greater the financial pressure, the more central governments were thrown back on the voluntary co-operation of the privileged classes and corporations. As early as the reign of Philip II, the Spanish government had been forced, by financial pressure and the incompetence and corruption of its own officials, to hand over recruiting and much of the administration and supply of the army to the provinces and cities. Olivares could not give up the monarchy's alliance with the Castilian nobility and was forced to adopt the plan of the Union of Arms which shifted the conflict from Castile, where the monarchy was strong, to Portugal and Catalonia, where it was weak. Since Olivares could not offer the Portuguese and Catalan ruling classes anything that they did not already possess, his political and financial demands inevitably raised against him the alliance of forces that rose in revolt in 1640.

In Naples, and perhaps also in Sicily, the Spanish monarchy was in a somewhat better position because it could offer more to the local nobility: rights of jurisdiction and administrative control over the provinces; even the collection of the rapidly increasing taxation. This alliance of monarchy and privileged classes did not work very harmoniously, and it placed such unbearable strains on the rest of the population that the consequent revolts were directed against both the governments and the nobility. This doomed these revolutions from the beginning.

The basic causes of the Fronde in France were essentially similar. In theory the French monarchy was absolute. Its legislative and executive authority and its almost unfettered powers of taxation were generally accepted throughout the country. In practice, however, the monarchy was limited by the virtually untouchable immunities of classes, corporations, and individuals and by the lack of effective central control over the large and heterogeneous bodies of royal officials. As everywhere else, the prosecution of the war demanded both greater centralization and made it more difficult to carry this out. Thus Richelieu had to give up Sully's and Marillac's plans to convert the *pays d'états* into *pays d'élections*. The *intendants*, the most recent and effective agents of royal centralization, were bitterly resented by the other royal officials for interfering with their prerogatives and privileges. At the same time, war finance had greatly increased an already existing ground swell of social discontent, doubly dangerous because it was often encouraged by the local nobility. The royal minority, after 1643, raised the question, not so much of royal authority as such, as of who had the right to exercise it and how far. It was over this very practical question that the civil wars of the Fronde were fought. Characteristically, the revolts were triggered off by quarrels over taxation and the universal hatred of the tax-farmers and government bankers. But, at bottom, the question of finance and taxation mattered relatively little to the privileged classes. Different parties were willing to use popular movements for their own ends but took great care not to commit themselves, or allow themselves to be committed, to social revolution, as had happened sixty years earlier with the Holy League in Paris. The different opposition groups—the *parlements*, Cardinal de Retz and his followers, Condé, Orléans, and the high nobility—always protested their loyalty to the principle of absolute monarchy (although in the case of Condé there was probably implicit a much more medieval view of the monarchy, in which the great nobles, especially the princes of the blood royal, formed the monarchy or state together with the person of the king). Nevertheless, their victory would undoubtedly have seriously weakened the monarchy as against the autonomous forces in the provinces and in the royal bureaucracy. Mazarin's eventual victory was necessary for the complete triumph of royal absolutism under Louis XIV.

The Netherlands had abolished their centralizing monarchy in their successful revolution of the 1570's. But in order to fight their long war against Spain they had found it necessary to set up a surrogate monarchy, the house of Orange-Nassau. The problems of the United Provinces were therefore still essentially similar to those of the great monarchies and they were even more closely linked to the pressures of war. It was when the war had ceased that they exploded into open conflict. Since, at least in the province of Holland, there was no significant noble estate, and since the religious issue, still so prominent in 1619, was all but dead thirty years later, the conflict came to be fought quite openly and starkly for political power. For financial reasons the estates of Holland demanded a substantial reduction of the army. William II saw this as a deliberate challenge to the power of the house of Orange. He had the backing of the other provinces and of the states general, and he tried to cajole and bully the cities of Holland to support him. An attempted military coup against Amsterdam failed, but the regent party was clearly losing the struggle. At that moment William II died (November 1650) and the Orangist party collapsed for want of leadership. For the time being the Orangist attempt to establish a centralized monarchy in the United Provinces had failed.

But the most successful revolution against a centralizing monarchy occurred in England, the one western country which had dropped out of the Thirty Years' War after its first decade. Yet even in England the years of unsuccessful intervention in Germany and against Spain and France had left bitter memories of national failure and had burdened the monarchy with debts which, during the long years of economic depression, forced it to resort to one unpopular financial expedient after another. Characteristically, it was the attempted assertion of the royal authority over an outlying kingdom which caused the first break in Charles I's system (1638)—although in Scotland the immediate issue was not financial, nor directly related to the war, but (as in Bohemia in 1618) religion. But it was the Scottish war which finally ruined Charles I's shaky finances and thus precipitated the conflict between king and parliament.

Revolution and compromise

The crisis of the European states at the end of the Thirty Years' War was a genuine crisis of societies and of their political constitutions. Even the Swiss cantons experienced it, when wartime prosperity had given way to postwar economic collapse. Then the remains of medieval democracy struck back against their patrician invaders in a peasants' war (1652–1653) and an intercantonal war, fought belatedly under religious colors (1656). At stake everywhere were the forms of patrician government and, sometimes at least, the existing structure of society. This structure was openly challenged from below in Naples and Palermo and in the *ormée* of Bordeaux. Elsewhere, as in England, only some parts of established society were challenged, and the challenge came primarily from the propertied classes. A very similar challenge had been successful in the Netherlands in the 1570's; but the history of both the United Provinces of the Netherlands and the English commonwealth was to show that the resultant changes produced their own political and social problems and that, to the surprise of contemporaries, they did not solve the fundamental political question of the age, that of the relation of a centralizing monarchy to the rest of the body politic. In France, in Portugal, and in Catalonia this was from the beginning the central question, just as it had been in Bohemia and in the Empire. But since seventeenth-century states were complex structures, with widely varying histories and traditions, the political problems were never posed in their pure form (except for the special case of the United Provinces in 1650) but were always entangled with a host of different social forces and personal ambitions.

The results of the revolutions were therefore very varied. The basic class structure of European society remained intact, was indeed confirmed. The genuinely popular and democratic movements were everywhere defeated. The privileged classes remained privileged. But within this very broad framework there appeared enormous differences. France, Spain, and the newly independent Portugal confirmed the absolutism of their monarchies, the special position of the Catholic Church in their social and intellectual life and, to a rather more varying degree, the preponderance of their nobilities. In both Denmark and Sweden the monarchies were soon to establish their royal absolutism by coups d'état at the expense of the nobility. In Poland, on the other hand, the monarchy had finally lost its long struggle with the magnates, and the king had become a kind of Venetian doge in an aristocratic republic whose nobility was more rapacious and autocratic than the absolute monarchies of western Europe. The greatest transformations occurred in the United Provinces and in England. There, compromse solutions were found: mixed constitutions, the emancipation of intellectual life from clerical control, and the development of open and flexible, even though highly differentiated, social structures. These were the differences which were to determine the course of European history for the next hundred and fifty years.

Index